Praise for

the Queen's path

"For millennia, we have been psychically trapped by the concept of the hero's journey as the only viable storytelling archetype. In ways subtle and less subtle, that has nudged our communal consciousness to continue on in the patriarchy by prioritizing, elevating, and admiring only those traits, mind pathways, and thought patterns most common to men. Stacey Simmons, with this work, liberates us from that paradigm. It is beyond thrilling to follow her mind and brilliance through an escape hatch and into a glittering field of what storytelling can be when the underlying structures are rearranged to accommodate and support feminine modalities."

— **Naomi McDougal Jones**, filmmaker and author of *The Wrong Kind of Women: Inside Our Revolution to Dismantle the Gods of Hollywood*

"I'm blown away by the ambition and the scale of *The Queen's Path*— this work is revolutionary for women-driven story. Women won't be relegated to second-class citizenship in the halls of heroes any longer! The world needs *The Queen's Path*, and it needs it now!"

— **Steven Pressfield**, author of *The Legend of Bagger Vance*, *The War of Art*, and *A Man at Arms*

"Every director and screenwriter in Hollywood is going to buy this book. It will take its place next to Chris Vogler's *The Writer's Journey*. I can't wait to assign it to my students."

— **Anne Hamilton**, writer and director of *American Fable* and professor at University of Southern California Film School

the
Queen's
path

the Queen's *path*

A REVOLUTIONARY GUIDE TO WOMEN'S EMPOWERMENT AND SOVEREIGNTY

STACEY SIMMONS, PH.D.

HAY HOUSE LLC
Carlsbad, California • New York City
London • Sydney • New Delhi

Cataloging-in-Publication Data is on file at the Library of Congress

Tradepaper ISBN: 978-1-4019-9352-8
E-book ISBN: 978-1-4019-9358-0
Audiobook ISBN: 978-1-4019-9385-6

10 9 8 7 6 5 4 3 2 1
1st edition, November 2024

Printed in the United States of America

This product uses responsibly sourced papers and/or recycled materials.
For more information, see www.hayhouse.com.

*For all those who have given me powerful words,
and most especially, my beloved.*

Contents

INTRODUCTION

Women in Captivity

Women are one half the world's population. And yet the world is hardly fair to us. We struggle with empowerment, but anyone offering a solution wants our money. Culture doesn't want us to own our sexuality, and yet we are expected to put it on display for everyone to comment upon. We are entreated to long for motherhood and partnership and then belittled if that is "all" we do. We are constantly lectured about how "emotional" we are, when historically it has been our job to put the feelings of children and partners above our own in almost every context. Life constantly tells women who to be and how to be it, and tells us what's wrong with us. And then it turns around and tells us to just "lean in" to the challenges we face. To understand ourselves, women must first look at not only our own hopes, dreams, and fears but also the systems in which we operate and try to realize those same desires and ambitions.

This book is about women. It is about women as we are taught to be and who we can become when we look beyond the options given to us. The path that women wind down is not a linear journey but instead an ever-turning spiral, one where we regularly engage with the same events from different vantage points. To know women is to understand the complexities that women endure. Most of us long to be who we were instructed to be: thin, powerful, in control, beautiful, brilliant, and effortless. The ideal of womanhood has become an archetype so far from what is attainable that many women ultimately reject the ideal in favor of the possible.

Most of us live saddened by that or are downright ashamed. No one seems to question whether these binary choices are real, good for anyone, or are simply based on a system of oppression.

This work is the culmination of years of research. The story of the Queen archetype and the worlds that she moves through are complex *and* elegant. Decoding the Queen archetype was only possible because there has been so much change in recent years. Women hold important positions in government, the media, academia, and business. The model described in these pages appears in story after story, regardless of the medium being employed to tell it. The model is intuitive; writers have been reproducing it for millennia. You will find the Queen and her model in everything from ancient Sumerian myths, to the Hebrew Bible, all the way to the present day in movies like *Frozen,* and television series like *The Handmaid's Tale, Cruel Summer,* or *Killing Eve.*

I have worked in and around entertainment most of my career, so it is natural for me to easily find the examples of these elements in movies and television. Inevitably, though, the same elements appear in any stories where women are prominent. This is true whether the authors, actors, historians, screenwriters, memoirists, or directors intended to follow an archetypal path or not. As we go through the steps along the Queen's Path, there are some familiar and unfamiliar paths we will place our glass slippers onto.

I am asked frequently if I am writing a woman's version of the Hero's or Heroine's Journey. This is a difficult question to answer. It would not have been possible for me to recognize the steps of the Queen's Path without the work of Joseph Campbell, Chris Vogler, Carol Pearson, and Maureen Murdock. However, I disagree with my esteemed colleagues Pearson and Murdock on the arcs that they describe. There are similarities between the Hero's Journey, the Heroine's Journey, and the Queen's Path. But I found my model by analyzing all kinds of narratives, from fairy tales and films to personal stories from my psychotherapy patients. I broke down the key elements long before comparing them to the work of other authors and researchers.

The biggest difference for me is that on the Queen's Path, the woman herself ultimately has to decide *how* she will combat the cultural expectations placed on her. These constraints are structural to her journey in ways that they are not for a Hero. Her path is marked by the individual woman's or female character's struggle with predefined categories put on women by culture or society. It is up to her to ultimately decide her own fate, and come to terms with her own sovereignty, in a world that would prefer that she fit into easy tropes that either keep her small and docile or punish her for becoming big and powerful. The Queen's Path denies that these tropes are the only options for her, but to overcome them, she must work *through* them. She cannot ignore them. The Queen overcomes these binary choices, becoming whatever version of herself is the most sovereign truth for her to run her own life according to her ideals, goals, ambitions, gifts, and talents.

Not a Heroine's Journey

A Queen doesn't take a Hero's Journey. That's not to say that some women don't take Hero's Journeys and that there aren't men who take the Queen's Path. This archetypal journey describes what women face in a society where they are not historically treated as equals. No one asks Clark Kent if his job at *The Daily Planet* will interfere with the expectation that he will want to marry and have children. No one tells Indiana Jones that to "have it all" he will have to sacrifice his masculinity and be better than, and subtly flirt with, the women at the university where he is a professor. No one tells Frodo that he needs to "lean in" to the troubles befalling him and be a better version than the female hobbits as he gets on the road to Mordor. No, as we read these stories or watch these characters' stories unfold, the assumption is that these male protagonists are already expected to be on a rarefied journey simply by being called to the quest.

We describe the quest in inherently male terms most of the time. Female characters have simultaneously been dissuaded from these quests and also subsumed in them. People are often uncomfortable saying that women are qualitatively *different* from men, and yet that is exactly how we are portrayed in a telling of the

Heroine's Journey. You will find descriptions where she eschews all that makes her feminine to be on the Heroine's Journey, taking on increasingly male roles and attributes. You will also find descriptions of the Heroine's Journey aligning her with a path through the underworld where she meets a goddess or god, and then *only* a supernatural encounter can ultimately free her. The problem with these descriptions is that the path of the female character in these stories is in relationship to a male protagonist, a presumed male experience, or to an assumed weakness of her sex. Women, whether in real life or as characters in stories, do not exist only in relationship to a man or to maleness.

The Queen's Path acknowledges that all women have to confront society's expectations of what women are. Individuality has been much more difficult for women to assert over the millennia. Each woman has to move through the realization that we are given a role. The reality of being a woman is that more than anything, culture (and by extension, jobs, families, spouses, and children) want us to fit the archetypal models more than they want us to be individuals. We hold ourselves to those ideals as well. It is not at all difficult to see that the interlacing systems of expectations will easily consume our individuality just to feed the machine of culture.

The struggle for women is that along the Queen's Path, we have to separate from the expectations of society. Before we can find ourselves at the end, defining our domain and being sovereign, we must first recognize the separation—the experience of being divided. Ultimately, we are expected to align ourselves within a set of parallel expectations. The possibilities for women are usually limited—we are "good" or "bad girls," "tomboys" or "ladies," "Madonnas" or "whores." All these are false dichotomies. Women cannot free ourselves from them without realizing that they are not handed to us as *personal expectations*. We must recognize that they are handed to us as uniforms that we are expected to inhabit throughout the course of our lives.

Society has attempted to make the story of women's lives about these polarities, attempting to force women into one of two damning choices. Either you are a "typical" woman or an "atypical" woman. You either love dolls and makeup or abandon them to be more *masculine*. You're either an ideal female, or not, which often gets truncated to simply being masculine. These binary choices are not representative of real women's lives. Nor are they representative of the characters' lives in novels, television, films, or sacred literature. How women navigate the complex performance of gender is only one aspect of women's lived experience. And yet, most storytelling models fall into these descriptions because it is the simplest and most acceptable representation of women.

Having said all that, to ignore the struggle of women and the far more complicated expectations placed on us by society, our families, and sometimes ourselves is to avoid the internal and external conflicts women face in the endeavor of becoming wholly ourselves. As children, we learn the expectations and struggle with how to break free of those structural chains. We learn very early the cost of being born into (or presenting) a female body. Most women struggle with these identities for the majority of our lives. The difference in the Queen's Path is that the model illuminates the expectations placed on the individual woman and reveals the way to overcome these expectations in favor of her deliverance. She unfolds as a sovereign being enjoying the full expression and liberty of her unique humanity.

The Queen's Path illuminates a trajectory for women to overcome the choices handed to us early in our lives. It teaches women that we have the ability, power, and agency to make our own choices, even in a world that attempts to constrain our identities and reduce our autonomy via biological determinism. The Queen's Path is a guide to write our own endings and to guide writers to create women characters who more closely adhere to women's lived experience.

The World Is Run by Archetypes

The world is filled with archetypes. A day doesn't pass where we aren't assailed by at least one archetype or symbol. In my therapy practice, these structures parade in and out of my clients' sessions, most days without a moment's recognition. Archetypes hold our most cherished ideals and sometimes our greatest fears. They tell us who we wish to be, and that tells us a great deal about who we are. Most often, archetypes come to us from culture. We learn them from our parents, teachers, religious leaders, and favorite stories. We take the archetype on, aligning with it, investing in it. We revere the symbols associated with it. Our Savior archetype becomes Jesus, our deified salvation. Our Father archetype becomes Yahweh or maybe when brought down to earth a bit, Liam Neeson in *Taken*. Our Mother archetype becomes the Madonna, Kwan Yin, or June Cleaver from the 1960s series *Leave It to Beaver*. When we struggle, we compare ourselves and the people around us with archetypal ideals that we mistakenly label "normal." The Greek origins of the word *archetype* mean "old type," but an archetype is so much more than just an arcane model of something. An archetype is a collection of behaviors and qualities seen and experienced together repetitively across cultures. Usually, these are personifications, but not always.

My world in the last several years has been punctuated by the work of archetypal psychologists and mythologists, all dedicated to revealing the work of these powerful psychological structures in culture and in the individual psyche. Marie-Louise von Franz, James Hillman, Marion Woodman, Joseph Campbell, and Carl Jung are responsible for our current understanding of archetypal psychology. We don't *create* archetypes; they are always there. At different times in our history, certain archetypes are favored over others, and they take up more of our intellectual and psychological attention. Archetypes in one form or another have been known to us since at least the time of Plato's *Forms*. Plato introduced the idea to explain that we all share some basic understanding of everything, from the simplest rock to the most elaborate throne. Most of the time, we are unaware of these archetypal powers and their influence on us, and yet we see them, reproduce them, and create expectations of ourselves and others based on their prominence in our cultures, families, and our personal goals and ideals.

You are probably most familiar with a related concept, a stereotype. A stereotype is a reduction of an idea into its most basic or culturally understandable form. Often, stereotypes are negative because anytime you oversimplify something, you risk reducing it to its most base attributes. Archetypes are similar, but the word itself suggests that the form you are looking at has been at work across a more profound time span, picking up nuances, influences, and definitions along the way. Archetypes also carry the possibility of deep meaning, and so they often (though not always) hold the "ideal" versions of the type. We can think of archetypes as holding the essential, expansive qualities rather than the most basic and simple ideas that we find in a stereotype.

Cultures build expectations for how we behave on archetypal patterns. Every culture has a Hero archetype, for example, though the individual hero may be different. The archetype is the "hero," not the name we give him. Once we give the archetype a name, it becomes a symbol. For example, the archetype of Hero doesn't change, regardless of the name he is given. He might be Achilles in Greece, Ogun in West Africa, or King Arthur in Medieval Europe. Every culture has a goddess of love, whether she is Oshun in West Africa, Aphrodite in Greece, or the Madonna in Western Christianity. An archetype carries the expectations of the culture. We place meaning in the archetype and use it as a touchstone for understanding. Sometimes an archetype has a negative association, like a villain, ghost, or embodied evil like a devil or demon. Archetypes always hold multiple levels of meaning, and they can cross cultural boundaries because they are not named and associated with any given place or culture.

When you think of the Father archetype, for example, you will likely have a powerful, strong, guiding, and sometimes dominating idea of what "Father" should be. When you think of the "Mother," you probably think of kindness, loving support, nurturing, and warmth. When you think of a Warrior archetype, you probably see some attributes of male, brave, honor, and ferocity. If you experienced anything different than archetypal behavior in your own life, then you likely compared that "other" behavior to an archetype.

As a psychotherapist, I see many clients who have experienced less than ideal parenting. It is a rare thing for my clients to not compare their experience against an ideal. It usually goes something like, "Why couldn't I just have *normal* parents?" or "Why can't I just have a *normal* family?" What they are expressing is how far from the ideal their experience was. My answer is almost always the same. There is no normal. There is ideal, and then there is how we realize the ideal in ourselves and our experiences. Most people cannot withstand the pressure of how they measure up to their ideals. In retaliation, they push against anyone or anything that reminds them of these failings, rather than examine those archetypal expectations. This is a painful and avoidable reality. Successfully navigating the space between the archetypal ideal and lived reality can be difficult, but it is the best way I know for building a happy life. To be capable of that negotiation, you have to first be able to identify the archetypes at work in your psyche, your world, and your relationships.

The Gendered Soul in Culture

We welcome children into the world with a sense of great joy. The entry of the new soul into our lives is seen as a gift from an unknown realm into the terra firma we see every day. The new person is not a zombie or a golem awaiting a soul's arrival. The soul is here, with the newborn, becoming itself, divine potential unfolding into flesh. In our culture, arriving at the threshold of puberty pushes children out of their cultural identification with innocence and into something often portrayed as dark and sinful: sex. This is an unfair attribution, one that associates secondary sex characteristics and sexual markers with corruption. In most cultures, when we start to notice these characteristics, our expectations shift. Characteristics that we associate with being successful at being a "man" or a "woman" become conflated with either claiming power or assuming a deference to authority.

In both sexes, appearance is judged, though for different reasons. Around age eight or nine, we start to expect girls to "act like a lady" and for boys to act tough or "man up." Children at this age start to identify with characters in games, movies, or television. Also, around this age, children begin to place themselves in the hierarchy according to the expectations and behavior of their family members. For men, the transition from boyhood moves the child into a track ascending from innocence to power. For women, this movement away from innocence gives women two prescribed options: move into social acceptance or social isolation. Acceptance means a loss of authority but belonging and protection, while being outside social norms provides the potential for more personal power but will mean the child finds herself isolated. In every way except emotionally, boys' options expand and girls' are constrained as they grow into adulthood.

The Rest Is Drag

I remember being in one of my earliest psychology classes and learning about the way roles become integrated into our individual psychology. We use roles to help us build identity. But if we never grow beyond the roles, we will find ourselves frustrated and stuck. Every role is a costume. Every persona we take on is a form of drag: executive drag, doctor drag, therapist drag, mom drag, best friend drag. If there's a role you're playing, there's a costume you're putting on for it. Whether you're showing up as a demure housewife, a butch lesbian, or a fierce mama bear, you're performing. In our culture, performance of any role will have a gendered component. Sex and gender are complex issues. Sex is what you are born with. Gender is what you perform in the world. In many cultures, these two are conflated, and any difference between the two is treated with disdain at the very least and violence at the very worst.

Cultural issues around sex and gender are complicated, mostly because of this conflation. When society can separate the cultural aspects of gender and sexuality from the biological issues of sex, we often find ourselves with more tolerant laws and cultural norms. These result in social expectations supportive of all people. Rigid and punitive cultures enforce the conflation of sex with gender. People are expected to stay in their gendered lane according to their biological sex. This can make people feel more restricted, and while it may make those with traditional expectations of sex roles feel safe, it makes anyone outside of those norms feel disempowered. Worse, under rigid social norms, regardless of the size of the group—from schools and churches to highly stratified monarchies and theocracies—there are very real risks for anyone who may deviate.

The performance of gender according to traditional sex roles is at the core of many conservative cultural norms. These inform everything, from stereotypes of what is considered feminine and masculine behavior to archetypal ideals of motherhood, fatherhood, marriage, family, and ideal work. There are dozens of archetypal models of female expectations we can examine: Mother, Witch, Wife, Nag; there are new ones that have entered our lexicon as well: Angry Black Woman, Hippie Chick, Karen. When working in any realm where we are interacting with other people, archetypes will be alive in the discussion.

The tumult over Hillary Clinton's e-mails and the general view of her as "untrustworthy" in the 2016 U.S. presidential elections wasn't about her as an individual; it was about her alignment with an archetype. She was a "bitch" and a "feminist." She didn't know her place. She had opinions and expected to have a voice in policy. Beyond having opinions, her husband cheated on her with a much younger woman, an intern. He chose infidelity with a woman who was clearly subordinate to him. The implication was that even Hillary's husband didn't want to have sex with her because of her "bitchiness." Her lack of submission was unattractive, undesirable, and unwomanly.

The more a group is vilified or subverted in society, the more the representation of that group will be dominated by archetypes and stereotypes. Similarly, if a group is losing ground in society, it will latch on to archetypes and stereotypes as easy simplifications of good and evil to make their message clearer, their cause more plain. Complexity ceases to be possible in the face of archetypes and stereotypes. Archetypes typically expand qualities, and stereotypes narrow them. Archetypes traverse cultures, whereas stereotypes often are limited to the society or culture that adopts them. Stereotypes can, of course, be transmitted across cultures, but they don't expand the categories as they do so.

Symbols are the next step in understanding archetypal ideas in culture. Archetypes tend to create categories. For example, every culture has a Savior archetype, Mother archetype, and Father archetype. The culture will assign a symbol to this archetype to connect with it and make meaning. In the West, Luke Skywalker is a contemporary hero. Luke is the symbol; Hero is his archetype. In the 2016 election, Hillary was the symbol; Bitch was her archetype. She has another, the MIPE (MEE-pay), an archetype we will dive into as we traverse the landscape covered in this book.

Recent History and the Hero

The Hero's Journey has become one of the most important archetypal stories of the last century. It has been used in historical analyses to examine how great men and women of history have made their way in the world. In psychology, it helps people navigate the travails of life. In literature, it codifies what makes a good story. This complex archetypal pattern examines the Hero's life cycle as he traverses the realm of life from being called out of the wilderness of the unconscious and into a life of purpose. In the traditional structure, the Hero is called to his purpose, refuses the call, is pulled, meets a teacher, goes on a quest, gives up or loses something important, learns something transformational, and ends up returning to the place of origin to share his wisdom. Depending on what kind of work you're doing, there could be anywhere from 12 to 17 steps along the Hero's Journey.

Joseph Campbell was the first to identify the Hero's Journey by examining myths that had been passed down across time through multiple cultures. His work was deeply influenced by that of Swiss psychologist Carl Jung. Culture makers have relied on Campbell's structure to give us our history, help us make sense of our present, and build a framework for our future. But the framework has never been robust enough to also hold the story of women's lived experience. Women's lives include decisions and experiences that are relatively universal to women but that the hero on his journey never has to confront. The hero never has to struggle with whether or not he is culturally acceptable based on his looks or has to deal with life-and-death issues that focus on marriageability, virginity, and fertility, for example. As a result, the Hero's Journey has been insufficient to describe the paths of women.

The Hero's Journey cannot fully hold the space of women's struggle with these realities. It cannot precisely reconcile the forces that push women into an identity that is almost always a reduction of the whole self, balancing the demands of desire and motherhood and the powerful role women struggle with in being the channel of life for the continuation of humanity. The different stops and struggles along the Hero's Journey don't include these aspects, and they cannot, for the Hero's Journey tells the story of men. Men's journeys usually don't preclude whether or not they are fathers, at least not archetypally. Whether or not a man gets married does not fundamentally change the arc of his story from a cultural perspective. No one assumes a married man has a different path to becoming a lawyer, banker, adventuring archaeologist, or Pulitzer Prize–winning writer than a single man. That is a very different calculus for women.

For a woman to be on a Hero's Journey, she must have already taken on the mantle of "outsider." Before she even begins that journey, she has had to navigate the archetypal path that is laid out in this book. I call it the Queen's Path. The traditional Hero's Journey does not address how women navigate the world. Women constantly balance reconciling multiple identities. Some are compromised in culture, others are empowered, and all are subject to cultural, gendered norms that assume women's subjectivity in the world. From a cultural perspective, it doesn't matter if a woman is the hero of her own story. Her story will always be less important in culture to a similar man's story. A female hero is almost always seen as an outsider at best and an imposter at worst. In the chapters that follow, I'll explain why.

The domination of male story patterns in our culture is constantly produced and reproduced. Cultures continue to repeat the Hero's Journey as an organizing principle found in sacred texts, fairy tales, and cultural myths. We find this structure in film, novels, and television. You'll find it in comic book heroes like Superman and Batman. You'll also see it in sacred literature from the Torah to the Gospels to the Upanishads. Psychologists use it as an organizing principle to help people make meaning in their lives by reframing the client as a hero navigating through their own Hero's Journey. Joseph Campbell called it a "monomyth."[1] In that terminology, he intentionally put the Hero's Journey forth as a universal story structure for everyone. Except he didn't include women. Campbell famously offered that women didn't need to take the journey; they were the center that the Hero was trying to get to.[2] This wasn't intended to be an insult; rather, Campbell believed that women occupied a sacred center and that by standing in that place, the world would come to us. But the foundation of that idea means that some women get to be the center and others do not. We will talk about that fallacy in the next chapter. The cultural norms that tell women we have a holy duty as mothers, or that we shouldn't need more than our families, or that being a bad girl excises us from our community, are all traps. Good girl or bad girl . . . if we adhere to one or the other, we cease to grow into women.

I have never fit into the easy expectations. I have longed to be a heroine and have worked hard to engage in that mythos. I have longed to prove myself through work—whether in my first job at 15 or in highly stratified organizations like studios and universities. Throughout my life, I was taught first by my family, and later by my culture, that my value was defined and confined to a slim body and pretty face. My intelligence, insight, spiritual longings, and sexual identity were not only unimportant but also unacceptable. From a young age, I had a visceral response to being silenced, likely a response to my mother's lack of a voice. I remained vigilant so that I would not fall into the same trap. But until I began this research, I couldn't see that I was on a path that didn't make room for a woman incapable of submission.

Women have our own archetypal structure, or to use Campbell's term, *monomyth*. Our journeys include the impact of the patriarchy as well as the way of overcoming it. I know many of my feminist colleagues see the world as rooted in patterns of violence and greater usurpations of power. I don't disagree with these points of view. Women's lives are mediated and punctuated by violence in ways that culture does its best to sweep under the rug or normalize. However, I don't think that at this particular moment addressing the problem from the point of view of women as victims is the most meaningful. Instead, I ask you to consider thinking of women and other people whose bodies and minds have been colonized as people who have been trained to believe that they must ask permission. I offer that the time for permission is over. Anyone who wishes to live their lives according to their own will rather than a narrow set of expectations is free to do so. What they need is a set of instructions.

Women are changing the world. We can make these changes for ourselves, our children, and men. First, though, we have to tell our own stories. That begins with an archetypal journey that focuses on women's experiences, not one that adapts a man's monomyth and tries to force a woman to ignore the cultural, social, familial, and biological forces that make her care about her role, her destiny, and her legacy. We are Queens, and by reclaiming our rights to our own unique journeys, we can remake the world. Like the pieces on a chessboard, the Queen has more power, more maneuverability, and more flexibility. She moves in ways that kings, bishops, and soldiers cannot. When we learn to see the game, and break it, we can claim a territory for ourselves that before this moment had only been available to a king.

PREPARING TO WALK THE PATH OF SOVEREIGNTY

CHAPTER 1

INVISIBILITY, EQUALITY, AND SOVEREIGNTY

It was 2007, and I found myself in that deep pain again. I had moved my mom in with me, my marriage was a wreck, and I worked in a stressful, toxic, and very high-profile university job. I had earned a Ph.D. focused on social and media psychology 5 years earlier and had been in therapy at that point for more than 15 years. I was tired of telling my story, "trauma, abandonment, betrayal . . . blah blah blah . . . death, guns, anorexia, drowning, rape . . . blah blah blah." My narrative had become boring, even to me.

Steve, my latest therapist, wanted to try something different. He complained that he had been doing cognitive behavioral therapy (CBT) for decades, and it only scratched the surface. He asked if I would be willing to be one of his first patients to try something called acceptance commitment therapy or ACT. He felt it could help break through the wall I had built. The intervention we would try required I identify and stop resisting my greatest emotional fear. He wanted me to name the feeling I would avoid feeling at all costs. That January day in 2007, something broke in me. I don't remember if I actually moved, but my memory is that I stood up in Steve's office.

My body felt foreign, and I felt . . . fear. No—terror.

The leather sofa held me up tentatively for a moment by pushing back against my calves. Was I really standing? Or was it one of the ACT exercises of watching a train go by? I don't remember it as my therapist's office. It *felt* like I was standing on a platform at a train station.

"What are you avoiding?" My jaw couldn't move, as though the entire apparatus of my mouth were made of concrete. My jawbones fused, silencing my voice. I felt away from my body, swaddled by a night sky, surrounded by pinpoints of light like stars. My mouth wasn't connected to my awareness, and I couldn't find the power to move my lips.

Steve took me back to an early trauma, a near drowning at age seven. I lay at the bottom of the pool, looking at what was happening around me, unaware that I was unconscious. Lifeguards pulled me from the deep end and gave me mouth-to-mouth. Moments later, I was spitting up water. No broken ribs, just a sore throat and raw nostrils from the chlorinated water. The lifeguards stood me up tentatively. I was dizzy but conscious. My mom looked me over. Unfazed, she decided that if I was breathing, I was okay. She went back to the conversation with her sister. I wandered away from her in pain, a yellow towel wrapped around my shoulders, my ponytail dripping cold water onto my back. My lungs hurt; my eyes burned. My skin stung, and everything in the world looked and felt different. I stared at the trees and the brick wall, my back to the pool and my mom. I couldn't bear to look at anyone or anything. It was too much for my little seven-year-old psyche to process.

I almost died, and she. didn't. care.

"What are you most afraid of feeling?" Steve asked, going deeper.

I felt a clutch beneath my jaw, my voice silenced, an invisible hand like a fist in my throat. There was no air. "I'll die," cracked painfully and almost inaudibly from the back of my mouth.

Steve pressed again, "What feeling makes you feel like you're dying?"

Deeper still. Abject terror. I shook my head, and then I felt a tiny eruption out of the most hidden place of my body, the smallness of the sound a betrayal of the depth of the pain.

(I can't speak.)

"That I am invisible," a barely audible crackle, and almost impossible to say.

(Death is right here, breathing in my face.)

"And what would happen if you let yourself *feel* invisible, for just a moment?"

I shook my head again, slow, the clutch at my throat holding the air just beneath my heart.

"You're safe. Let yourself feel it, just a little bit. I'm right here. I want you to say it but louder this time, *'I am invisible.'*"

Through a wall of resistance, out it came: "I am *invisible*." And with that utterance, a hurricane of tears, sadness, anger, confusion, and rage erupted like a tsunami from the seat of my psyche. I hadn't known there was so much feeling in my body. My unconscious had been holding back the ocean for decades. I was so terrified of being invisible that I had buried it. Invisible was my reality. Covered in the detritus of shame, anger, pain, and multiple abandoned dreams, I had tried to make a mountain of accomplishments, degrees, notoriety, and success so high that no one could ever make me invisible. But it was a lie. I was nowhere to be found on that mountain.

I was under it.

And the higher I built it, the more invisible I became.

Discovering Invisibility

My experience of being invisible is not unique. Almost every woman I know has to battle "invisible" daily. For women of color, it is even more pernicious. For trans women, deathly perilous. In depth psychology, we are taught that unnamed, invisible archetypes are the most dangerous. They hide in the shadows. They haunt places that reject the light of discovery. Invisible archetypes create psychic prisons—in individuals and culture at large. I had felt invisible for a long time, imprisoned in expectations and roles. I could not locate myself in anyone's gaze. No one saw me. They only saw the roles I played.

The Invisible Woman has been explored in many different genres, from books, and movies, to comics. Women patients have described their invisibility to me in various ways. Sometimes their pain, either physical or psychological, is ignored or diminished, rendering it invisible. Sometimes invisibility shows up simply as a wall that ostracizes. There is an invisible wall separating us from the life others have, enchanting us as "other." Other times, invisible is in our experience of being ignored or silenced by our families, our religious organizations, or our jobs. Can you illuminate invisibility in your own life? Do you hold your tongue when you want to express your outrage? Do you conceal your brilliance to avoid attention? Have you chosen clothes, jobs, friends, or partners based on how you will be seen?

Some parts of the world consider women's invisibility virtuous, covering girls in yards of fabric as soon as they reach puberty, or they cloister women out of public view. In the West, we often pretend that women's invisibility isn't happening—ironically laying invisibility on top of invisibility. Sometimes we describe it in euphemisms about our experience, like "the glass ceiling," an invisible barrier that we bang our heads against but can never break through. Other times it happens when we are reduced to a function: "wife," "sex-symbol," or "nasty woman." The individual woman is swallowed up by a broader force anonymizing her.

It shows up in the increasing morbidity of women in childbirth. Invisibility is what causes the systemic medical problems of under-treating the symptoms and physical pain of women of color in hospitals and doctor's offices. Invisible is the experience of women in boardrooms when male colleagues take credit for their ideas right in front of them. It is in the mansplaining that women experience.

Women have had to endure these forces for so long that we no longer see the hand of culture deftly moving the influence and expectations around us. We are blind to the reality that invisibility is the consequence of *a process*. It first shows up at a point in women's lives between childhood and adulthood. Women internalize the idea that we are supposed to be "effortless" in our performance of beauty, housekeeping, childcare, and other traditionally gendered ideals. Women are our roles first, handmaids to a patriarchal culture. Our existence is functional. We are human beings second, sometimes even third or fourth to the roles we fulfill.

My therapist had opened a secret door. I didn't know the door or the space behind it even existed. I didn't know that there was a place in myself I wasn't allowed to go. And now that it was open, I was terrified of what it would mean. That day with Steve was the first in my many years of therapy that something unmediated came out of me. In every other form of treatment, I learned to intellectualize my pain. I could describe it. I was able to connect the dots to earlier trauma. But I could barely *feel* it. Sure, I had cried in therapy before . . . a *lot*. But I had never felt the deepest part of myself. I had never *felt* my deepest fear.

Frozen and *Maleficent*

Years later, I was in a fully new life. I had abandoned my home and academic career and was going back to graduate school to become a therapist. As part of my studies, I had to write a master's thesis. The academic years were intense, so I decided to focus on something familiar and beloved. I wrote about animation. The *Frozen* franchise persuaded millions of children to "let it go." The story surrounds the relationship between sisters. Elsa, the eldest, wields magical powers allowing her to control ice and snow. Her younger, nonmagical sister, Anna, has no powers of her own but isn't jealous of her sister's magic. As children, Anna thrilled in the fun they had in the film's first act. But soon, Elsa's power is out of her control, and Anna suffers a magical injury. Elsa is forced to hide her powers thereafter. The two are separated from each other until they reach adulthood, when Elsa is called to become queen of Arendelle. Soon, magic again drives Elsa from her domain when she accidentally displays her power during the coronation ball. Elsa runs to North Mountain, and Anna, suddenly understanding their years of separation, goes on an adventure to reclaim her sister and bring her back to the castle.

The story celebrates the bond between sisters, turning the "true love's kiss" story on its head. *Frozen* redirects the idea of true love as being between family, rather than focusing on romantic love. In the end, it is the nonmagical Anna who saves Elsa from certain death at the hands of a bad man. The story celebrates women's power and pokes light fun at the idea of "happily ever after."

We've all seen the memes and viral videos of little girls and grown women singing the film's power ballad, "Let It Go." It's the ultimate freedom song, the lyrics reflecting the feelings we all want to celebrate. In it, we are reminded that women have the right to own ourselves, even when it is difficult. We are entreated to choose our own power over the idea of settling for the "warmth" that comes from giving into cultural expectations and perfectionism.

The songs, costumes, creativity, and artistry made for an incredible film. But more than anything, audiences responded to the empowerment of the sisters relying on, and connecting with, one another. There was no "evil queen," though in early Disney storyboards Elsa's character exhibits the traits expected of a Disney villain akin to the film's original inspiration, the title character in Hans Christian Anderson's "The Snow Queen."[1] But as the story developed, the cultural moment of women coming together in sisterhood rather than competition developed, likely because of the influence of co-director Jennifer Lee and because so many of the creative team were women.

The story of family love showed up again in 2014's *Maleficent*. In Disney's original 1959 version, *Sleeping Beauty*, Maleficent is an evil fairy who curses an infant Princess Aurora because she wasn't invited to the baby's christening ceremony. In the 2014 live-action version, the eponymous fairy queen is portrayed as a magical creature betrayed by her lover, Stefan. The bond they shared as young lovers becomes Maleficent's torture, as it is "true love's kiss" that enabled Stefan to mutilate Maleficent, cutting her fairy wings from her body. Stefan takes the wings and presents them at the royal court, a tribute to win the favor of a childless king. Having succeeded in his quest, Stefan becomes king after the old king dies, and Maleficent in her fairy kingdom becomes his mortal enemy. The betrayal sets the stage for her to take revenge on her former paramour by cursing his newborn daughter to a life of servitude and sleep until she is freed by "true love's kiss," a clear reference to his betrayal of her. Maleficent says these words in a mocking tone before the whole court, showing her disdain for the betrayed promise of true love.

But Maleficent isn't a cold-hearted monster; she feels bad that she cursed a child who had done her no harm. Magic cannot be reversed, so she finds herself acting as Aurora's guardian, protecting her from the curse after the child is sent far away from the kingdom to live in seclusion. When she reaches 16, Aurora inevitably falls under the spell of Maleficent's original curse and pricks her finger on a spinning wheel, putting the princess into a deep sleep (a not-so-subtle acknowledgment of domestic servitude's ability to turn any woman into a zombie). Distraught, Maleficent attempts to find a prince to love Aurora, hoping the caveat in the original curse would save the princess after all. When the princely kiss doesn't awaken Aurora, Maleficent kisses her forehead with a mother's love, giving her a heartfelt apology and vowing to always take care of her. Aurora opens her eyes, free from the curse. True love doesn't always mean romantic love.

A pattern emerged in watching these films. In both stories, there are two bonded women characters. In *Frozen*, they are sisters. In *Maleficent,* it is a mother-daughter bond. I noticed that one character was magical, and the other one was without power. The magical creature was an outcast. The powerless one was always trying to connect. I noticed that the characters followed almost identical arcs in each film. They start their lives in innocence and then experience a curse of some kind that leaves a scar or a mark. After, each is pulled onto a forked path. They will either become an "acceptable" passive woman always seeking relationships, or they will live their lives magical, isolated, and unprotected.

It wasn't as simple as seeing that one character was a "wicked witch" and the other was a "princess." No, there was a much different binary being shown in these characters. Most importantly, in both films, there was a queen that emerged at the end. This queen was not power hungry; she didn't seek to destroy her sister. No, in becoming queen, she gathered the lost parts of herself back and ruled with confidence in her own power and authority. She gained sovereignty over herself.

I wrote my thesis, presented it, and thought I was done. But soon, I started to see this pattern in other places. I saw it in the lives of my clients as they talked about the expectations put on them and the roles that they were pushed into. I saw it in television shows like *The Handmaid's Tale* and *Killing Eve*, and in films like *Practical Magic* and *Promising Young Woman*. I saw it in comedies like *Legally Blonde* and dramas like *The Color Purple*. I saw it on Broadway in *Wicked* and *Waitress*. I looked backward to older films and found it in *My Fair Lady, Imitation of Life, Out of Africa*, and *Gigi*. I looked even further and found it in the Bible, both the Old and New Testaments. I found it in ancient myths about the *Descent of Inanna* from ancient Sumer and the *Rape of Persephone* from Greece. This pattern was everywhere, and it had been right in front of me, in front of all of us for thousands of years.

What was I seeing? Ultimately, I realized that I was seeing an archetypal model that represented the lived experience of women. It is an analog to the Hero's Journey, but it is not derivative of it. I named it the Queen's Path, because it reflects what women experience as we traverse the world of expectations, roles, marriageability, sex, accomplishment, desire, motherhood, and, if we are lucky, sovereignty—the ownership of our bodies, minds, and lives.

Sovereignty and the Divide

To unlock the mystery of following the Queen's Path, we must understand the two most important aspects of this research. These are the ultimate goal, *sovereignty*, and the thing that keeps us from it, *the Divide.* I cannot count the number of times younger women, students, or patients have sat in my office and argued (or struggled) with the belief that the problems of equality have been solved. There is a deep desire in our culture to believe that the structural impediments of the past are historical relics, and that everything keeping us from achieving our most ideal versions of ourselves is squarely within our individual control. Psychologically, when confronted with a difficult problem or threat, people default to what is within their power. Either "nothing is in my control" or "every-thing is in my control." The truth is much more nuanced.

I have discovered in my research that there is a way to think about these ideals that keeps the individual responsible for herself and takes into account the difficult ways the culture snags against her unique rights. That idea is sovereignty. Sovereignty is different from equality. Equality is expected to flow from one person to another or from a society to the individual. Equality is an external system that is mostly executed between people. In order for equality to matter, the parties involved must *value* equality. But what if you are dealing with someone who doesn't value it? What if you work in a toxic place that denies equality, and you need to keep your job until you find another one? What if you are in a difficult romantic relationship with entangled finances that have to be disentangled in order for you to be free? The answer is sovereignty. Sovereignty is the belief in my right to own myself and acting in accord with it. Where equality is an external system that flows between people, sovereignty is an internal system that flows outward.

If you want to understand women or a woman character, you will need to make sense of her unique path over the terrain of the Divide, and whether she ever achieves the coveted experience of owning herself. It is at once disorienting, disconcerting, and ephemeral. Girls are presented with one clear option for becoming women. Be a "good girl." In almost every patriarchal culture, this means that a woman is defined by her ability to be silent, passive, dutiful, obedient, fertile, and motherly. But what happens to the women who don't or can't become that? They become "other." But this second group isn't "othered" randomly. Their *othering* follows a pattern. The "other" woman when generously portrayed is seen as powerful, sexy, intelligent, assertive, and unafraid. When the portrayal is not kind, she may be seen as sexually perverse, hungry, evil, power-mongering, and emasculating. For these traits, she often must be silenced. So much so that we don't even give her a real title in patriarchy. We rely on the unconscious to find her, as she is banished to the netherworld where we have named her evil, witch, or bitch. To be *other* as a woman is to haunt the underworld.

The journey into the Divide starts when we are little girls. If we learn to be quiet and obedient, take polite turns, and defer to authority, we have the option of becoming the idealized passive feminine. If we don't learn these things, or if we have circumstances or trauma that keep us from becoming that idealized version, we are relegated to second-class womanhood. In either case, we become divided. This is not because as a woman I chose the Divide. Rather, as a woman, I am given two invisible paths. I may get pushed into the first, and if I fall off the ideal path, I am relegated to the second one. Some of us never get the choice. We end up on the second path of the Divide against our will.

The path of the *ideal* I call Maiden in Search of Relationship (MISOR, pronounced MEE-sohr). Women who walk this path understand the power of submission. They know that to get by in patriarchy, you have to look and play the part. You can become a professor, doctor, or even a Supreme Court justice as long as you play the role of the dutiful mother who defers to authority. If you get pushed onto the second half of the Divide, you take on the part of Magical, Isolated, Powerful, and Endangered (MIPE, pronounced MEE-pay). The MIPE is always "other." Her magic doesn't always refer to true magical powers but rather to things that make her "surprising" to those around her. She may have great artistic talent, intellect, or athletic prowess or be extraordinarily beautiful. The MISOR's power comes from family or marriage, while the MIPE's is her own, and as a result, she is unprotected by parents, a spouse, or culture.

If you start to look for these stories, you will find them everywhere. Some are fairy tales, like the story of Snow White; others are more sophisticated, like the depiction of June/Offred in *The Handmaid's Tale*. They may be fun and still move audiences with deep meaning, like in 2023's *Barbie*, directed by Greta Gerwig. One thing is consistent. All women are placed on the path of the Divide. As a result, we all *become* "divided." We are all set up to become either MISORs or MIPEs. Whether you wanted to be one or the other, if you are a woman, you will have been placed on this path. It is the Divided Woman that separates the Queen's Path from the Hero's Journey. At no point in the hero's quest does he have to contend with whether or not he is marriageable or attractive. He never has to worry about fitting into the expectations of proper sexual conduct. The hero cannot be made lesser by not adhering to the same social norms that confine his female counterpart.

The Divided Woman

The Divided Woman is not just a literary trope; she is also a regular character in real women's self-reported narratives. Here are some of the titles my therapy clients have used to describe her:

Suzy Cupcakes	Stepmonster
Bitch	Stepford Wife
Dragon Lady	Lady in the Streets
Tiger Mom	Ho in the Sheets
MILF	Bad Mom
Wicked Witch	That Bitch

Any of those sound familiar? Probably all but Suzy Cupcakes—a client made that one up on the spot. The client I'm speaking of is named Susan, and she is a total badass. She has an MBA from Harvard and a law degree from Columbia Law School. Colleagues describe her as a genius at complex international banking laws. On a recent work trip, Susan traveled to several countries in Europe while working for an international law firm, where she supervised some of the most challenging financial law anyone can master. She came home accomplished and exhausted, having successfully negotiated treasury agreements across several multinational banking conglomerates.

She arrived at LAX on a Thursday, got an Uber home, took a bath, and collapsed into her bed. Her husband came home an hour later and immediately went to the bedroom, trailed by two screaming children, and asked, "Can you please make dinner tonight? I'm exhausted and need a break." When she arrived at my office the next morning, I thought Susan was going to explode out of her skin. She ranted for almost 30 minutes, pacing the floor in my office and regaling me with the complex details that she had negotiated (that I didn't understand). At the end of her seething, she finally screamed, "Who the fuck does he think he's married to, Suzy Cupcakes?" She collapsed on the sofa in tears. Here was an accomplished woman with multiple high-level degrees. She spoke three languages and was, by every account, including her husband's, an amazing person. But in the moment when her husband could have come home and seen her as a tired, overtaxed human being, he saw her as a wife who had been missing for the previous eight weeks, and he wanted that wife back so *he* could have a break.

This is the Divide. Women don't get to choose which side we're placed upon. We are given a track, and we follow it, often not realizing that we've been placed on it at all. We believe we are following a path of our own making, but chances are pretty good that we aren't. We are on either the path of the MISOR or the MIPE. As challenging as this can seem, the Divide is not the end of the story. All over the world, women are standing up to the Divide. By traversing the Queen's Path, we are reclaiming our power. Women are claiming our queendoms at a scale that has never been seen. Deep down, we know sovereignty is our birthright, and women are standing in their sovereignty, sometimes without the words to describe it but just the innate sense that they can no longer tolerate the alternative.

The Archetypes

All women are set on the path of the Divided Woman between the ages of 8 and 12. We arrive by cultural design, not by choice. Culture tells a little girl that she can have anything she wants . . . but as she gets older, she learns that she can have anything, just not that one thing over there. Oh, and not that other thing behind it. Oh and wait a minute, that juicy one too—nope. No, she can desire all she wants, but she must conform. Desire is a complex puzzle, even a trap. And if she doesn't conform, she'll be ostracized—cut out of the body politic, the clique, or the tribe.

The Divided Woman is a newly *defined* archetype, but she is not a new archetype in the world. If you look at the history of story, everywhere we look, we find the Divided Woman. Just investigate mythology—she shows up in the relationship between the Sumerian goddess Innana and her sister, Ereshkigal, keeper of the underworld. You'll see her in the dyad between the goddess Athena and the human who challenged her to a weaving contest, Arachne. She's in the Hebrew stories (the Talmud and the Torah) of Lilith and Eve. She is in the Bible's Book of Esther, the story of the Jewish Hadassah becoming a confidante to the Babylonian king and defeating an evil advisor, eventually becoming Queen Esther. She appears in the Christian Bible as Mary of Nazareth and Mary Magdalene.

Different authors have come close to discovering the Divide, only to land just shy of it. Women have been defined as wounded, betrayed, or ignored by writers trying to include women in the role of hero or heroine. But these definitions remove the structural component of women's lived experience in favor of varying degrees of agency and responsibility. Cultural expectations are absolute; either fall in or fall out. While men can choose between warrior, king, lover, or hero, for women there are only two options. We typically define them as "Good Girl" or "Bad Girl." But the reality is that there are two primary subarchetypes to the Divided Woman, the MISOR and the MIPE, and all female archetypes fall into one of those two categories except the Queen, (more about her later).

If you have doubts, think about how women are frequently expected to fulfill the following opposing expectations:

- Be available/be unobtainable
- Be pretty/be serious
- Be effortless/work hard
- Be agreeable/be mysterious
- Be likable/be confident
- Depend on someone for security/make your own money

The Divided Woman resides at the center of the entire model. As I looked further into the stories we tell about women, I found that there was a more subtle structure underlying the stories. In every one of them, the woman starts out in the world of "Once Upon a

Time" filled with promise, potential, and desire—she is *undifferentiated*. We are set on a path at a tender young age to either be the idealized, helpful, passive feminine MISORs, or we are cast aside and forced to inhabit a role where we can have our brilliance, sexuality, or unique abilities—but we are not allowed to be both, at least not in the beginning. Women are only offered the preferred version, and anything else is doomed to being "outside" the norms and standards, even when these are unachievable or undesirable. In mythologies from movies to sacred literature, power is not for those born to become women. Women who seek power become MIPEs.

The MISOR woman acts in a way that fits our stereotypes of passive femininity. MISORs are pretty, maternal, allowing, and often perform being demure. They want children and a family or at least know that is the key to acceptance. They understand the need to be of service to men and patriarchal institutions. The MISOR is the only version of female behavior that is valued in patriarchy. Meanwhile, the MIPE is the odd one out. She may play with boys as a child. She may long for a career in fields traditionally occupied by men. She values her intellect, her body, her power, her work ethic—likely all these. She is baffled by finding that the more she uses the powers given to her—intelligence, strength, magic, intuition, sexuality, cunning— the more she is pushed away from the center of power, whether that's as a daughter, wife, professional, or member of a community.

The Divided Woman Arrives for Brunch

I spent a fortune on quiche. More than a hundred tiny pies the size of a silver dollar covered the sideboard. I'd never seen so many mini quiches in my life. I definitely overbought, but also didn't want anyone to go hungry. I stacked them in pyramids according to their flavors: quiche Lorraine, tomato and mushroom, broccoli and cheese. They reminded me of a fourth-grade social studies project on Mayan pyramids. Nervous, I ate a few stray pies as I put the finishing touches together. I handwrote the flavors on tiny wooden signs with a chalk pen. I laid out the china, reminiscent of the place settings my grandmother bought in Italy on her honeymoon. The plates and their gold-painted edges brought back fond memories of parties at her house. Graceful flutes for the champagne and cloth napkins were all there for the taking. Champagne and orange juice sat next to the towers of quiche on my sideboard. The champagne chilled in a steel ice bucket, while the orange juice waited in a fancy glass pitcher built with a special ice bath to keep it cold. There were other goodies all around: fresh fruit, turkey bacon, scrambled eggs, bagels, lox, cream cheese, tomatoes, capers, Greek yogurt, fresh berries, and challah French toast with organic maple syrup.

The food was a pacifier. Research has shown that hungry people are more critical. Trial judges reportedly give more harsh sentences just before lunch and more lenient ones after.[2] I was hoping for a judgment but didn't want it to be handed down too harshly. I had been working on the theory outlining the Queen's Path for two years, and this Sunday morning, I was going to put it in front of some of the smartest people I knew. A doctor, two lawyers, several writers, two former students, animation professionals, and a cardiac nurse, several of them colleagues from graduate school, graced my house with their brilliant minds. I invited them to tear the theory, and me, apart. If the ideas weren't well received, I at least wanted to impress my guests with the spread. I'm a sixth-generation New Orleanian, so hospitality and good food are in my DNA. I hoped they would enjoy the menu enough to smooth over harsh words with thoughtful critique.

I had an idea about what to do with the research, but it seemed so broad that I was intimidated by the scope. I wanted my friends and colleagues to help me figure out how to make it less academic and more accessible to the people I wanted to reach: storytellers, therapists, women—anyone who had a stake in what it means for women to construct narratives or for anyone writing women's stories themselves.

I spoke quickly to my guests about the discovery—that wicked witch and princess were prescriptions, options based on what sort of desire women are allowed to pursue. The women stared at me. I became nervous, not sure what was happening in the group as they noshed on their quiche Lorraine. I learned later from every woman there that hearing my theory was shocking; they described it as though someone had finally locked the missing pieces of a puzzle together. But in the moment, the stares and drawn breaths seemed like boredom or disdain. Rachel sat back in her chair. Patricia sat forward, focused on me. Merle took notes on a yellow legal pad, as did David, but his were in a hardbound notebook. I scanned the room and had nearly everyone's attention. I couldn't tell what anyone was thinking, but no one made me more anxious than Sandra.

My friend Sandra shifted in her seat uncomfortably. I met her in graduate school at Pacifica Graduate Institute. In our tiny cohort, she was one of the smartest. She had conquered nursing school, imaging programs, yoga teacher training, and another master's degree by this point. Small and strong, she always seemed to me like her soul was too big for her body, as though it was desperate to take up more space—but didn't dare. Sandra stared at me with an intensity I mistook for anger.

I explained the core ideas. I spoke to my guests about examples from mythology, literature, film, and theater. The longer I talked, the more uncomfortable Sandra became. When I had gotten through my presentation but before the group was set to ask questions, she excused herself and said she was feeling ill and would send me her notes. I was relieved that the look I saw from her might be that she was physically unwell and not a response to my work. Sandra left, and I continued with my other guests in very productive discussions for two hours, discussing holes in my presentation and answering questions about the MISOR and the MIPE.

We discussed why the theory mattered, who it was for, and how it could be used. My friend Patricia argued that calling it "The Queen's Path" was a bad idea. She had grown up in Scotland in council housing when Margaret Thatcher was prime minister. Trisha's idea of a Queen was someone who took from you without caring if you were safe or well-fed. She felt that I'd need to change the name to appeal to readers in the UK. Several people asked me why I didn't use archetypes everyone understood already. I explained that the existing titles were packed with so much baggage, it would be impossible to discern the new ideas from the old structures. Most of my guests gave me excellent feedback, had thoughtful questions, and suggested important edits. I was deeply grateful.

When everyone had left, I felt very satisfied and only mildly beaten up. I went to my office to write up some notes and found that I had a long e-mail from Sandra. In it, she outlined that my presentation had made her see why she had been so confused and sad for the majority of her life—constantly struggling with depression. She described how, as the oldest of four children in her family, she had always been given a great deal of responsibility. Sandra had struggled to understand that no matter how much she pursued education, degrees, and financial success, her family rarely acknowledged her. They shamed her for being too "manly." They constantly asked her why she wasn't married with children and berated her despite her many accomplishments. She pursued men who wanted families and children, mostly because it aligned with what her family wanted for her and what she was raised to want for herself. But every man she dated wanted her to do less, be less, and make herself smaller so that she didn't outshine him. She saw in my presentation that she had been a MIPE in a world that only recognized the MISOR. And she wanted many things that are traditionally associated with the MISOR. She wanted a family and children, but she had been trying to be part of the MISOR world with her MIPE credentials. She couldn't negate her intelligence, strength, and ambition. She reported that she had spent her life hoping to be recognized by her family and chosen for her accomplishments. But her family and the men she had dated wanted a woman who didn't have any talents, gifts, or accomplishments. They all wanted her to find her sole meaning and purpose in serving her partner and her family.

It was in this moment that I understood the power in naming the Divided Woman. Sandra had done everything she felt was right and meaningful to honor her intellect and abilities while trying to be a "good girl." She had wanted to "have it all." Sandra was a MIPE and had never realized it—constantly doubling down on her authenticity. She used her MIPE talents and skills in hopes of scoring MISOR points. The more her parents and family pushed her, the more she used her innate gifts—her intellect, ambition, and even her athleticism. Sandra's family expected her to use those gifts to achieve the MISOR goal of marriage and family. Anything else was unseemly.

Sandra wrote that she was grateful for the research and that it would be a little while before she'd be ready to discuss it again. She was going to take this insight to her therapist and try to better understand how she had internalized the expectations put on her as she struggled to be authentic to herself while also acquiescing to her family. She wrote that she finally understood why she had to live thousands of miles away from them. She was sad, but she offered that she finally had the clarity that she had struggled to find for the last several years. I broke into tears at my desk. I hadn't quite realized the impact of my discovery until I received Sandra's e-mail.

Invisible and Divided

The Divided Woman is one of the central parts of this research. The archetype is complex but easy to recognize once you learn her attributes. When she is in her divided state, she appears as either powerless or magical. She arrives either a Maiden in Search of Relationship (MISOR) as the familiar damsel in distress, princess, or cheerleader or she appears as Magical, Isolated, Powerful, and Endangered (MIPE), someone with power outside of the norm, like a witch, intellectual, or warrior. The Divide takes an undifferentiated girl and places her on the track of one of those two options.

I get asked a lot why I created new names for these archetypes rather than rely on ones that everyone already understands. The answer is implied in the question itself. There is too much baggage in the titles we have already defined. The assumptions about MISORs and MIPEs using existing archetypes are already very biased. We think of Cinderella or Snow White as innocent young maidens, incapable of harm. We wouldn't naturally put Snow White in the same category as Regina George from *Mean Girls*. But both are MISORs using beauty, passivity (even if performative), and availability to get resources, attention, relationships, or protection. Meanwhile, we associate the MIPE with the Wicked Witch of the West, Elphaba from *Wicked*, or Villanelle from *Killing Eve*. But would you think of Diana Princess of Wales as a MIPE? Or Margot Robbie's eponymous Barbie from Greta Gerwig's *Barbie*? What about Offred/June Osborne, from *The Handmaid's Tale*?

I chose these descriptive acronyms precisely because they don't come prepackaged with the overly positive and negative attributes that *princess* and *witch* already bring to the table. A MISOR can be an antagonist, and a MIPE can be the protagonist. A MIPE can bring out as much compassion as a MISOR. Contrary to our automatic assumptions, the princess-like MISOR can long for a life filled with power. A MIPE, whom we would normally align with the wicked witch, can long to be a mother.

According to archetypal psychologists Carl Jung and James Hillman, archetypes aren't created, they are eternal—they always exist. It is how we name them that changes—the symbols that emerge from those spaces morph over time. We have been living with two archetypes that fit together like puzzle pieces for thousands of years. We have treated them as though they are enemies of one another, and indeed they are often portrayed that way. But they are two halves of a divided being—a woman being told that one side is acceptable, and the other is not. How she navigates those definitions is the core work for any woman following the Queen's Path.

MISOR or MIPE?

Throughout this book, I'm going to ask you to reflect, write, and maybe even draw. A journal or notebook will be helpful. This first exercise will help orient you on your first steps of the Queen's Path. One of the gifts of Frank L. Baum's book, *The Wonderful Wizard of Oz,* is the notion that the word *witch* isn't only for those women who would use their magical powers maliciously. In the 1939 film version, Dorothy arrives in Oz having accidentally dropped a house on the Wicked Witch of the East. Glenda the Good Witch of the North asks her, "Are you a good witch or a bad witch?" There had been few depictions in popular culture of magical women having any "good" potential. For the first entry in your journal, I have an exercise that will set the stage for you to understand your own journey through the Queen's Path. Similar to Glenda's question to Dorothy, with a slight twist, are you more MISOR or MIPE? No woman is 100 percent either—indeed, that is the point of this book. All of us are placed into the role of one or the other, despite the fact that each of us contain traits and display behaviors of both. How we reconcile this, and overcome it, determines our own personal expression of the archetypal Queen's Path.

For your first exercise, let's look at whether or not you tend more toward the MISOR or MIPE.

I've prepared a quiz to help guide you along the path. It's not meant to be all-encompassing but to give you guidance as to whether you lean more toward the Maiden in Search of Relationship (MISOR) or Magical, Isolated, Powerful, and Endangered (MIPE) archetype. No woman is all one or the other, but every one of us gets placed on either the MISOR or MIPE track. Recognizing that track puts us on the Queen's Path to sovereignty. Let's look at where you may be more likely to find yourself.

For each question, respond with a yes or no. At the end we'll tally up the scores and determine if you're more in the camp of the MISOR or MIPE. Sometimes it helps to read the questions aloud. At the end, we'll tally up and look at some interpretations.

- Growing up, I had the freedom to do what I wanted with very little parental intervention.
- In my childhood, I liked playing with dolls and "girly" things.
- I feel comfortable when I defer to someone else's authority.
- Looking feminine is important to me.
- Sex is something I do for my partner, it's not really for me.
- I prefer to be in a support role rather than a leadership position.

- I believe women should be protected from certain types of work.

- My faith tells me I should defer to a higher authority, and I agree.

- If I must choose between being liked or respected, I prefer to be liked.

- People often tell me I'm intimidating.

- Having a husband or parents to support and protect me is important to me.

- I'd prefer to be a stay-at-home mom than a working mom.

- I believe innocence and deference are desirable characteristics in a woman.

- I'm okay with earning more money or having more authority than my romantic partner.

- Romantically I prefer to be pursued.

- In most situations I feel more comfortable being the leader.

- I often feel like I'm behind and need to catch up to peers or people I admire.

- I believe men and women have different roles and responsibilities for a reason.

Subtract the number of yes responses from the number of no responses. Above 0 toward a score of 8 means you are more likely to see yourself in the MIPE archetype. If you score below 0, you are more likely to see yourself in the MISOR archetype.

MISOR vs MIPE scale

-8	PURE MISOR
-6	
-4	
-2	
0	
2	
4	
6	
8	PURE MIPE

Sovereignty Redefined

Sovereignty is defined as the right to authority, ownership, or rule. The word has been reserved for governments and historically has been tied to regents, kings, and queens. Being sovereign over something means to have absolute ownership, and thus the right to do as you please with what one is sovereign over. In respect to modern governments, sovereignty is recognized as the right of a defined nation to determine its own destiny without interference from other sovereign nations. However, with the publication of the Universal Declaration of Human Rights by the United Nations General Assembly in 1948, the idea of sovereignty gained a new dimension. It put forth the idea that the sovereignty of nations is *derived from* the sovereignty of the individual. Governments exist in service to their people, not the other way around.[3]

But sovereignty for human beings inside the state has been difficult to achieve, most often because self-sovereignty is not in the best interest of those who have greater access to resources, whether we are talking about money, food, water, land, or power. Women's rights as autonomous human beings haven't been enshrined in culture for very long, and they aren't protected equally across the board. Only 14 countries in the world have full legal protections for women under the law. Belgium, Canada, Denmark, France, Germany, Greece, Iceland, Ireland, Latvia, Luxembourg, The Netherlands, Portugal, Spain, and Sweden all have explicit legal rights of equality granted for women.[4] That's just over 7 percent (7.2 percent) of the world's 195 countries that make up the United Nations. It's even less when you consider that there are 243 sovereign nations in the world, reducing the percentage down to just under 6 percent (5.8 percent). The United States doesn't make the list, having no formal enumeration of rights for women, only the tacit understanding that women are included in the protections of the U.S. Constitution.[5]

Women's sovereignty is not a new concept. The 14th-century poet Geoffrey Chaucer, author of *The Canterbury Tales*, wrote about women's sovereignty in *The Wife of Bath's Tale*. Politicians and members of the clergy have debated the rights of women for millennia. Women have rarely been included in the historical determination of our rights. Cultures that have repressive attitudes toward women's sovereignty point to long-held cultural beliefs to justify the disenfranchisement of women from the right to education, meaningful labor, voting, work, self-sufficiency, and reproductive freedom. But just because something is culturally defined doesn't mean that it cannot change.

The history of women as handmaids to patriarchal cultures is long. It comes out of the development of war as a means of rule, which has been ongoing for thousands of years. Colonization and conquest require violence as the force that keeps people under the control of the conquering power. The more complex the society, the more we depend on violence or the threat of violence to maintain order. When societies are smaller, there is no need for hierarchies based on the threat of violence.

Equality is a threat to the idea of conquest, because it gives a higher-level imprimatur to the protection of women and minorities. The bottom line of sovereignty is that every individual of the age of majority has the same rights as every other. They enjoy (in principle) the same access to resources. That is not to say that there is no competition. But rather that basic human rights are to be assumed, and any one person's ability to expand their wealth or capacity through their own creativity is in and of itself a sovereign right. There are, of course, some legal limits—that's what happens when people live in a society together. My sovereign right to self-determination doesn't allow me to commandeer your new Ferrari and call it my own. That would be me infringing on *your* sovereignty. The concept can be tricky once we get into how the state may intervene when some rights are enumerated and others are tacit. But the bottom line of sovereignty is that it is the right of every individual to own herself (or himself) without fear of infringement and with the expectation of equal treatment under the law.

As a result, sovereignty becomes an individual practice. Women (and minorities) can engage in behaviors that protect their sovereignty. They can create protections and organizations to align their concerns before government bodies. Sovereignty can become a practice in the community. It becomes a practice at home, when we teach our children that they have the right to decide to whom they give physical affection. It becomes a practice when women and men in relationships decide the division of labor in their homes, rather than relying on old gender stereotypes. Sovereignty becomes a practice when violence is no longer a default that keeps some people in submission and others in power over them.

Sovereignty is thus an internal system based on an external, international acceptance of the rights of the individual. A woman who lives under the rule of a violent system can hold an internal knowledge that though she may lack the power to oust her oppressor, she can find the places of sovereignty within herself. She gets to guard her personal thoughts and beliefs from anyone who might wish to replace her internal beliefs with external authority. She can cultivate an internal expectation, that may one day open the door to her breathing the full air of her liberation. When a woman (or any oppressed person) has achieved this internal knowledge of her true nature, she has sovereignty over herself.

The symbol of sovereignty has universally been depicted as something worn on the head, usually a crown. One could argue, though, that while some forms of head covering have been linked to submission (a nun's veil, the hijab), they are just as easily transformed into symbols of sovereignty for the women who reclaim their meaning to determine their own destiny. Women who became nuns in the Middle Ages usually did so to be free of marriage and childbearing to focus on learning and service, and the veil for them was simultaneously a symbol of service to God and freedom from the service of marriage and reproduction. For many devout Muslim women, the hijab is a symbol of their autonomy, symbolizing their sovereign adherence to faith, not their blind obedience to it.

Sovereignty will be expressed by different women in different ways. That is what this book is ultimately about. Though each woman's sovereignty will be different, her path to get there will have an archetypal dimension. Archetypes exist whether we believe in them or not. According to Jung, we most often live out archetypes when we are not aware of them. The more we attempt to stay out of the archetypal realm, the greater its force will be upon our lives.

How can all women navigate this archetypal pattern that I have named the Queen's Path? We may not be able to rout out all the negative impacts the cultures of conquest have created for our world. But we can free our minds and hearts to create a more just world so that all women can experience sovereignty as their birthright.

What's Next

We will wind through the Queen's Path with an eye on both internal and external narratives. A word of caution, though: This model explodes the idea of women as heroes or heroines. It's not that women cannot be heroes or heroines, but rather that without sovereignty a heroine is always going to be an outsider, a MIPE. That means that even if she is on a heroine's quest, she must also take the Queen's Path. She may succeed in her goal, but she will fail in her hero's quest if she doesn't first gain sovereignty. This model, like many before it, can help organize stories from screenplays and novels to personal essays or psychotherapeutic reflections. As an archetypal model, it is a guide, not an absolute. Gather up your notebook and colored pens, and let's set our glass slippers and pointy shoes along the first steps of the Queen's Path.

CHAPTER 2

THE DIVIDED WOMAN

In *The Prince,* Niccolò Machiavelli described what he called the "mathematical sense," a strategy of war first made known in the West by the Greek king Philip of Macedonia. Machiavelli called it *divide et impera,* better known in English as "divide and conquer."[1] The words have become hollow after centuries of use, as we have become somewhat detached from their deepest and most nuanced meaning.

In the current political climate, we see it in the division of people into factions. We maintain our ties within groups based not only on what we collectively agree upon but also on excising those who do not meet standards of purity with regards to group ideals. But the meaning of Machiavelli's phrase proves even more sinister, implying that the best way to wage and win war is to separate people from trusting in themselves and *then* ruling over them. Confuse them. Make them doubt themselves. Replace their own internal sense of knowing with an external authority. Divide et impera can also be translated as "render and dominate."

Deep within the framework of fairy tales and children's films, I uncovered a set of feminine archetypes that are the result of divide et impera, hidden in plain sight for thousands of years across the Western canon. I didn't expect to find them, and yet there they were, staring out at me as I first dove into innocent fairytales and children's films, modern retellings of *Sleeping Beauty* and *The Snow*

Queen. I saw over and over again that if we look at almost any depiction of femaleness, whether it is in literature, religious texts, film, or television, we will see a girl being forced into one of two paths. She is either groomed for a safe, domestic life of service and childrearing or banished to a life of magic, isolation, and power.

In both narratives, the girl is cut off from one side of herself and grows up separated from her counterpart self. If she accepts the role of the domestic life, she is welcomed into society, albeit in a prescribed role. She learns never to expect power or sovereignty. But she may enjoy protection provided by her family or partner. If instead she embraces the role of power, she is promised a life of enchantment but can't necessarily expect love or a family. In almost every place I looked, I found a girl or woman cut off from her whole self. I found her in Disney films from 1937's *Snow White and the Seven Dwarfs* through 2013's *Frozen*. I found her in traditional films like *Gone With the Wind, Titanic,* and *Thelma and Louise,* and in iconic fantasy characters like Daenerys Targaryen and Cersei Lannister from *Game of Thrones.* I found her in popular television characters like Sydney Bristow from *Alias*, Samantha and Serena from *Bewitched*, and Serena Joy and June Osborne in *The Handmaid's Tale*, and many more. I found her on Broadway too, in plays from *Wicked* to *Waitress.*

Does a woman learn to be demure and quiet to gain the favor of powerful people around her? Maybe these are parents, teachers, or members of her religious community. Or does she follow a desire to identify with her body, or her intelligence, and defy the power that surrounds her in favor of a power within her? If she follows her own will, she is likely to have to go it alone. If she stays in the lane prescribed for her by culture, she may never fulfill her potential. Every woman holds both possibilities, so it is unfair to consider that any individual woman would be 100 percent MISOR or MIPE. The secret is that the Divide is itself a trap. We are pushed to be 100 percent in one camp or the other. The truth is that while we may fulfill those roles exceptionally well, no woman is all role and zero human. To reclaim herself, every woman must account for how much she has given away in her attempt to belong to the roles prescribed to her by culture.

Whether she is a MISOR or MIPE, when she is reunited with her counterpart, she becomes sovereign. In stories, she is usually then depicted as a Queen either literally or symbolically. In the film *The Woman King*, General Nanisca saves her country and her sister warriors, eventually ascending the throne. In the animated feature *Moana*, our eponymous leader successfully staves off a famine. In the end, she dons a crown of flowers and captains the fleet to explore new lands. In the life of Malala Yousufzai, she survives an assassination attempt and goes on to attend Oxford University and become the youngest recipient of the Nobel Peace Prize in history. In these and thousands of other stories, women characters successfully navigate the Queen's Path.

When they reach the final stage of their journey, they overcome the prescriptions of cultured gender norms. In this stage, they are almost always depicted wearing something on their heads. The journey to sovereignty allows them to ascend the throne of self-determination. In my original research, I called the character reconnected from the rendered halves the United Queen, because she was rent asunder early in her life and is brought together again and made whole. In being reunited, she enjoys a new set of qualities that make her unique in her self-sovereignty. She has experienced the division of her identity, and as such has a new, wise, and deep perspective on humanity.

In her human form, the Queen owns herself. She is her own imperator in life, she is in command, no one has her under their rule, she is no longer divided or conquered. She fully decides the *imperative* of her life, and this drives her forward without having to become secondary to any societal model of ownership or childlike dependence. Discovering her and her multiple constituent parts has completely changed my life, in most ways making everything better. In some ways, discovering her has made me profoundly sad. Avoiding the Divided Woman for myself, my friends, my mother, my daughter, and my patients has proved impossible. Mostly, discovering her has healed my own divided self.

This archetype offers a model of hope to any woman who has endured the experience of being rendered, divided against herself. In the last several decades, there have been many movements to rediscover her. Different communities of women have created rituals and reading groups to help women find an archetypal model of empowerment. You can find her at the Sacred Table, the Red Tent, Cakes for the Queen of Heaven, the Full Moon Circle, the Croning Ceremony, or anywhere women gather to know themselves better. Where you find Her, you will find your Self. You will find her in these pages; you will find her in your own heart and in your own history. Through your journey to bind the rendered space, you will climb the steps to your own throne, and you will touch your hands to the crown that is your feminine birthright and become the Queen of your own sovereign life.

No woman starts out a Queen. She gets there through a journey that illuminates her path within cultures that seek to define her. In no culture on Earth do individual women have the sole responsibility for that definition. The next pages will introduce you in detail to the MISOR and the MIPE, the archetypes of the Divide, and will follow up with some recognizable examples. My purpose is to underline the role the Divided Woman plays in every woman's life. We are not placed on this road by accident. We do not put ourselves into the Divide. We tread the path innocent and unknowing of what lies ahead, blind to the Divide that will consume us. We all know the Divide, but no one names it for us. No one tells us about it, mostly because our mothers and grandmothers were kept in the dark about it too. They didn't know its terrain, but they can describe the scars they received walking it. Don't blame your foremothers; they didn't have a map either.

Maiden in Search of Relationship (MISOR)

We know her, the pretty girl. She's the cheerleader, the homemaker, the princess. She is demure, lithe, and deferential. She is one of the first versions of woman we are taught growing up. She lies behind the constant pressure from our parents and teachers to "be nice!" She represents the ideal feminine in most of the world. In fairy tales, she shows up as Cinderella, Snow White, and Sleeping Beauty. In Christianity, she's the Blessed Mother or Virgin Mary. It's this version we want to be when we play with our Barbie and Skipper dolls. She's the one our grandmothers encourage. She's the one that teachers endorse. She's polite and well-behaved and shows off her manners.

As children, girls are expected to be courteous and polite. We are taught young to tolerate bad behavior in favor of keeping the peace. As teenagers we are taught to align ourselves with other girls in support of the boys and men in our communities. We are admonished to not walk alone, dress modestly, and idealize virginity. We are given purity rings and directed to not give into our own desire or pleasure, saving these for one lone man who is supposed to fulfill our every longing. Sex is for men, not for us. We are taught that we are "pretty" for a reason. To be looked at is a gift of attention we should foster, encourage, and be responsive to. Being a "good" woman means that we don't mind objectification; we know that it's just part of culture.

Writing this section proved difficult. The more I engaged in the research to support this chapter, the more I struggled to make sense of my conflicted feelings. The MISOR ideal is everywhere. I studied some of the writers who espouse these ideals wholeheartedly. I read books by antifeminist commentators. I attended a debate between conservative and progressive women about whether the sexual revolution had failed. It is often difficult for me to see where these women are coming from. But the reality is that they represent a version of womanhood that is real and valid. I don't always understand or agree with them. I have after all, been a MIPE most of my life. My dreams, hopes, and ambitions have been defined by being outside of the MISOR ideals. However, to do feminist justice to all women, I must endeavor to look past my biases as much as possible and hear what the MISOR women have to say about themselves. I let them tell me their story. I will do my utmost best to represent that here.

It isn't surprising that many of the MISOR ideals permeate our culture. The MISOR ideals of beauty, nurturing, deference, submission, and likability show up in stories about and research on women. In 2017, the Pew Research Center, a leading think tank in Washington DC, published a report on gender differences in the United States. The report was compiled from survey data of Pew's American Trends Panel (ATP). The ATP is a collection of survey participants who have been recruited over several years to report on nationwide trends. In the 2017 study, participants were asked a series of multiple-choice, scaled, and open-ended questions about the place of gender in American culture. There were 4,573 respondents who took part in their study on gender differences.

The study examined attitudes about how men and women are viewed in society. In it, the highest attribute associated with being a woman was being attractive. Seventy-one percent (71 percent) of women in the study reported that they felt social pressure to be attractive compared to less than 30 percent of men (27 percent). In the study, both male and female participants ranked attractiveness as the social value that was most desirably associated with women (35 percent), with empathy, nurturing, and kindness coming in second (30 percent). The Pew study found that only 32 percent of people in the survey looked up to "feminine women." Of that 32 percent, an outsize percentage within that group (83 percent) reported that they found this to be a "good thing." Women also reported that it was important for women to be seen by other women as feminine, with over 50 percent (52 percent) reporting that it is at the very least "somewhat important" to be seen as "traditionally" feminine.[2]

The MISOR is the version of womanhood that cultures across the world have held up as the ideal of female virtue. Chaste, pretty, and demure, the MISOR can be found throughout mythology, sacred literature, and our everyday experience. Author and homemaking expert Alena Pettit describes this ideal in her book, *Ladies Like Us*, as being "ladylike." She describes this idealized version as "bright, sweet-spirited, kind, reliable, modest, sensitive to people's needs, and always honest." She also describes this as a "princess ideal" and encourages women that regardless of their social position, they can become princesses.[3] She assures her readers that "we all want to be princesses." She claims, "We want to be beautiful, to be treated with respect, to not have burdens or cares about the harsh realities of life. To live in comfort, security, and to be adored for who we are and our radiant beauty."[4] Alena Pettit writes books and teaches classes on traditional homemaking. She sees herself not as an ambitious entrepreneur but as a dutiful wife and homemaker who is sharing her expertise with other women who want a life like hers.

The MISOR has enjoyed a bit of a resurgence in the last several years. Women around the world idealize her as the path to security.

There is a contemporary movement that crystallizes this aesthetic. Whether as a response to the failures of contemporary feminism or as an outright rejection of it, the Traditional Wife or TradWife movement has become very popular in the last several years. Women who espouse these principles proudly call themselves homemakers and extoll the relationship benefits of being submissive to their husbands. Primarily the space of Christian women who want to live their traditional values, the TradWife movement started to show up around 2020, but its origin story begins much earlier, in the mid-20th century.

In her 1963 book, *Fascinating Womanhood*, author Helen B. Andelin explains that to have the kind of life women want, we must understand what *men* want. She encourages her readers to consider that women need to think of themselves as merging both angelic and human aspects. Her book explains that men want to admire women and be admired by them. While the book itself is considered a tome of modern anti-feminism, it demonstrates a critical principle that I have named the Divide. In Andelin's examination of what makes an "ideal" woman, she describes the need to be angelic in the sense of being "above the fray," divinely inspired toward her duties and not engaged in behavior that would embarrass her or her family. On the flip side, her human nature can come out in being sensual, desirable, and demanding respect.[5] While Andelin and I might disagree on what those divided pieces mean, or how to reunite them, she clearly saw the Divide at work.

A devout Mormon and mother of seven children, Andelin's work asserts that the ideal between a man and a woman is "celestial love." She affirms that this love will inspire men to behave in a manner consistent with their ideals and that this will (mostly) protect women from bad behavior. She extolls her readers to accept men "at face value." By doing so, the woman expects no change from her partner, for that "breeds resentment, destroys love, and causes problems in the marriage."[6] In the end, she posits that trying to change a man just doesn't work and leaves both parties frustrated. Change from him will come organically by his own will, or not at all. From a psychological perspective, I cannot argue with this. Change only comes from within by those who desire it.

Andelin's work has become a touchstone for the TradWife movement. A TradWife stays home, raises children, engages in homemaking tasks, cooks meals, and decorates. She might manage a household budget, but the husband has all the authority in the home. TradWives idealize representations of the 1950-60s TV housewife who made homecooked meals, kept an immaculate home, and always had fresh-baked cookies at the ready. Their images can be found all over social media in perfectly coiffed hair, neat aprons, and pretty dresses. These women assure other women through social media, books, and websites that women and men are equal but have different responsibilities. They insist that it is in these responsibilities that women should submit their will to their husbands. Women who participate claim that after embracing the TradWife lifestyle, their homes are peaceful, whereas prior they were filled with acrimony. Most ascribe this to the belief that their attempts at working and balancing a home made them resentful of their husbands and the workplace. By staying home and taking on a traditional role, she no longer worries about the outside world. She doesn't have to fight about sharing household responsibilities because there is now a clear division of labor.

TikTok star Estee Williams claims that her purpose in life is to be a good wife to her husband. She sees her job as keeping a beautiful, clean home and serving her husband delicious meals. She performs these duties in hopes that he will consider himself lucky to have her. She somehow also manages to record these activities and post them on social media while looking like she's got a hair and makeup team just off camera. While she wears dresses that are reminiscent of June Cleaver of *Leave It to Beaver* fame, her performance and persona embody more Marilyn Monroe. With her bouncy blonde bob haircut and voluptuous frame, Estee Williams embodies the MISOR ideal, easily realized in Andelin's combination of angelic and human.

You need only watch a handful of Williams's videos to get the TradWife vibe. With over a million views and multiple articles and controversies, Williams is the current social media star of the TradWife movement. Her videos range in content from cooking videos and sweet moments with her husband to social commentary. In MISOR fashion, her videos often feature her just "looking pretty" and posing while her captions tell the story she wants to convey. In other words, she is often silent. One video in particular starts with her looking innocently into the camera, while a caption reads, "Society wants me to go work for someone 9-5." Her demeanor shifts into a knowing and slightly bemused look, while the caption changes to read "What they don't realize is that my husband works for me."

The implication of course is that her role is as an object of worship, not one of scorn. Indeed, the whole message of this movement as described in the books of Alena Pettit, Helen B. Andelin, or the videos of Estee Willliams is that women and men are equal but have separate and very different roles and responsibilities. Men's roles are to be protective and to work for money outside of the home. Women's roles are to be helpmeets to men, keep a home, and raise children. As such, ideal women are deferential and elevate homemaking and childrearing. Any desires outside of their roles are secondary. Careers, vocations, or artistic endeavors are not as important as upholding the role of idealized feminine partner.

The TradWife movement is a modern example of how the role of the MISOR is produced and reproduced in culture. While this new incarnation may help make her more noticeable, the ideals of the MISOR have been around for a long time. Finding them is not difficult. The MISOR's familiar traits include the following:

- Looks or appears innocent
- Focuses on relationships
- Is available for the needs of those around her
- Power is attached to a man or her family
- Idealized as a sexual object, but is not supposed to be sexual
- Is intuitive and understanding
- Needs protection
- Is likable
- Submits to authority
- Is demure and obedient

In looking for the modern MISOR, I found her everywhere. She's easy to find in film, television, mythology, and literature. But I also needed to find her in the real world, in places where women live and struggle to make sense of their experiences. In the United States, the place where the real-life MISOR turned up the loudest was in evangelical Christianity.

I researched many voices in Christian women's circles. All shared messages for women to lead lives of meaning in faith. Some voices seemed more generous than others. Some of these women's work moved me, and some of their messages appalled me. Two Texan evangelical sisters stood out for me as examples of the MISOR ideals personified. Blonde, bubbly, and making it clear they want to connect, Kristen Clark and Bethany Beal burst through my screen as MISORs in human form. The sisters have a social media–driven ministry with content across YouTube and Instagram. They have written books and have a website filled with content. Their messages are heartfelt, though there are some red flags and gross misrepresentations that show up from time to time, like their assertion that feminists want abortion on demand up until full term, a patent falsehood embraced and promoted by the religious right. The sisters assert in the bio on their website, girldefined.com, that they "dabbled in the modeling industry" before launching their ministry in 2014. This idealization of beauty as a profession lines up very well with modern MISOR identities. The rejection of objectification for money is also 100 percent in line with the MISOR's message. This is how they describe themselves:

> Since launching Girl Defined Ministries in 2014, our goal has always been the same—to help modern girls understand and live out God's timeless truth for womanhood. In a day and age when girls and women receive so many conflicting messages about their value, purpose, and identity, they desperately need to know that the only one who can define them is the One who created them.[7]

The MISOR message is replete through this one statement of purpose. The words *girl* and *woman* are used interchangeably, a common vernacular in the Southern United States but one that keeps women infantilized in discourse. They connect their "Girl

Defined" with "God's timeless truth for womanhood." This reflects back on the MISOR ideal of women's power being under an authority external to her. For the sisters, the authority they rely upon as a means for defining womanly virtue is the Christian Bible. They claim that only God can tell a woman her definition, as she is ultimately a *subject,* in this instance to God. A woman cannot define herself because she has been given a set of instructions by the Creator himself. Anything less is sacrilege at worst or misinformed feminism at best. They don't discuss if men are expected to adhere to the same requirements.

Watching their videos and reading their books shows that their desire to connect is palpable. They are sweet—endearing, even. Kristen and Bethany clearly believe in their message. They tout their Texas credentials; everything is bigger in Texas—even faith. Their presentation is 100 percent the recognizable MISOR: thin, pretty, helpful, and sweet. Just a cursory view of the topics on their website reveals their MISOR priorities. There are a mere 6 posts on addiction, 12 on college, and 17 on boundaries. Meanwhile as of this writing, there are 62 posts on beauty, 42 on body image, and 106 on femininity.[8] They make an honest effort at transparency, always mediated through the lens of faithful service to God. Their writing focuses on how to live a MISOR life through the lens of contemporary evangelical Christianity.

Most troubling about the sisters' message for me was the absolute certainty with which they approach their topic. They see what they call the "cultural checklist" as the problem. Defined as the constantly shifting expectations given to women by culture, their critique feels appropriate. The cultural changes that yank us around are certainly unkind to women, the goalposts always changing to fit the moment. Their response, to look to the authority of the Bible as the touchstone for femininity, gender, and behavior, aligns exactly with the MISOR message. The MISOR is always subject to the authority of someone else. Family, institution, scripture, husband, culture . . . they all have a claim on her before her own desires. Kristen and Bethany write that they had to consider their goals as though they were aiming at a target.[9] To hit the target, they had to have the right tools. For them, the ultimate tool is the authority of the Christian Bible. The MISOR always defers to an authority greater than herself. It is in this deference that she is empowered. She borrows authority from the power she is submissive to. Her power is not her own, but comes from a family, scripture, husband, or religious belief.

Scripture is one of the first places we encounter the expectations put upon us by culture. In the Christian and Hebrew texts, there are clear messages about how to be a "good" woman, with multiple examples of appropriate behavior or punishment for any possible transgression. The overriding messages to the MISOR are "be compliant" and "accept the authority over you." On the surface, there is nothing wrong with the MISOR. She strives to be kind, generous, beautiful, and thoughtful. But can a woman achieve her true fullness if she is a subject to authority? Kristen and Bethany would likely argue that the answer is yes, if it is God's authority you submit to. However, how does any woman come to know herself if submission is all she knows?

Another place to find the MISOR is at home. She is Disney's Snow White keeping house for the Seven Dwarfs. She is Celie in *The Color Purple,* her superpower being cleaning and organizing Mister's messy home. We find her in Dianne Wiest's Peg, the helpful suburban housewife in *Edward Scissorhands.* She's June Cleaver in *Leave it to Beaver,* and Serena Joy in *The Handmaid's Tale.* We know the MISOR by her comfort in the home.

The MISOR feels comfortable taking care of a family and children and making a welcoming and peaceful home. She may enjoy the tasks associated with domestic life like cooking and caring for children. Even if she doesn't enjoy these tasks, a MISOR sees these as "natural" extensions of being a woman. She likely has a health regimen that keeps her attractive and healthy. She participates in her children's schooling and educational community. She plans meals, birthday parties, vacations, and welcomes guests for holidays and events. She is often a gifted hostess, cooking or catering meals. She looks out for her community in these ways, bringing gifts of food for a potluck or sending a homemade dish to a community member in mourning or need.

An unmarried MISOR will likely live at home with her family or with other women. She may like an orderly and clean space. She will idealize peace and ease in her relationships and may sublimate her desires in service to the expectations placed on her through family, culture, or community. The MISOR at home will keep the peace. She'll try to make everyone happy, but that doesn't mean she can't be stern. She will follow the rules and expect others to do so as well. She may impose rules on those around her, with the intention of not conflicting with greater cultural expectations, social ideals, or religious rules. She wants to be seen as the "good girl" by her family, community, and in her own expectations of herself.

If a MISOR is working, she likely has to. You'll find her in a profession that feels safe for a woman. She's a teacher, nurse, waitress, pediatrician, social worker, or family attorney. She is someone who follows the rules. She wants very much to be treated respectfully. But she will defer to authority, whether that's her immediate supervisor, a doctor, a judge, or the CEO of a company. She is compliant and rarely will make waves unless there's some mistreatment happening. The MISOR at work is there to earn money to contribute to her family. While her work gives her meaning, she likely sees it as secondary to her role as a wife, mother, daughter, or any of those roles combined.

The MISOR who has a job isn't there for glory. She's there for service. And she knows that the way to keep her job is to be liked. She is diligent, not because she's climbing the corporate ladder but because it is the right thing to do. She is dutiful and likely very loyal to a boss or mentor. She might be ashamed of any ambition she feels in her job. A frustrated MISOR will be snarky to or about co-workers. She'll critique others who don't "follow the rules" or those who refuse to understand the way the hierarchies operate. She'll expect other people to carry their own weight and do things "the right way" (which is usually the way she does things). A frustrated MISOR is on the path to sovereignty too. She'll look for ways to double down on her service. She'll align with people who have power and authority. She truly believes that if she is just good enough, she'll be rewarded for her goodness. And yet we frequently find that on the path to sovereignty, we cannot give ourselves over sufficiently to another so that we are made free. This is a funda-mental challenge for the MISOR, whose life has been shaped by her belief in and dedication to authority.

One of the hallmarks of the MISOR is relationship; the word is in the descriptive acronym of who she is, Maiden in Search of *Relationship*. In stories, the MISOR is the one looking for connec-tion. She's good at relationships. Depending on the story, it can be a romantic relationship, friendship, parent-daughter relationship, or sibling relationship. She wants to belong; she may not realize that she's part of the "in" crowd, but she's usually at least adjacent to popularity, if not downright popular.

In romantic relationships, the MISOR wants a partner who leads. She feels safe being deferential to someone who can hold their own. Her partner should be powerful or should be poised to take power. The MISOR expects her partner to know her worth. In a romantic relationship, she will expect to be treated "like a lady." Chivalry is expected. She expects (or at least idealizes) remaining chaste until married. She will demonstrate how strongly about these convictions she feels. She wants to be the center of her part-ner's world. She gives deference in exchange for being beloved. She may be jealous of the parts of her partner's life that don't include her. Her behavior will follow traditional models. For a MISOR, that means communication and investing in relating. That usually means conversations. The communication doesn't have to always be deep. To be fair, these are good ideas for *any* relationship, roman-tic or otherwise, but they are the sure way to win and maintain a MISOR's heart and fidelity.

A MISOR will expect consideration and protection. She will want to know that her partner shares her values. She will want the deep intimacy that comes from knowing someone profoundly. She will be loyal and defend her partner to anyone and everyone if she has their protection. Sexual relationships for the MISOR can be complicated. Some MISORs don't see the point after a while. Sex is something that they give like a gift to their partner, and if the part-ner's attention wanes or they breech the trust in the relationship, sex is the first gift to be withdrawn. Earning it back is challenging.

The Blessings of the MISOR

Women are idealized across many cultures as the embodiment of motherly nurturing. Women are expected to be the ones who soothe our pain. It is why professions like teaching and nursing are culturally seen as "women's" work, (which is a multifactorial problem). People feel comforted in the presence of female therapists. Most people seeking therapy want a woman to be the one listening. For a long time, I thought this was because most people, both women and men, felt more comfortable talking with a woman. I reasoned that this disparity exists because women talking to one another is one of the first social skills little girls learn. But as I have honed my therapeutic skills, I have learned that the truth is deeper. Women hold the feelings in our culture. Men are allowed only four emotions: lust, accomplishment, pride, and anger. Anything else should be held back, stuffed, or ignored. But the thornier a problem or feeling, the more challenging it is to bury. The more life one lives, the more these feelings aggregate in the psyche. The next best thing is to give any of those unwanted emotions away, and the cultural expectation is that you give emotions to *feeling* people: women. If a man is lucky enough to have a MISOR as a partner, she may be capable of containing some feelings for him. If he has a woman therapist, he can share them with her, and while she might therapize him, he still gets to let go of those difficult emotions, even if it's only for an hour. If there's a trusted woman around, men will unconsciously feel safe not holding on to those bothersome feelings.

The MISOR is submissive and deferential. She knows how to make and keep the peace. She is a good cook. She has good rapport with children. She is good at relationships. She makes people feel welcome and wanted. The MISOR looks and acts young. She's innocent and attractive. She doesn't take male attention personally, accepting it as the currency of being receptive. She upholds the standards of virtue. She is polite. Basically, all the things that culture sets forth as womanly ideals are the blessings of the MISOR. If a woman can embody a large percentage of these, she will be seen as someone worthy of social support. She can expect to be respected as a "good" woman. If she marries well, she will be financially supported. If she remains athletic and pretty, she will be upheld as an "aspirational" ideal for other women. If she raises successful children, she will be presented as a model of motherhood. If she defers to her husband, family, or other sources of authority, she will be seen as humble, poised, and dignified. If she is seen as "good," she can expect to receive the protection of the culture. Most MISORs are respected as embodying feminine ideals. Men idealize the MISOR as the ideal wife: deferential, attractive, and hardworking at home. Other women idealize the MISOR as an aspirational vision. She looks great and makes it look easy. The MISOR embodies beauty, receptivity, effortlessness, and submission. She knows how to make things beautiful. Whether creating a home or a perfectly catered meal, the MISOR is the one who makes the ordinary beautiful and appealing.

The Dangers of the MISOR

The ideals of the MISOR sound pretty good. Indeed, most women have wrestled with them in one form or another at some point in their lives. The problem is that ideals rarely join reality. A bonus (in American culture especially) is that when people fail to live up to an ideal, we often blame the person for not achieving the ideal, rather than blaming culture for an impossible standard. The dangers for the MISOR are easily deduced when comparing ideals to lived experience for most women.

The beautiful MISOR can become vain and self-referential. She can become self-serving, expecting the world to revolve around her. The MISOR may feel entitled—after all, she has given over all her desires to fulfill a role. She may have exacting expectations of the relationships that she so deeply values. The MISOR may be too trusting and keep herself willfully naive, never learning the skills to navigate the world on her own. She may never develop her own sexual identity, seeing sex as a service she provides. As a result, she may be inexperienced at the least or frigid and punishing at the worst. She may become dependent on a partner. And should that partner die or leave, she can be left with no marketable skills, limited work history, and possibly the added burden of children to provide for. In a culture that values dependent mothers, a mother who loses a partner becomes a wife to the state, which is seen as undesirable, and immediately casts the MISOR out of her former place. A MISOR may become anxious, her worth always defined by how she adheres to the role assigned to her. She may struggle with her own identity, having focused on what the outside world thinks of her rather than what she thinks of herself. Deference can become manipulation. If a woman is dissuaded from using her voice, she will get her needs met using indirect means.

I lived this reality as the child of a MISOR. My mother was the quintessential model of the baby boomer MISOR. She was beautiful, sophisticated, and believed wholeheartedly in her femininity. She believed in being a "good" wife. She kept a beautiful home, had two children, and stayed home to try and live the ideal. But she underestimated the culture changes that were upending her way of life in the 1970s and '80s. She was unprepared. My dad owned a small business, and this exposed him to meeting very different people than those my mom met at church, PTA meetings, and the country club. Where we lived, there was a building boom, and my dad's business was for a time very successful. My mom, disoriented by my dad's success and the rapidly changing culture, was blindsided when he fell in love with another woman and left our family. To be fair, she shouldn't have felt blindsided. My dad had been a bad actor for a long time. He had multiple affairs, partied a lot with his friends and customers, and would sometimes disappear for days on end.

My mother believed, down to the core of her soul, that if she was a good and dutiful wife, if she forgave him every time he hurt her, then she would win the long game. She would tolerate his frequent petty self-indulgences. She was often hurt by the ways that he would talk to her, shaming her for the baby weight of a pregnancy, telling her to make him dinner two days postpartum, or calling her stupid because she didn't know some obscure fact. To be clear, my mother was not at all stupid nor ugly or fat (not that it matters, but to honor her, I include the distinction). She responded to everything he said thoughtfully. If he thought she was fat and needed to lose baby weight, well, then she dieted and went to aerobics. If he called her stupid, she would read a book he recommended. He didn't like her nose, so she got a nose job. She believed that if she asked for less and submitted to his demands that she would win in the end. Except she didn't.

He decided that he wanted a different life, with a different woman. My mother was devastated. She resented his life after her from the time they divorced in 1982 until the day in September 2017 that she left this world. That is 35 years! The saddest part was that she always loved him, and she refused to believe that there was anything wrong with her role. She was heartbroken and often bitter. She resented having to work. She resented having to raise two kids on her own. She married again, twice. Both marriages failed. One abused her physically, and the other used his faith as a whip to always place her in submission to his will—even when he was wrong. All three of them saw her as someone they could rule over. She chose men who claimed they wanted a "wifely" woman. She liked being a MISOR, and she was good at it. But the possibilities, especially in the time of history where she was trying to live those ideals, made it impossible for her. My mom died a MISOR, and while she and I disagreed on a number of things, I can never fault my mother for not living up to her ideals. She made every effort. She knew what she wanted. The problem was that the thing she wanted could only be granted by a man who wanted the same things and knew himself well enough to struggle with temptation and come back to his traditional life and wife. While I know men like that exist (I am married to one), my mother could never get there. It makes me sad for her to this day.

Though the dowry system in some parts of the world over the last 200 years became a "bride price" paid to a husband, that is not how it started. The dowry was originally a transfer of money, livestock, land, or goods to a daughter upon her marriage. It was a protection for the woman in a patriarchal system that guaranteed that a woman didn't become a slave in a marriage. Should the marriage go downhill, the dowry guaranteed a woman could have a means of independence. For MISORs today, I highly recommend

> considering a setting aside of funds that is for her protection alone. A trust or some other financial protection that guarantees that she will not be dependent should her relationship fail to live up to her expectations.

In her memoir, *Untamed*, author Glennon Doyle refers to the MISORs who permeated her school days as "the Golden Ones." She recounts the story of her homecoming court at high school. In her story, Glennon was adjacent to this rarefied group of teenage girls, but she never felt she belonged, a common refrain from women who we all thought were part of the popular group. She describes how she idealized the beautiful, effortless girls in her peer group. In thinking about homecoming as a snapshot of the teenage petri dish, she describes how the decisions are perpetuated to keep the status quo reproducing the same expectations:

> *Our job is to judge ourselves against the standards they set. Our existence makes them Golden, and their existence makes us miserable. Yet we vote for them year after year, because the rules control us even at the privacy of our own desks. Vote for the Golden Ones. They have followed directions perfectly, they are what we are all supposed to be, so they should win. Fair is fair.*[10]

Glennon captures how most of us feel about the people we admire in life, those we hold up as standards against whom to measure ourselves. The problem is that in our culture, we usually take out the measuring stick, measure how we align with the ideals, and in response to whatever small way we fail to measure up, change our grip on the yardstick and use it beat ourselves into submission.

Glennon Doyle is one of the most prolific and honest writers about the inside experience of trying and failing at living the MISOR ideal. She talks about bulimia, addiction, and the vertigo of a high-wire act performed for everyone else's opinion and comfort. Her raw accounts of eating disorders, alcoholism, and finding a voice in writing are an inspiration and a perfect example of how the Queen's Path can be traversed by everyone. Glennon, in all her Golden Ones, Momastery, Christian idealist, lithe, thin, blonde, and bubbly identity could not outrun the Divide. Like all of us, the Divide came for Glennon. The only way out was to get on the Queen's Path and trudge her way toward her own personal version of sovereignty, making her own unique map along the way.

Playing this game is dangerous. Whether you play what I call "the Girl Game" or you intentionally set out on the Queen's Path toward sovereignty, you will face danger. But ignoring the battles within the archetypal journey keeps us perpetuating the war as though the war is acceptable, normalizing it. While these journeys may be pervasive, there is nothing appropriate about six-year-old girls internalizing impossible standards about beauty and submission. There is nothing endearing about discounting women's voices in the name of hegemony. Women who are not popular, or who can't fit the MISOR ideal for whatever reason, often feel that if they could just be _(insert MISOR adjective here)_ thin, pretty, athletic, and so on, then their lives would be better. Their female existence would make sense. But most women cannot become one of the "Golden Ones." We aren't effortlessly skinny, submissive, or demure. We laugh too loudly, are too smart, have a few extra pounds, or want to be noticed for being who we are, rather than on how closely we meet a standard.

Most of us spend our teenage years navigating or battling male attention. In my teenage clients, I see various strategies: embracing, rejecting, exhausting. The important reality, though, is that these young women are never free of the presence of men and boys. It is an uncomfortable dance for me as an adult woman to articulate with these young clients the unfairness of the world they inhabit. And yet, it is necessary for me to do so. And so, I spend my time listening to these young women and encouraging that they simultaneously have a right to their own bodies, their own sexual pleasure and identities and simultaneously reflecting back to them that the culture they live in is unfair and unkind to them. The culture will not protect those women in the same ways that boys and men are protected. They will be objects if they do nothing. They will be judged whether they do something or nothing. And they will internalize rejection and attention in ways that become existential to their identity as a result. By the time they arrive in my office, they have likely already developed some set of skills in interacting with male attention. Because of their age, it is likely ineffective. In an article in *The Guardian*, journalist Moira Donegan describes it perfectly:

> Those early experiences of male sexual aggression are maybe one of the most reliable rites of passage for female children. It's more common than any of the other rituals that signal impending adulthood ... by the time a girl reaches any of these milestones, she has likely already developed a skill set for navigating the unwanted attention of adult men, and started to learn the delicate balance of signaling their own lack of interest, or of curtailing men's interest, without escalating. . . . The message that all of this sends to young girls is that womanhood is a state that consists largely of receiving unsolicited male attention, much of it benign, but much of it threatening, exploitative, or hostile, and that their ownership of their own bodies, their ability to peacefully occupy public space ... can all be abridged by the whims of a man's desire.[11]

Consent is not the same as control. Women often feign consent to maintain a personal sense of control. Consent is not protective in daily life. No amount of protest will keep a 200-pound man who believes "hard to get" is a game from raping a 120-pound woman who says, "No!" over and over again. Women know it. We develop elaborate strategies to convince ourselves that rape is not rape. Our culture encourages this double-speak, and we all internalize it. What is "nonconsensual sex" but rape? What is sex with an "underage woman" if not (statutory) rape of a child or adolescent? What is it that happened to the client who believes she consented though she said nothing at all, while she let a man have sex with her out of fear? How is that not rape? We see consent implied in language. Yet, that implied consent is not at all representative of women's lived experience and the twisty acrobatics we engage in to protect our psyches from the onslaught of our place in the world.

What does this have to do with the MISOR? She inhabits this world and either doesn't see a problem or accepts the problem as just "how the world works." She, of course, is not wrong about the world. But because of her MISOR ideals, she doesn't find it seemly to engage in battle. Battle and war are for men, not women. The MISOR is both an idealist and a pragmatist. She believes that the world should be a place where she is safe. Men should be protectors, and women should expect that of them. Ladies deserve chivalry. From the pragmatist side of her values, she sees that the world of men is real. Women don't have a place in it, so why fight? Fighting is beneath her. Instead, she works within the expectations on her to make the most of her situation. Some women succeed with this. If they are pretty and deferential and have chosen a partner who shares these values, then she may succeed in fulfilling her MISOR ideals. However, she is living in a bubble of her own experience. The danger of the MISOR's willing submission is that the world is not filled with chivalrous men. That isn't to say that those men don't exist. But they are the minority, not the majority. The MISOR's submission makes it look like the world of chivalry is available to women and girls for whom it is not an option.

The MISOR is not the enemy of feminism nor is feminism the enemy of the MISOR. Blaming either the MISOR as an archetype or feminism as a movement misses the point. The reason feminism exists is for the women who cannot live the MISOR life. I am not idealizing that life, but if it truly worked, then there would be no need to question it. The expectations placed on the MISOR are not there to empower her; they are there to keep her subordinate. The division between the MISOR and the MIPE is fiction. They exist to divide a woman from herself, to always have her chasing an impossible set of conflicting expectations. This expectation of women's submission makes the world a dangerous place for women like Glennon Doyle, my mom, and any others for whom submission wasn't or isn't an option (which is most of us).

Magical, Isolated, Powerful, and Endangered (MIPE)

We think we know the MIPE. When we see the Wicked Witch of the West in *The Wizard of Oz*, Elphaba in *Wicked*, or Evilene in *The Wiz*, we recognize her. We see her in Snow White's stepmother, the character who doesn't even warrant an actual name. She's only known as "the Evil Queen." We recognize her in Sleeping Beauty's nemesis, Maleficent, whether she's the 1957 version who shapeshifts into a fire-breathing dragon or the 2015 version starring Angelina Jolie. The MIPE appears less obvious in other roles, but we still recognize her archetypally. We see her in Shug Avery in *The Color Purple*. We recognize her in Josie Geller from *Never Been Kissed*. She is obvious in characters like Harley Quinn from *Batman* and her other starring roles in movies, books, and sacred literature.

Recognizing the MIPE outside her representation as the "bad girl" can be a little more challenging than seeing the MISOR. We are raised with the MISOR ideals and values. The MISOR shows up in the expectations that women are compared against on a daily basis. The MIPE can become the "catchall" for every characteristic that doesn't fit the ideals we expect in the MISOR. Most of the time, we know the MIPE by the *behaviors* she engages in that don't reflect the MISOR ideals. How does she behave when challenged? Does she behave like Aldys, from the film *Never Been Kissed*, standing up to the bullies in her Denominators sweatshirt? Or like Janis Ian in *Mean Girls*, dressed in gothy black and calling her former friend a lemming? Does she support the resistance, spiriting children out of Gilead like June Osborne in the television series *The Handmaid's Tale*? Or perhaps she's more recognizable in real life as the former First Lady and Secretary of State Hillary Rodham Clinton looking bored as her detractors drone on for 11 hours in a politically motivated hearing?

Whenever a woman is described as "unlikable," "bitchy," or "powerful," you will find the MIPE archetype. This is the easiest way to identify her. Most of the time, she inhabits the unconscious. The more someone ignores their unconscious, the more negatively they will view the MIPE (and anything else in the unconscious). Think about the conscious and the unconscious like a building with a long elevator shaft. The conscious is at the upper level, the penthouse. This is where all our conscious ideals and loftiest goals live. It's where we *believe* we operate from every day. But that assumption would be incorrect. The deepest part of the unconscious lies in the lowest part of the basement. The foundation supports the penthouse and all the lofty ideals. But we avoid the unconscious, not wanting to look at the foundation. We don't like the darkness, the rattling pipes, the humidity. We like to pretend that the basement isn't where everything is supported. The more focus there is on the penthouse and the top of the building, the more the lower levels and the basement will be ignored. Soon, the foundation of the building and the elevator's mechanics are at risk because the unexamined contents are falling apart. Machinery starts to break; the plumbing starts to create problems. The more you ignore the unconscious, the more ugly and fearsome it appears. This isn't because the contents are actually frightening, but because like any ignored space, the cobwebs and old broken things start to take on a sinister hue. Broken pipes and mechanics in disrepair are dangerous for anyone walking around in the darkness of the basement. The basement, the foundation, begins to feel haunted in the absence of care.

When the MIPE is ignored in culture, in the psyche, in relationships, she can become a demonic force, a succubus, or witch. People will fear her. Stories will portray her in a negative light, invoking frightening symbolism. In communities when women stray beyond the norms set for us, we are often threatened with being seen this way. The associations alone are enough to scare us into submission. Even now, in communities where there is change and anxiety that no one wants to attend to, there are witch hunts. This is true in religious communities in the United States, and it's true in places like rural India and Africa where social change threatens traditional norms.

In rural India, there have been thousands of deaths of women accused of witchcraft since 2015. Journalist Suhasini Raj chronicled the story of one such accused witch named Durga Mahalo in *The New York Times*. Mahalo rejected the sexual attention of a powerful man in her village. Rather than deal with the fallout of her accusations, he accused her of witchcraft. This successfully set the town against her. The powerful man didn't have to navigate the complexities of his infidelity; he successfully got his wife to participate, realigning their bond. Even Durga's family turned on her.[12] Making a vulnerable person a scapegoat is a tried-and-true means for aligning a community. When there is strife, find a person or cause to organize around. In social psychology, this is a well-worn method for managing social stress.

The MIPE has for the longest time been the symbol toward whom a community can point their ire and organize their opposition. Whether we are talking about the 17th-century witch trials in the colony of Salem, Massachusetts or the 21st-century maiming and murder of women accused of witchcraft in sub-Saharan Africa, the MIPE is a familiar symbol of noncompliance. The worst aspect of this cultural reliance on her in that role is that the accusations don't have to be founded in any reality. They can be focused on a woman not meeting a standard as simple as the length of her dress. She can be accused of spectral visitation, coming into someone's dreams, and her real-life human counterpart will be considered responsible.

This compounds the unconscious nature of how we see the MIPE. The MIPE is whomever we don't want to be responsible to or for. She is the one we don't want to pay attention to. It is the MIPE we ignore; we are encouraged to look away from her. And it is in her lived experience of vulnerability, invisibility, and endangerment that she draws her cultural power. The MIPE who figures this out will often become embittered and power hungry. She will rail against the powers that would isolate and endanger her. The magic and power associated with her come from her connection to the unconscious and how far and deep we have to push her in order for her to be safely buried there and out of our sight.

In every religion, there is a version of the MIPE. In the Christian tradition, she is Mary Magdalene, Lilith, Salome, and Jezebel, to name a few. In Islam, there are fewer women named, but there are a handful who fit the MIPE, like Zulaykah, who tries to seduce Joseph when he is enslaved in Egypt, and the Queen of Sheba, who maintained her pagan rites. But one need not have a named character to represent the MIPE. Indeed, any woman who doesn't fit the narrow definitions of what an ideal or "good" woman is by default will take on the MIPE's mantle. Every religion, and every denomination and subculture will have their specific definitions that include being modest, obedient, chaste, and motherly. All these common expectations align with the MISOR, and anyone who cannot uphold the expectations set by them falls into the realm of the MIPE.

The MIPE will work hard for financial security to ensure that she has control over her own life. She would prefer to not be beholden to anyone at all if possible. She fantasizes about a big financial windfall so that she has no commitments that would force her to compromise her identity. The MIPE has very high expectations. She will build a life that supports those expectations. If she values education, she'll commit to college or graduate school. If she values financial security, she'll work in a role that pays well—or that will eventually. If she values freedom to travel and move as she pleases, she'll have a ready passport and resist any temptation to be held down.

The MIPE will value her looks only in as much as are relevant to what she wants in life. If she wants to be an accomplished athlete or a supermodel, she'll prioritize her body or beauty. Otherwise, she'll succeed based on what she is good at doing. If she doesn't think she's pretty, she will work around it. If she feels that pretty gets her the wrong kind of attention, she'll downplay her looks. If she doesn't think she's beautiful, she'll focus on an attribute that makes her feel powerful or valuable. If she works out, it will be because it makes her feel good or because she has a goal like running a marathon or climbing a mountain. A MIPE's relationship to her body is complicated. As a young woman, she may be a perfectionist, struggling with eating disorders or athletic goals. The danger for both the MISOR and the MIPE is separation from her body. While the MISOR will give her appearance over to external expectations, a MIPE will likely let her body become less important than her mind or her accomplishments. This may be true even for MIPEs who are athletic; the body may be pushed like a machine, rather than treated as a supple and breakable seat of identity. This tendency to dissociate from her physical being has much greater consequences as the MIPE tries to navigate the Queen's Path. She may attempt to control her body out of fear. She may long for embodiment but not trust it, as the body has usually been the perceived territory of the "pretty girls" the MISORs or it may have been the terrain of assault or abuse.

A MIPE gets loads of personal meaning from her career and ambitions. In addition, she values the independence that money brings. She knows financial independence is a critical piece of her freedom. Being dependent on anyone makes her uncomfortable. Despite the MIPE's love of independence, she will want validation from her work. This can cause problems as she seeks to please bosses and co-workers. She will work herself to the bone for workplace recognition or validation. If she hasn't found her calling or ideal work environment, she will be even more motivated by pleasing her immediate supervisors, customers, or clients. She may start her own business and depend emotionally on the value she brings her customers or their positive view of her. In a more traditional environment, the MIPE can get into trouble by not respecting the chain of command. Motivated by recognition, she'll show her value to people in the decision-making roles of her workplace. She will likely struggle to see the political environment she operates in, expecting the meritocracy to advance her for being smart, dedicated, and a problem solver. Where the MISOR values the protection of service, the MIPE wants the recognition and validation of accomplishment.

I have a client, Philippa, who works for a big entertainment company. By all accounts within the company, she is very good at her job. Just a few months after assuming her current role, a #metoo scandal surfaced that implicated her immediate supervisor. He was abruptly let go, and this threw the whole division into chaos. The team Philippa was on had the lion's share of the responsibilities for getting the division to a new milestone, and suddenly everything was on her shoulders. She worked extra hours and made sacrifices of her time, sleep, and health to make sure the milestone was met. There were thousands of moving parts across multiple teams to manage: marketing, development, design, art, post-production, and many more. When the milestone was met, she expected to be rewarded with praise, a promotion, and a raise. But soon after meeting their deadline, Philippa was brought into the office of the newly appointed supervisor, who told her that she was going to *fail* her performance review. She had saved the deliverables but made enemies in the process. Her peers didn't like that she was so driven. She rocked the boat; she made demands of other teams to meet the company's goals. She didn't have time to waste; there was a real deadline with huge financial consequences for her company if they didn't meet the timeline. Her supervisor told her point-blank that she wasn't likable and that her performance review was being determined by the feelings of several of her colleagues who saw her as a "bitch." She was in a no-win situation. Had Philippa not driven the team to meet the deadline, the company would have blamed her for being ineffective, but by making demands, she was too pushy. Philippa recently left that studio and found another company where she is more appreciated.

I don't know a woman I'd consider a MIPE who doesn't have a story like this. Indeed, we need only look at some of the most famous women in our recent history to see this type of storyline in action. I think of Hillary Clinton after her husband became president. Hillary Clinton first set into motion the idea of universal healthcare—that was in 1993! When she became First Lady, it was the number one agenda item on her to-do list. The establishment in Congress didn't like this uppity woman coming in and telling them what their legislative agenda should be. They quickly decided that she was unlikable. They found her behavior unladylike. She was too much. The powers of DC politics quickly put her in place. America's First Lady is supposed to be the ideal MISOR, not an ambitious woman dedicated to social change.

If you're the MIPE at work, notice that you might come off as abrasive to people. Don't be alarmed by it, just notice. This may escalate if the workplace is challenging or if there is a lot of pressure in the work itself. When the MIPE is unsatisfied in her work or feels that she is being treated unfairly, she can become bitter and vengeful. She will point fingers at those whose work isn't up to par. She'll be frustrating and short with colleagues. If she doesn't feel that she has a path to success, she may dedicate herself to blocking that path for others, especially other women. The important thing to make sense of in a workplace where you are the MIPE is whether or not you are being held to MISOR standards for fitting in and whether that works for you as a MIPE. If it doesn't, then perhaps a better-fitting environment would be in order.

People are often intimidated or afraid of the MIPE. Co-workers fear she will outshine them. Bosses feel she will outperform them. Everyone sees that she is ambitious. She may also be seen as capable. Together, ambitious and capable are a threat. In instances where peers and bosses are threatened, they will pile on the responsibilities, assuming no one could possibly keep up. They underestimate the MIPE. She will work harder. Doubt and restrictions often make her double down on her resolve and dedication. Her desire for more security or greater authority isn't a power play; it's just part of her identity to challenge herself and expand her capabilities.

As an archetype, the MIPE has a history of difficulty relating to others. She usually leads with her skills, knowledge, or power, thinking that these attributes will demonstrate her value. Of course, this never seems to work out for her. The MIPE doesn't understand when she's rejected for the very thing that brought her to the relationship to begin with. If you met her at a marathon training class and then she always tries to relate everything back to running, she'll be confused as to why this is a turnoff. If you're in a romantic relationship, she'll be shocked and hurt if you keep expecting her to "get smaller" by taking on a more domestic role. She may try to please you, but she'll resent it and then be filled with frustration if you don't do the same. If your best friend is a MIPE, she will value loyalty and consideration in your friendship. She'll expect you to think through problems and hold you to a high standard around integrity and consistency. She'll be more easily hurt if she feels rejected, and she'll never tell you because she believes she's not supposed to expect much of others, though she desperately wants to.

The Blessings of the MIPE

The MIPE teaches us to trust the power inherent in our being. She connects women to the body and to all the pathways we have to explore our gifts as individuals. She doesn't feel inferior. She may experience moments when she feels insecure or unsure, but that's not the same. The MIPE invests in and defends her intuition and knowledge. She believes her point of view has merit. The MIPE is dedicated to learning and making any situation better than how it was when she found it. She'll dedicate herself to the goals of an organization, group of friends, or sport. She challenges herself and will always want to do better. She will expect it of herself and thinks this is normal for other people. She's often tired and exasperated by other people's lack of motivation. Once she has had even a small taste of success, she'll be buoyed by the feeling of accomplishment and will use it to inspire more motivation, whether for her own goals or to encourage others.

The MIPE values work and power. She will fight for what she believes in. She stands out, and while it may surprise her that she stands out in the first place, it doesn't make her uncomfortable. She is simply baffled by the fact that other women (and men) aren't standing in their power and feels that it is her place to stand where they will not, or cannot.

The MIPE has no choice but to become resilient. She may hate that doing so is necessary, but she will do it nonetheless. The MIPE teaches us to dig down deep to find our strength and power. She teaches us that though the world will work to break us down, we can find reserves of power that are outside of the approved definitions. She demonstrates that power for women is greater than the power that we would be given and exists in ourselves in places where we need only claim it.

The MIPE delights in the complexity of the world. She feels drawn to power. She may want power for herself or want to be near it to feel normal. Don't presume her need to be close to power or wield it is something sinister. It is likely just the way that she makes sense of her place in the world. She cannot play small. The sure way to break a MIPE is to deny her authentic voice or being. Does she have delusions of grandeur? Maybe, if they're delusions . . . or they may just be who she is called to be in the world. The MIPE will always make her partner or friends think. She'll expose them to new perspectives. She'll challenge them, in ways that they need and sometimes hate. She will dedicate herself to finding the best way.

She'll work hard, hoping to prove herself. She will appear magical, otherworldly, incandescent. She'll be a bright light that attracts a lot of attention. The MIPE will fascinate and enchant those around her. She'll appear powerful, and with that can come attention and success in many domains, especially career and anything in the public view. But the MIPE's visibility can also be a curse. While the MISOR often is given a curse, the MIPE is often the source of curses. Whether she intends it or not, her power comes at a cost. Her power can become sinister to anyone who has a reason to distrust her.

The Dangers of the MIPE

Any woman who wields power is suspicious in the world. This is the legacy of our cultural inheritance. With the exception of a handful of tribal spaces or isolated communities, there are almost no places left in the world where matriarchies exist. By and large, the world has been made and remade by conquest. Hegemony fears a woman with power. I believe this is because patriarchal cultures know that their ways facilitate the abuse of women, children, animals, and the Earth itself. As a result, women are overdue for a little retribution. Those who love conquest are often the most afraid of women with power. No one wants to be on the receiving end of the MIPE's revenge.

Medusa, one of the most famous MIPEs in mythology, was cursed by the goddess Athena. What was the crime she was cursed for? Being raped by Poseidon in Athena's temple. The beautiful Medusa in her original form was cursed for being the object of the God's desire. Athena was angered that her temple was defiled, and rather than taking out her anger on her uncle (who is after all, a god), she cursed Medusa, his victim. As a result, Medusa became monstrous, with her once glorious and beautiful hair taking on the form of living snakes. The contradiction of a beautiful face and a monstrous form transformed anyone who looked upon her face into stone. The symbolism clearly gives us the message that monstrosity combined with sin and beauty, even if it's not the fault of the monster, turns one to stone . . . hardens the heart. Clearly, the message is that the rape victim turns anyone who looks on her fate to stone. Don't look at her! Don't look at what she has become as a result of her curse. She is left to haunt the underworld, the conscious world is stone-faced to her suffering and pain. As a result, the victim is left to manage on her own, alone, and she can turn anyone to stone, just by looking at them.

The MIPE is an easy scapegoat and is frequently blamed for what befalls her. If she is raped, it is her fault for how she dressed, where she was, or what she looked like. If she is unpopular, it is because she cannot meet the standards set for her, regardless of how unrealistic they are. If she is poor, it is because she doesn't work hard enough. Her place as a MIPE will be seen as a choice. If she's an outcast, it will be because of some rumored transgression. If she's burned as a witch, it's because some power or malfeasance is attributed to her, whether the injury is real or perceived.

The MIPE can become bitter for not fitting in. She can be easily hurt by how the world responds to her inability to live up to the standards expected of the MISOR. The MIPE's complaints aren't false; they're culturally sanctioned. We are taught that it's okay to beat up on the girls who don't fit in. Kids are encouraged to bully the fat girl, the ugly girl, the weird girl. Women who grow up with these experiences are often surprised to find themselves in an adulthood that still adheres to many of the principles that they couldn't live up to in childhood. Women clients in therapy so often wonder aloud whether or not they will ever break out of their childhood curses. Even if they achieve their ideal body or get the dream job, they still feel haunted, disconnected, and endangered. They long to have a "normal" life and experience of relationship or friendship. Few notice that what they are calling "normal" are actually the MISOR ideals. They long to belong in the same way that the MISOR does, but they cannot perform the submission necessary to get there, not authentically anyway. The MIPE is by definition isolated. She often feels alone and misunderstood. She longs for deep friendship and a capable partner. She believes that belonging will make her feel "normal" and accepted.

To make things harder on the real-life woman who inhabits the MIPE archetype, she really is isolated and ignored. The MIPE lives in the unconscious, and as such, we will often find ourselves ignoring her out of habit. We ignore her out of what she means to culture. We cannot bear the experience of looking at our behavior and our expectations of women. As a culture, we don't look. We rail that she must have done *something* to be treated this way. People aren't this awful; children aren't this mean. We let her get bullied. We make excuses for her abuses. We participate in victim blaming. If only we could get her to just stay in the light instead of wandering into the unconscious! If only she could embrace the standards, then we wouldn't have to go down into the scary basement.

To the world that embraces the standards and norms expected of women, the MIPE is a threat. She holds the negative expectations we try to deny as a culture. Patriarchal cultures believe that a matriarchy would behave in as damaging and evil manner as patriarchy—specifically that women are just as likely to seek revenge and do to men and boys what has been done to women and girls for millennia. While I understand where this sentiment comes from, there's no evidence for it. What little we know about earlier and the one or two extant matriarchies is that they are primarily cultures where the sexual mores are not as punitive, children are cared for in common, and punishment for crimes or transgressions focuses on making restitution. The presumption that a matriarchy would look like a female-led version of patriarchy speaks to the deep unconscious of patriarchy—that the system is profoundly aware that it is founded on domination, pain, and abuse. No one wants to fix it, and there is little appetite to correct it. If we correct it, it is an admission of our collective, social guilt.

From the outside, the MIPE appears most frequently in the form of a wicked witch. However, in stories, she can take many other forms: a murderess, bitch, whore, fallen woman, sinner, loudmouth, comedienne, demon, vampire, goddess, charlatan, soldier, genius, or feminist. But the world sees the MIPE primarily as someone undesirable. She doesn't accept authority, and for that she is seen as dangerous to the status quo. The MIPE is often depicted as a woman who accidentally follows her curiosity or ambition and then falls into a role that transforms her into something or someone powerful, evil, or perverse.

Consider the 2018 Jennifer Garner film *Peppermint*. In this film, the protagonist's husband and child are murdered by a drug cartel. Garner's character, Riley, is pushed into successive corners by the powerful forces of the cartel. The cartel has infiltrated the police force, district attorney's office, and local courts. Riley can't get justice, so she becomes a vigilante instead. The film follows her on her road to exact retribution for the loss of her family. She is a transformed woman. Having lost her innocence as a MISOR, she takes on the mantle of the MIPE, becoming a different kind of woman. She has power. She learns how to shoot, fight, and make bombs. She lives in places where she can stay under the radar. She focuses on her goal of bringing all the corrupt men who failed her to justice.

Culture treats the MIPE as someone to be feared and avoided. Often portrayed as evil, you'll find her in wicked witches and murderesses. She can appear ambitious like Annalise Keating from *How to Get Away with Murder* or Alex Forrest from *Fatal Attraction*. She can be magical and powerful like *Xena: Warrior Princess*, Diana of Themiscyra (*Wonder Woman*), or Angela Bassett's Marie LaVeau from *American Horror Story: Coven,* season 3. She is my client Phillippa who got the creative project to the finish line but who pissed people off by being authoritative and demanding.

The MIPE is often aligned with feminism, especially the version that people revile. Founders of Girl Defined ministries, sisters Kristen Clark and Bethany Beal paint feminism as the worst thing to happen to women since Eve and the apple. They assure their followers that feminism "acts like *all* women want abortion, autonomy, careers, power over men, and more." They specifically call out feminism as "anti-Christian," and say explicitly that "we obviously don't believe feminism is the answer to our womanhood questions." They follow up with the assertion that while feminism has "done some good over the years," it hasn't helped women as much as it has made things more challenging for us. In other words, it makes the MIPE more attractive and makes it more confusing when women are aware of the Divide.

The Real Purpose of the Divided Woman

Regardless of whether you find yourself on the track of the MISOR or the MIPE, you're locked in a metaphor created to keep you in submission. Being a MISOR means you accept the authority that would lock you into submissive roles for the rest of your life. It puts you in danger of being dependent, having fewer resources and less time in the workplace to build skills and expertise. But embracing the MISOR also means you build a world and life for yourself where the role of motherhood is central. Nurturing, caring, and homemaking are valued. This world is protective under ideal circumstances. The MISOR lives a life of submission and protection. Meanwhile, the MIPE lives a life of power. She may find herself jet-setting across the world to fantastic destinations. She has her own money. She decides who is in her life and how she wishes to live. She submits to no one. And yet she may find herself profoundly lonely and hurt at her lack of relationships or family. Further, she'll risk being vilified, maybe even persecuted. Her power will be distrusted.

The Queen's Path isn't about elevating either the MISOR or the MIPE but rather in noticing that each path is there to confine us as women. When you stay in your lane, you're running someone else's race. The Queen's Path will show you how to get off the track altogether, whether you have been on the track of the MISOR or the MIPE. When you leave the competition and repudiate the rules that keep the MISOR in submission or the MIPE isolated in her power, you'll find the steps to your own sovereignty. It is in sovereignty where you will make the decisions about how to navigate the world that has been given to you. You may choose to stay in the world familiar to you, whether that is the MISOR's church groups and PTA meetings or the MIPE's partnership climb or ambitions to become the first woman president. But as you navigate the Queen's Path, you'll find that you get to decide which of the pieces of each track you want to adopt, adapt, or reject. You'll reassemble the pieces into a beautiful tapestry that is unique to you. You'll stand in the power of your female body, as the queen of your own domain. You'll gather the people around you who can see your power and who aren't put off by it. You'll be crowned in sovereignty, deciding for yourself what your life, family, and future look like. You will reign your life.

These are heavy ideas. Spend a little time reflecting on what being either a MISOR or MIPE has meant to you. Here are some prompts for writing in your journal.

- Was your mother a MISOR or a MIPE? How did this impact you?

- Have you found yourself sad, frustrated, or depressed because you've been passed over for promotions or creative opportunities? If you look back, can you see expectations of MISOR or MIPE around those environments?

- Has your family expected you to behave either as a MISOR or a MIPE? How has this impacted your romantic relationships?

- Have you ever experienced an unknown malaise around your role(s)? Has it ever occurred to you that you made a choice because it was expected (e.g., getting married, having a baby, taking a job, going for a particular career or position), not because you wanted it?

CHAPTER 3

THE QUEEN AND THE DIVIDE

She walks across the parquet floor in any direction she chooses. She feels at ease chatting with everyone. She speaks easily to a young soldier flummoxed to find himself in the royal court. He is nervously checking his uniform; she encourages him that he belongs. This powerful beauty then moves across the room to speak to an army general about strategy in a brewing conflict. Her presence next to him reminds the room that the Queen is more than a sexual conquest. The Queen then moves slightly off to a corner to rebuke a clergyman whom others suspect might be plotting against the realm. She speaks in harsh but hushed tones until it's time to join her partner on the royal dais. The Queen's power is not to be underestimated.

This is almost always how I consider the Queen in a game of chess. She moves across the board with purpose, always aware of her power and influence. Your opponent in a game of chess always has their eye on her. According to Marilyn Yalom in her book, *Birth of the Chess Queen*, the Queen became the most powerful piece on the chess board in Spain during the reign of Queen Isabella, sometime in the late 15th century.[1]

What changed? When chess was first invented in the 15th century, the queen was not so powerful. The piece that held the powers that the queen now possesses belonged to a piece called "the vizier."[2] That piece represented the king's closest advisor. It was relegated to the role of the bishop on the board, and the role of the queen took on new powers. As women gained a greater voice in politics and worldly affairs around that time, the role of the queen became more critical, and the game of chess reflected how wars and politics were being influenced by the powerful men and singular woman who could change the course of the game.

Six hundred years before, Chaucer wrote *The Canterbury Tales* and answered the question that men continue to ponder aloud (but have ignored) for thousands of years, "What do women want?" In his tale of the bawdy Alyson, Chaucer explains to his contemporaries that what women want is "sovereignty" over themselves and in some instances, their partners. Chaucer weaves for the reader a story about a knight of King Arthur's Roundtable who rapes a young woman he encounters on the road. The court is scandalized, and King Arthur turns the fate of the knight over to the women of the court, including the queen, Guinevere. She sends him on a quest to save his life. He must learn the truth about what women want. For over a year, he travels the land, asking women and men what women want. He gets so many different answers, he despairs he will fail in his quest and be executed.

The knight encounters a group of magical women, but they scatter as he approaches. As he gets close, the only one left among them is a lonely old hag. This woman recounts the life of a woman who has been raped, beaten, and subjugated by abuse and neglect. She tells the knight that she will give him the answer if he will pledge himself to her. Faced with the dire possibility of execution, he agrees. She agrees to provide him the answer, but only if before the court, he agrees to marry her. Appalled but without options, he agrees.

Bawdy Alyson tells him the secret, that women desire sovereignty, primarily over themselves, and in some matters, over their husbands. As they are preparing for their first night as husband and wife, the knight is looking glum. The old woman asks him why he is so upset. He shares that he is ashamed to have an old, low-born wife. She then explains that as a magical creature she can turn into a beautiful young woman. He can choose. He can have the old hag, and she will be good, kind, and faithful. Or he can choose the younger model, but she cannot guarantee her fidelity. She will be young and coquettish. Remembering her answer before the court, he says that she should choose for herself. The knight learned the lesson. The woman chooses for herself and decides to be young *and* faithful.

Scholars have studied and analyzed Chaucer's *The Wife of Bath's Tale* for hundreds of years. The tale scandalizes and challenges readers—describing a woman widowed multiple times, open about sex, and who owns herself because of her wealth and age. It stands as a parable on multiple topics: social class, marriage, women's sovereignty, feminine behavior, "real life" characters, and independence. In addition, the story provides commentary on the pursuit of inner beauty (rather than focusing on outward appearance), and on medieval fears around women's power, especially during a time of plagues and wars.

What do the queen of the chessboard and Alyson, the Wife of Bath, have in common? They emerged around the same time. We can see in this development the emergence of a public woman, describing herself and telling her own story. Granted, the story ultimately is being told by a man, Chaucer. But Chaucer gives the character a voice of her own. She speaks for herself. Her experience reflects the lived experience of merchant women of the period, a member of a class that emerged as an unexpected power. The economy shifted from a landed economy, where wealth was measured in the size of one's estate, to a cash economy, where wealth was measured by availability and liquidity of funds. In other words, in this time, cash had new power. Women having that power was revolutionary. It gave women like Alyson a new platform and authority for speaking their minds. Chaucer's *Canterbury Tales* explored lived experience. By examining biography in this vein, Chaucer exposed audiences to reflect on the lives of individuals, and that included individual women.

What can we learn about women and sovereignty from Chaucer or the queen's role on the chessboard? The first lesson, one of examining history, is to look at what was happening around these stories during those time periods. Those times, like today's were filled with vertigo-inducing social change. Everything was being upended. Wars were changing both the landscape and the borders. Colonialism was changing fortunes everywhere—and there was a race to determine which royal nations could subdue the greatest portion of the world. Because of wars and colonialism, the economies were shifting. Cash was needed to pay soldiers and buy ships. And because of wars and the death of men as soldiers, there were more women than men at home. These women often were dependent on husbands and families, and there weren't obvious ways for them to make a living for themselves or take care of their own needs.

Finally, there was increased international trade, part of the purpose of expanding colonial powers. This expansion brought diseases like small pox to new colonies via trade ships. Colonialism returned home with new diseases like the plague. The conflux of problems, while complex, is relatively easy to look at historically. Living it in real time would have been difficult to untangle, as we can examine in our own time with the complex of world-altering realities we are facing in the 21st century.

It has only been 30 years since the Internet completely changed how the world works. It's only been about 15 years since the arrival of social media. Over the last 50 years, traditional church attendance has diminished. People travel more than ever, changing the landscapes of places far from their homes. As a result, there is an increase in personal liberty and a backlash against progressivism in all parts of the world. We have seen the arrival of multiple pandemics over the last 50 years. Wealth has continued to flow upward to the few, leaving large swaths of people the philosopher Edmund Burke called "the Great Unwashed" to scrap between themselves for whatever is left.

These types of social and cultural change are not new. They happen every 200 to 300 years, with big upheavals or social problems enduring sometimes for centuries. Poverty, sickness, discrimination, racism, sexism—these are problems that have endured, not because they cannot be solved, but because solving them alters the balance of power in unpredictable ways. Typically, societies prefer predictability over freedom, and they prefer war over change if they are fighting to maintain that predictability.

What does this have to do with sovereignty? Women have been subjects to men and society writ large for thousands of years. We need only look to the centuries when witch burning was a law-and-order issue to see that the motives for accusing (mostly) women of witchcraft centered on power and control. Ostensibly, the fight against witches pitted the powers of the church and state against sorcery. But under closer examination, the battles were against women's rights to self-governance and fear of change in a time of cultural and economic upheaval. Women shouldn't have access to power—money—so witch hunters went after widows for their estates. Women shouldn't have more respect in the community than doctors and clergy, so go after healers and midwives. Women shouldn't dress provocatively, so go after those who can afford fancy clothes. Women shouldn't say prayers that aren't authorized by the church, so go after those inclined to poetry and song.

The unpredictability of forces that couldn't be codified by the ruling powers caused a great deal of conscious and unconscious anxiety at both the individual and societal levels. How do the ruling powers keep women under control in a time where the men are off fighting and dying in wars, women have no codified ways of making their own living, and the economic base is shifting from an agricultural, land-based economy to a liquid-cash economy?

In a cash-based society, money is an equalizing force. Women, minorities, immigrants, and marginalized people can "buy" their independence if they have enough money. Societies that seek to curb the abilities of these groups to participate in the public sphere, to reduce their capacity to "buy" their independence. If a marginalized group cannot participate in public life, then they are effectively cut out of the body politic, and power remains in the hands of those who control access.

Our culture is experiencing the effects of standing at the crossroads of tradition and self-determination yet again. We are experiencing the effects of a power struggle between those who want a "return" to what they dub traditional values, where traditional hierarchies are preserved—unsurprisingly, this supports following the expectations of restrictive religions and white men. The members of the generations born after 1981, (technically a millennial or a member of generation Z if born after 1997), have lived in a world where self-definition precedes community definition. The Internet, parents, and the educational system took the American ideals of individualism to a new level. Individualism has become the absolute right to determine your experience of the world. This idea, while in many ways laudable, also has some inconsistencies. In this view, the individual's identity is expected to be wholly self-determined. It does not consider or, at the very least, privilege the observer's view of the individual, except where that view goes against a cultural norm or is disrespectful of the individual's rights or a previously defined marginalized group's rights.

That is not to say that these two groups don't struggle with the pressure of outward appearance, bullying, or other problems. They do. Their orientation to them is different. They have been raised to believe that how they define *themselves* matters first and foremost. The constructs handed down by culture were not given to them in the same way that they were given to anyone born before 1980. If you were born before 1980, cultural definitions were given to you as absolutes. Any variation from the absolutes of Black, white, woman, man, gay, straight, good, bad, hero, villain, and the like, had to be fought for.

From 1790 to 1950 in the U.S. Census, a census taker who visited your house determined the race of the person being counted. Beginning in 1960, a person had the right to identify their own race.[3] It's only since the year 2000 that people have been able to identify more than one race for the census (and thus other means of "counting" people, like job applications). Until the 1960s, by the "one drop" rule, if someone had a nonwhite ancestor in the distant past, it was enough to be counted as nonwhite in many parts of America.

What does this have to do with women's sovereignty? There has been a fight going on for decades about the role of feminism in society, especially in groups and subcultures who promote women's roles as homemakers, mothers, and helpmeets over those of independence, working in careers, and so on. It's amazing how much of a bad rap feminism gets. I have been told by many men (with a straight face) that feminists want to kill men, that they want men to be castrated. Antifeminist women have said things to me that are equally shocking, that feminists want to kill babies, especially male babies, and that women have a sacred duty to submit to their husbands and bear children.

While I have seen one video of a crazy woman calling for men to die and leave the world to women, this is not a majority view. It's not even a minority view. It's a single outlier. And yet in our current climate, outliers are treated as evidence. Women on the whole don't want a "matriarchy" in the style that men's rights activists promote. Those activists fear a system like the one we have now but turned on them. They believe that women would want to be as dominating as men have been for the last thousand or so years. That is pure fear mongering. Study after study suggests that women (and most men) already believe that women should be paid equal to men for the same job, that women should have equal opportunity in the workplace, and that women should be free from sexual harassment and sexual assault.

Why would these ideas be controversial? They're not. What *is* controversial is the route women take to get to those outcomes. The vision of the angry feminist donning short hair and spouting angry rhetoric while burning her bra is fearsome. Why? Because it stands in place of a version of women's sovereignty that is "given" and instead takes a place that is combative. Women fighting for—demanding—our rights is unseemly to many people. But to do otherwise implies that the rights are coming from somewhere other than ourselves. The implication that women can and should fight, demand, argue, and engage in dismantling systems of oppression reminds us that there are systems of oppression to begin with. It points out the obvious: that if I have to be given my rights by someone else, then they aren't mine at all. They are determined by someone else and thus can be taken away, limited, curbed, protected, or earmarked by someone else.

The argument against women's sovereignty is that it upsets the predictable order. It is the same argument for all cultural change. People on the whole distrust ambiguity. This is based on basic biology. If I have to think about you for longer than a moment, if I can't just react to you, it feels like fear. The hesitation feels like indecisiveness. When you live in a warring society, where threats are everywhere (because that is what keeps certain groups in power), then you don't have time to think about the person in front of you. You need to make a decision about them instantly, or it could mean death. That's the fear circuit in the brain warning people of danger.

Fear sells. Fear is the basic currency of our society. Women know this better than men, because we are typically the target. We are trained to go places in pairs. We learn to carry our car keys laced between our fingers. We don't walk alone into alleyways. We don't get into elevators with men we don't know. We are trained to be worried about our reputations more than our intellect, our attractiveness more than our emotional well-being, our likability more than our self-worth and personal ambitions.

We are taught from the time we are little girls to not trust strange men, even while we are encouraged to hug uncles, cousins, and family friends who are more likely to become our predators than strangers. Women are taught from a young age that it is our responsibility to police the men around us. We must learn to thread a difficult needle where we don't tempt a man while appearing to maintain his dignity as a predator. Being a "good" woman means not questioning a man's motives or desires, and simultaneously not giving into them, unless we "belong" to them and only them. Fear underlies this pattern: fear of being rejected, fear of being an outcast, fear of losing resources, fear of being vilified. We rarely ask if we want to live in a society where we are afraid of everything. We never ask if this system of beliefs is just or if it is simply what we have inherited.

Sovereignty is most commonly discussed in the realms of political science. A "sovereign" country is one that defines its own rulers, government, culture, and political future. A country's sovereignty is usually discussed in disputes. The sovereignty of a country being disrespected, as in an invasion or a breach of territorial waters, is often seen as an act of war. There are also movements in the United States and other places to define "sovereign citizens," individuals who claim that no government has the right to infringe upon them and their desires. It is striking to me that it is usually these same types who are most opposed to women's rights to sovereignty. Their claims are for men—and often specifically white men alone.

Sovereignty is different from equality. I can demand equality, but you don't have to give it. Equality comes from someone else. It is based on comparison. I had a client named Carolyn once tell me that she had figured out what was wrong with her and that she felt that her therapy needed to shift to address the problem caused by this fundamental flaw her mother had created. Carolyn's mother had taught her to be, in her words, "a cis white man." This client figured out that all her pain in her job, her relationships, even her friendships was that she expected to be treated in every endeavor as though there were no "female tax" on her behavior or expectations.

Sovereignty is something anyone can act upon. In it lies the expectation that regardless of how other people see you, you will behave in accordance with your beliefs, values, morals, and ethics. You will determine your own future, and you will work within the system as much as you see fit—using it where it serves you and ignoring it where it does not. Sovereignty presumes equality; it doesn't need to demand it. In situations where our sovereignty is challenged or compromised, we can choose to leave or stay to take advantage or wait for an appropriate, strategic moment. When you are sovereign, you are not a victim. When you are sovereign, you are not subjugated.

Sovereignty flips the idea of equality around. Don't wait for equality; stand in sovereignty. When you position any argument as one of sovereignty, not equality, it is much harder to bait and switch. Why should a woman be paid the same as a male counterpart? She has as much responsibility for her well-being as a man, she often has fewer social protections, and she needs to protect her career/body/future as much as anyone else. She has the right and responsibility to own herself as much as anyone else. She is paying the same to be educated, to own a home, to own a car, to pay for health insurance, then why on earth shouldn't she have the right to determine her own destiny by claiming the right to own herself and her decisions in the same way a man would?

As a result, women en masse can use sovereignty as their own individual and personal means to move forward. We can use sovereignty to create networks with other women. If we as individuals demand our sovereign rights, it will be more difficult for the equality argument to be offered to us piecemeal. If women doctors, for example, form their own group practices based on sovereignty, then there is no one to tell them how to govern as "women" doctors. They are just doctors. If women lawyers start their own firm, they can create a firm that interprets the law according to the principles of sovereignty for their clients and don't have to worry about sexual politics entering their boardrooms and offices. In other words, women can determine their own futures as individuals or in groups, should they chose to do so. Wherever possible, their personal sovereignty can guide their choices.

How Do We Get to Sovereignty?

There is a road map to sovereignty. It isn't easy, but it is predictable. In the next several chapters, you will learn how we as women can make sense of the path to sovereignty in a world that has made every effort to cut us out of that equation. The biggest obstacle to sovereignty is an archetypal pattern I wrote about in the previous chapter that I call the Divide. Explaining this critical aspect of the Queen's Path, and thus the road to sovereignty is the linchpin for the rest of the journey. Without understanding the importance, structure, and ubiquity of the Divide, the rest of the journey will be more difficult to make sense of and even more challenging to navigate.

You can think of the Divide like a ravine that splits in front of you. You have to walk along one side or the other, because the line becomes the route along which you walk. When you're little the Divide feels small, but as you get older, what was a tiny crack becomes as wide as the Grand Canyon. The work of sovereignty is to bridge the Divide, building structures and resources along the way. If you don't do so consciously, then when you encounter the steps along the Queen's Path, they will feel like punishment or personal failure. Carl Jung famously wrote, "When an inner situation is not made conscious, it happens outside as fate."[4] In memes and other popular treatments this has been wordsmithed as, "If you don't endeavor to make the unconscious conscious it will rule your life and you will call it fate." What that means is that if we don't endeavor to be in relationship with the unconscious forces in both our personal and collective lives, everything that happens to us will feel like an outside force pushing us around. We won't be living consciously. Our unconscious will run the show at both the individual and community levels. The more unaware we are, the more mysterious that force will be and the more power the unconscious will exert in our lives and world.

When we encounter the two tracks along either side of the ravine, we will be set upon one or the other. We might get to choose, but it is much more likely that we are given a set of expectations to live up to. Almost all of us are taught that one track is better: the track of traditional, approved female behavior. Women should be docile. Women should be demure. Women should be mothers. Women should be attractive. Women should . . . women should . . . women should . . . When a woman can't live up to those "shoulds," she risks falling onto the other side, where she is dark, sexual, powerful, and therefore dangerous.

CHAPTER 4

THE HERO STANDS ALONE

Luke Skywalker emerges from his Uncle Owen's house to gaze out on the setting of Tatooine's two suns. The sky is a beautiful blend of deep purples, blues, and reds as our hero looks out onto the horizon. The lowest sun on the horizon glows a bright orange. It reflects the slow burn we feel in him. We, the audience, see in his eyes a steely longing for more. His uncle wants to keep him safe, small. Luke wants more, bigger. He wants an adventure. He will soon find himself not only on an adventure, but on the hero's quest, a sacred campaign to understand the meaning of life and an expedition scouring the far reaches of the galaxy to explore the limits of one man's power. Luke's journey doesn't disappoint the audience as he guides us on our own quest. We take the journey with him.

George Lucas completed the original *Star Wars* with the aid of Joseph Campbell's 1949 book, *The Hero with a Thousand Faces*. The movie follows the symbolic structure of Campbell's mythic structure to the letter. Audiences fell in love with *Star Wars* and its unique brand of movie magic. We follow Luke Skywalker because he represents us, the viewer. He is me. I am on a quest. I must find my way to master the force and kill the evil and broken inside of me that longs for power. And then I must redeem that evil, and having done so, return to my home and share this boon with my community.

Except . . .

My mom says I can't be a Jedi because I'm a girl.

My eight-year-old brain screamed, "Garbage! I can be anything. There absolutely would be girl Jedis! They don't live on Earth. Jedis live all over the universe. Why wouldn't there be girl Jedis in worlds that have very different rules and customs than ours?" But in the original 1977 film, there are no girl Jedis. In fact, there are only two women of note: Princess Leia, who is one of the lead characters, and Luke's Aunt Beru, who we only meet for a moment. Neither are Jedis. So, <sigh> my mom was right.

Yes, in later films, there are women Jedis walking around, in council meetings and so on. But in the 1970s, there were none. If we look at the journey that Princess Leia takes in the original *Star Wars* movie, she is neither a hero nor a heroine. She goes through two different states in the film. She is a damsel in distress needing to be saved, and later she is a feisty military operator, butting up against a scoundrel/pirate to return the stolen plans of the Death Star to her people. When the hero's quest is over, she presides over a royal ceremony to honor Luke Skywalker, Han Solo, and Chewbacca for saving the Alliance.

What were the different experiences that Leia and Luke were living out on screen? Luke is the orphaned hero who is cast out from his family's protection onto the road of the quest. He is aided by a magical teacher, Obi-Wan Kenobi, and meets several helpers along the way. Leia is aided by Luke, Obi-Wan, and Han Solo as well. But her journey is not to gain a secret, but freedom and sovereignty for herself and her people. Luke is a hero. Leia is not a heroine but a Queen.

The Hero's Journey has become pervasive. The idea became part of modern storytelling parlance in the late 1980s thanks to the work of Janelle Balnicke, Phil Cousineau, William Free, Bill Moyers, and Christopher Vogler. Their books and films examined the different aspects of Campbell's influence. Their works skyrocketed the Hero's Journey from an abstract concept in mythological theory and philosophy to an organizing principle across multiple domains from filmmaking to psychotherapy. In the last several years, a "science of heroism" has emerged based on the Hero's Journey. The program isn't quite a flighty woo-fest; it's part of the curriculum at Stanford Graduate School of Business.

Like other areas where the male default doesn't quite fit women's stories, the Hero's Journey doesn't match the contours of women's experience. Where is the part of the journey where the hero has to fight off unwanted sexual advances? How about the part where the heroine has to convince the reluctant crew that she knows how to sail a ship or captain a star cruiser? What about the pregnancy scare after a night of romantic conquest? In the heroes' lives we are familiar with, we never see these played out. Alfred doesn't turn to Batman before a night of vigilante justice and say, "Do you really need that donut?" Perry White doesn't turn to Clark Kent and say, "Do you really want to work as a reporter here? Won't it interfere with marriage and kids?" Spiderman isn't told to smile more. The aforementioned Luke Skywalker doesn't have to worry that his pursuit of mastering the force will make him unmarriageable. When Zorro takes on the colonizing Spanish nobility, no one double-checks him to see if they really are cheating the peasants, and no one presumes that Harrison Ford can't carry an Indiana Jones movie at 80 years of age.

The hero has his own mythic structure. Campbell himself called the Hero's Journey the monomyth of human experience. Except, it's mostly the man-o-myth experience. We know the structure well. Depending on which expert on Joseph Campbell's original work you follow, there are anywhere from 9 to 17 steps in the Hero's Journey. Campbell himself characterized it rather simply in discussing the overall structure.

> *A hero ventures forth from the world of common day into a region of supernatural wonder: fabulous forces are there encountered and a decisive victory is won: the hero comes back from this mysterious adventure with the power to bestow boons on his fellow man.*[1]

Simple, right? Boy leaves home for adventure, boy encounters trials, boy has losses, boy makes manly decision(s); boy is transformed, becomes man, and teaches other boys how to become men.

Because the story of the hero is the story of men in patriarchy, women in patriarchy are not obvious heroes or heroines. There have been many women writers who have attempted to adapt the Hero's Journey structure for women. The sentiment is in the right place, "Wait, women are important! Women need adventure! Women can bring back just as much meaning as men!" My answer to these protestations is that they are correct in their critique. Women are certainly capable of anything a man can accomplish. But it is the question that is wrong. It's not because women aren't capable but because the title of hero is not won through personal trial and subsequent success in the quest. The title of hero is given to the person who *through* the quest acquires a truth, and then *shares it with their community.* And in most cultures, women aren't trusted to bestow a boon or share the elixir of life. In our stories, and in our lived experience, men don't want the women around them teaching them the ways of the force or showing them up in a glorious pursuit. If you need an example, let's examine one of the world's oldest stories of the Divide, the myth of Atalanta. This is my version, pieced together from multiple retellings from the classical Ovid and Aelian to the modern Adrienne Mayor.

Atalanta and Fierce Freedom

In the kingdom of Arcadia, there was a minor king whose wife was with child. The king was a very proud man and was certain that his first child would be a son who would take after his father, eventually inheriting his throne. But when the queen delivered her baby, it was a girl. The king was so disappointed that he instructed his servants to take the baby to the forest and leave her to die. Unwanted babies were often left in the woods or on the sides of cliffs to die of exposure, a cruelty that offended the goddess Artemis.

The baby was found in the woods by a bear whose two cubs had been killed by hunters. She picked up the babe and took care of her until she was old enough to walk on her own. Raised by a bear, Atalanta grew into a curious, ferocious, and strong child. Further, she learned no shame in being female. When a group of hunters happened upon her, they realized that though she was ferocious and formidable, she was a human living in the wild with only a bear for family. They captured her and brought her back to their community to be raised as a hunter. The hunters recognized the hand of the goddess in the girl's fate and revered her as one of their own. Out of respect for the goddess, they spared the bear. The hunters taught Atalanta, whose name means "equal," to take care of herself and hunt, wrestle, and ride horses. They supported her natural fearless disposition. Atalanta never forgot the wild and caring ways of her bear mother. From the moment she returned to the world of humans, she dedicated herself to the goddess Artemis who had brought her and her wild mother together.

Atalanta made for herself a beautiful cottage deep in the forest. She was happy away from the world and took care of herself, hunting and enjoying her home. One day, two centaurs saw the beautiful and athletic young woman hunting in the forest. Centaurs were known to be lustful, driven by their sexual passion and need for power. They made a pact to capture Atalanta and rape her. But the young huntress was as cunning as Artemis herself, and before they could capture her, she shot both centaurs with her bow and arrow, killing them instantly. As a result, her fame and renown grew far and wide.

When he heard about her exploits, the king who had ordered her to be left to die in the forest called for Atalanta to be returned to her family. Reluctantly, the princess returned to the family who had abandoned her. The royal life didn't suit Atalanta. She longed to hunt and be free. Women in Greece were not free to follow their own wills. They were expected to be ladies and to leave the world of ability and adventure to men.

In the neighboring kingdom of Calydon the king, Oeneus, had a dilemma and called to all the heroes in Greece to help him. A wild boar was marauding throughout the cities and countryside, killing people and wreaking havoc. People throughout Calydon were fearful of the boar, grinding public life to a standstill. There was no one to work. No commerce was taking place. The king had offended the goddess Artemis and the roaming, murderous boar was her punishment.

When Atalanta heard that the heroes of Greece were assembling to hunt the Calydonian boar, she thought she could be useful because of her hunting skills. She knew that because of her experience and her respect for the goddess Artemis, she had a better chance at killing the boar than anyone else. The king had a son named Meleager; he had been selected to lead the hunting party. When Atalanta presented herself with the other heroes, they scoffed. They had heard of her exploits but underestimated her ability to kill the ferocious boar. They dismissed her, but Meleager was intrigued, and sensing the disdain of the other hunters, encouraged her to hunt alongside him.

The day the hunt began, the boar's strength and ruthlessness were in full display. The boar killed several of the hunters. Atalanta watched as the boar seemed to pick its victims when they were least expecting it. The boar would charge and turn, confusing the hunters, then gore them violently with its enormous tusks. Atalanta showed Meleager how they could work together to kill the boar. The other hunters had wanted the glory for themselves, and this devotion to their own reputations made them much more vulnerable. They each wanted to kill the boar on their own, without help. Each hunter wanted the glory, for his name to be remembered for this magnificent feat of bravery and skill. But Atalanta knew that the boar was so ferocious that a single hunter would not be capable. The boar's skin was too tough, its tusks too dangerous. Her observations were rewarded as she noticed how the boar turned in its attacks. Atalanta positioned herself so that she could wound the boar and then drive the animal to Meleager, who would deal the final blow.

Atalanta drew first blood, and then cornered the boar on its deadly trajectory toward Meleager's spear. Atalanta and Meleager killed the Calydonian boar together in collaboration. As was tradition, having drawn the first blood, Atalanta was presented with the boar's hide as a trophy. But the other hunters were incensed that this honor would go to a woman, regardless of whether she demonstrated greater skill than the other hunters. Meleager defended her right to the prize and the glory. A bitter fight ensued, pulling many hunters into the fray. Meleager and several other hunters were killed.

Despite her success with the Calydonian boar, Atalanta was not welcomed home as a hero. She returned to her father's house heartbroken by the loss of Meleager, the first man who saw her as an equal. She was angry at the waste of life in the hunt of the Caledonian boar. Glory and pride didn't seem worth the loss. In her despair, Atalanta eschewed all forms of love, but especially romantic love. Because of the perceived disgrace over the Calydonian boar, Atalanta's father insisted that she marry.

Atalanta didn't believe in love and had no desire to marry. She wasn't interested in being someone's kept possession. She didn't believe that a man could love her. She saw only their vanity and desire for glory. She concocted a plan. Atalanta knew that no one could outrun her. So she told her father that she would challenge any suitor to a footrace; she'd even give the suitors a head start. She further raised the stakes, declaring that any man who lost to her would lose his life and any who beat her would win her hand in marriage. Her father agreed to the terms. Despite the stakes being so high, many suitors thought that they could beat the athletic Atalanta. They laid their lives on the line to prove her wrong and claim her as a bride. Led by their hubris and vanity, all the suitors set out to prove that they could outperform the capable Atalanta. They died one after the other. But one man chose instead to observe her rather than subdue her.

Hippomenes had been a student of the wounded healer, Chiron. Though Chiron was a centaur, he was the child of Titans and as a result had a more thoughtful nature, not moved by lust or diversion. He also had an eternal life and as a result invested in mentoring Gods and heroes. Those tutored by Chiron learned his thoughtful, patient, and curious way of being in the world. In hearing of the capable and athletic woman, Hippomenes felt he had to see her for himself. He studied her and knew that he would never win against her in a head-to-head match. She was too fast, too athletic, and too disciplined to beat.

Through his observation, Hippomenes fell in love with Atalanta. He knew that he could not get her attention in the footrace through his own athletic talent, as hers was far superior. To capture her heart, he would have to slow her down, using his intelligence and powers of observation. Hippomenes sought the assistance of Aphrodite, the goddess of love. Aphrodite was annoyed with Atalanta for her rejection of love and agreed to help Hippomenes. She gave him three golden and enchanted apples and instructed him to leave them in her path. Their magic was that they were so beautiful and alluring, anyone would yearn to eat them. They were so delicious that anyone who ate them would revel in the pleasure of their taste.

Though she gave him a head start, Atalanta would gain on Hippomenes. As she did, Hippomenes would roll one of the beautiful, enchanted apples toward her. Their golden magic would capture her attention, and Atalanta would be slowed down, giving Hippomenes time to move ahead along the route of the race. As Atalanta would gain on Hippomenes, he would roll another one of the enchanted apples toward her. She delighted in the apples, and this gave Hippomenes the advantage. He won the race.

Atalanta wound up falling in love with Hippomenes, not because he bested her but because he saw her true nature and treated her as an equal. The two were married, and their passion for one another grew. Atalanta and Hippomenes would make love with abandon whenever their passion was aroused. One day they were consumed by their desire in the temple of Ceres. The goddess transformed them into lions. Some of the ancient writers call this a curse, and others remark that it was not a punishment, but a way of making their love eternal. As lions, Atalanta and her beloved Hippomenes were free to hunt and make love as equals forever. They no longer bore the constraints of humanity and culture to limit their passionate natures.

What the Myth Tells Us

A MISOR can't be a hero; she's bound to the domestic life. She doesn't learn to ride horses with the men or hunt better than they do. She stays home with her mother and sisters. She learns to cook and sew. She defers to authority. A MIPE can't become a hero. The men don't want her in their ranks, competing for the glory or spoils.

They will fight and kill other men to ensure that women don't compete in their domains or steal their glory.

Atalanta was called a "heroine," but she never got to live in the halls of the hero. She didn't occupy the same mythic space. Her journey was not that of the hero. She was not allowed to share her boon with humanity. She didn't get to go on a quest. No wise teachers came to her aid, though she did have magical connections to nature and animals. When love came her way, she didn't trust it. She didn't want the domestic life, preferring to be on her own in the woods. When she tried to use her talents, she was pushed aside for being a woman. Her skills and abilities didn't matter; they weren't enough. The Hero's Journey is not a meritocracy.

Atalanta knew her worth. She saw that she had skills and tried to use them to be of service. She didn't feel the need to make herself small. She was cunning and made sure that any man who wanted to own her would pay the price with his life. To fall in love, she had to be tricked into seeing that at least one man would see her as his equal. The world is a bitter place for women. Knowing this, Ceres, the goddess of agriculture who tames the wild things and makes them domestic, saw that Atalanta would be best served by being her wild self forever, and transformed her and her husband into lions that would be wild equals for eternity.

In the prologue to her book *The Amazons: Lives & Legends of Warrior Women Across the Ancient World*, writer Adrienne Mayor describes a ritual called the Arkteia (translated as she-bear) that young Athenian girls participated in before they could be betrothed.[2] In this ritual, they took on the story of Atalanta, pretending to be bears, acting out the story. They raced each other on foot. They worked out their wild sides. The time in the temples preparing for the Arkteia were meant to help the girls express their untamed Atalantean side before they settled down as docile Athenian wives. They had to divest themselves of any expectations of fierce freedom before they could marry. The MIPEs had to be tamed into obedient, docile MISORs.

Presuming that women can go on a hero's quest in the same way that men do is shortsighted. Women aren't welcome on the Hero or Heroine's Journey. To be a hero, you have to leave the safety of home and strike out on your own. The MISOR won't do this, and the MIPE is punished or ostracized for it. Standing in the hero's place is something that women are not expected to do, and in our culture, we don't really want them to do it. As a result, they will always fight the Divide on the Hero's Journey. A woman must first overcome the Divide, or she can never become a hero or heroine. She must examine each role in her world, the MISOR and the MIPE, and reject both. Only then is she free to decide what pieces of those roles actually matter to her. She then chooses what to leave and what to keep. When she does this, she re-centers and ascends the throne of sovereignty. Whether the world wants what she shares or not doesn't matter. Her worth is determined by her alone. Her value ceases to be defined by how well she fits a role or how well she diminishes herself to be liked. She cannot be made larger or smaller by how hard she works for recognition. Her work, her joy, and her commitments are for her, and her alone.

Arguments for Women Heroes

People want there to be a path for women to be heroes and heroines. I get that. My work will not eliminate the vernacular use of the word *heroine* from our description of women protagonists in stories. But the Hero's Journey as a model for women's narratives is challenging. It simply doesn't meet the lived experience of women. It's not because women can't do the hero's work. It is because culture expects very different behavior from us. The woman who steps on the Hero's Journey is an outsider from the outset. She doesn't fit the model of what the world expects of women. Yes, she is there to change that. But she can't do that work the same way Luke Skywalker or Indiana Jones does it. While we may place women in similar roles and in similar jobs, the vast majority of people, men and women alike, don't want to see women in those roles (for an examination, see the Melissa McCarthy–led *Ghostbusters* reboot and the backlash). A woman can be a hero or heroine, but she *first* must take the Queen's Path and achieve sovereignty—otherwise, she's just an interloper on the Hero's Journey.

86

I've had this argument many times with people who aren't familiar with my work and disagree. Almost every time, it is because people don't want to believe that they have different expectations of women than men. These folks are well meaning. A few people who have confronted me about this model are writers who write female characters. They argue passionately for the role of women heroes. But for me, it is not that the women aren't capable; it's that society doesn't want them there, and this is the exact experience of the Divided Woman. A woman who finds herself called to the quest must first eschew all the tropes and expectations and determine her own sovereign path. She must free herself before she can free anyone else. The presumption that women take the same road is to ignore the different structural impediments that men and women face on their road to self-realization.

In giving talks and presenting my findings, there are women who finally say, "Yes, I get it!" And there are also women and men who engage me in passionate arguments to prove that I'm wrong. It takes a lot to offend me, so I typically wait patiently until the arguments come to an end. There is usually a long list of female heroines that are spat at me as though those characters fit the Hero's Journey and not the Queen's Path. Here is the usual list of heroines I am given, in no particular order:

Katniss Everdeen	The Bride
Moana	Ellen Ripley
Daenerys Targaryen	Princess Leia
Arya Stark	Eowyn
Mulan	Galadriel
Scarlett O'Hara	Lisbeth Salander
Clarice Starling	

My critics presume I haven't done my homework or that I don't understand the Hero's Journey well enough to place these characters there and see how ill-fitting the environment is for them. So I'll pick a couple. You'll find others discussed in different chapters. The underlying argument is not that women aren't capable of being heroes; it is that culture doesn't want to see us that way. And ultimately the role of hero is to go and learn something profound and deep that you then *share with your people.* If no one wants what you're sharing, the Hero's Journey isn't meaningful. It's not a Hero's Journey; it's just a trial of misery with no meaning.

Katniss Everdeen from *The Hunger Game* starts out a MIPE. Set in a dystopian future, every year, tributes from the conquered states are required to provide young people to fight in the Hunger Games. A skilled hunter who poaches to feed her family, Katniss has a recurrent dream that haunts her. Soon her fear becomes reality as her sister Primrose is selected as the tribute from her district in a lottery known as The Reaping. With no survival skills and being only 12 years old, Prim would certainly die in the televised spectacle. Afraid she will lose her little sister, Katniss steps forward to replace her. Bam! we are in the Divide. Katniss is an extraordinary person; she has great intellectual and physical power (Magical and Powerful). She leaves her home and everything she knows (Isolated). She can't avoid the games; she must play them (Endangered). She is put in a position to have to fend for herself. We know she must be wary of her fellow competitors—we have the Magical, Isolated, Powerful, and Endangered (MIPE) qualities very clearly. Yes, she gets a call to—are we going to call it adventure? A quest? She doesn't really have a choice. She gets help from a mentor. She enters a new world. She has trials in the form of the games. So sure, we may call her a hero. But she's more than that. She is on a quest to resolve the Divide within herself. She is seeking sovereignty, not fame, glory, or the elixir of life.

The eponymous Moana starts out on the path of the MISOR, Maiden in Search of Relationship. She feels the pressure of taking the throne for her family and living under the authority of their legacy. When her grandmother dies, she feels she must save her people from starvation and annihilation by returning the heart of Te'fiti, the plentiful goddess of life. She finds Maui, the demi-god, and they reluctantly set out together to accomplish this goal. But the task turns out to *actually* be the reunification of the Divided Woman, well, Divided Goddess. We learn that the demon Te'ka is the same goddess as Te'fiti. Without her heart, Te'fiti is a burning volcano who destroys everything that comes close to her. Moana shows the wailing Te'ka that she has the heart, a green stone imbued with the magical power of creation. Moana says to her, "I see who you truly are," and returns the heart to the goddess. Te'ka is transformed back into the goddess Te'fiti, and the world is returned to the place of creative beauty it was before her heart was taken. When Moana returns to her island of Motunui, she takes the mantle of Queen. She changes the goals of her culture, returning them to the seafaring people they had been generations before.

The Silence of the Lambs' Clarice Starling is a MIPE. She is intelligent, brave, (Magical and Powerful) and has nothing to lose. She has no family (Isolated). She strives to prove herself, something that the murderous Dr. Hannibal Lecter easily sees in the young woman seeking his assistance. Clarice's task is to save Katherine Martin, the daughter of a powerful senator, a damsel in distress (MISOR). To reunite Katherine with her family and save her from being murdered and mutilated, Clarice must reunite the pieces of herself that have been rendered through her childhood traumas. She is pursued first by Dr. Lecter and then by the murderous Buffalo Bill (Endangered). At each step toward healing herself, Clarice earns more clues from Dr. Lecter. She is uniting the disparate pieces of the Divide to reunite Katherine with her family.

In each of these stories, there is a clear Divided Woman image. In every one, the main character reunites the broken pieces to have sovereignty over herself. This isn't prescribed or random. Each future Queen unites the pieces according to her will, character, and ethics. In doing so, she is finding her way along her own unique Queen's Path. While her work is personal, it is in response to the pressures put on her by her place in the world. She is overcoming the limits and definitions that would keep her preserved in a role in favor of living as a fully authentic human being.

As you traverse your own unique journey along the Queen's Path, I want to encourage you to reflect on the places and times that may have presented you with inconsistencies. So many women are met with either MISOR discouragement or MIPE dismissal. Women who identify as MISORs often hear things like "Why are you doing that?" "That's too big." or "Why not make it easier on yourself?" Or on the MIPE side, perhaps, "You're wasting your time." Or "No one is going to care about that," or "Who do you think you are?" I think the saddest part of these is that so many women internalize these voices. Almost every woman I know has had to battle an internal voice that has taken all those messages from culture, parents, and partners and created an internal limiting structure. This set of internal strictures does additional harm, because when women face the world's harsh words or punishing uphill climbs, the internal voice matches the external obstacles. The harmony of the internal and external messages makes it more challenging for the individual woman to battle the forces that would keep her small. Sovereignty is the only force that can break the internal voice, so that an individual woman can find the resilience to battle the external pressures that would keep her "in her place."

We have spent the last few chapters preparing for the journey. Now we stand at the threshold. From here on out, everything changes, just as it always does when you take any trip. Transformation is the result of every journey. As we prepare to enter the steps of the Queen's Path, spend a little time with your journal and reflect on what is important to you. Think about what sovereignty means to you, not just in abstract way. What do you believe would change if you were able to live from a place of sovereignty for yourself? Would anything change for your career? Your relationships? Think and feel deeply about it and spend some time with your journal putting those thoughts in words or images.

THE QUEEN'S PATH: THE WORLDS AND THE TIME PERIODS

In this section of the book, we are going on our own adventure through the Queen's Path. We will start at the beginning and wind our way along through the treacherous and rewarding path that leads to sovereignty. We will discuss some stories and recent films as we go. I hope you've seen most of them. If not, maybe put one or two on your viewing list. I'll be referencing 2023's *Barbie,* 2022's *Promising Young Woman,* 1985's *The Color Purple,* 2017's *Wonder Woman,* 2022's *The Woman King,* 2001's *Legally Blonde,* 2013's *Frozen,* and 2014's *Maleficent.*

In most stories, we aren't paying very close attention to the place and the time that things are happening in the character's universe. We do care about setting and the plot. But that the character is at the end of high school or about to start a new job are usually context. If a woman is in the midst of a career change or is struggling to raise her children, that is not usually the focus of how her internal struggle is portrayed, whether in stories or in the personal narratives of real women.

In my therapy practice, individual women focus primarily on what they can do. These patients often come into their first appointment believing something is "wrong" with them. They almost always come into therapy to "fix" something that they think will make the important people in their lives like them more, believe in them more, communicate with them better, or love them more deeply. Popular stories focus on how a character finds herself. Is she pretty? Fat? Is she too smart? Is she awkward? But in thinking archetypally, we have to think about where things happen and when they happen. Every story has a structure. Most stories follow a formula that is familiar so that the reader or the audience can feel comfortable in the story.

The first part of the story structure in the Queen's Path is the "world" structure. This isn't the setting of the story, though that is important, and if we weren't speaking of archetypes, the subject of worlds in story would be a very different discussion. Archetypally, the world is a fixed thing in this story structure. It reflects the roles that the person or character is experiencing. Where in her psyche does the journey take her? Where does she begin? In which aspect of the archetypal world does the story commence? Do we meet our protagonist as she is starting a new life in New York City after a divorce? After college? These place her on the Queen's Path in a specific way. Is a new psychotherapy patient seeking support because of a divorce? Is she starting a new career? Maybe she has moved across the country and is feeling alone. All these help us to understand where in the Queen's Path we are.

The Times, Worlds, and Quadrants of the Queen's Path

In our journey, the woman begins in the World of Visible Power and Form. If you look at the above figure, you will see that the World of Visible Power and Form is the upper half of the circle. Her journey begins in the upper right quadrant. Look at the circle as though it is a clock face. The journey begins in the Undifferentiated Quadrant, which is in the World of Visible Power and Form. It is like starting the journey at midnight and moving toward one.

The World of Visible Power and Form

The upper two quadrants, Quadrant I and Quadrant IV, make up the visible world. They are the world you can see, the world of decisions and direct action. This is the world of the every day. The world of power, where there are clear hierarchies. The world of the beginning and the end, where everything makes sense. You may have heard of something similar in regard to the Hero's Journey, where the hero has to leave the "everyday world." While there is an element of that here, it is not the same. In the World of Visible Power and Form, the woman sees the systems that operate around her. In Quadrant I, she is inside these systems but doesn't understand them. She is undifferentiated. In the fourth quadrant, after her cycle through the path is complete, she has become differentiated and has overcome the divided self. She has become a Queen, meaning that in the World of Visible Power and Form, she has emerged in sovereignty. She now has power in this world. She owns her domain and doesn't have to fight against the structures of culture, family, or role-bound expectations. She is free.

Quadrant I: Chimaeric Time

Look at the diagram as though you were reading the face of a clock. The first quadrant falls between 12 and 3—that's Quadrant I. It is appropriate to draw the analogy of a clock, because this is the earliest part of the story. It is where the character herself is undifferentiated. She is unaware of what is about to begin. It has not occurred to her that she is about to be forced into a lane the same way that all women are forced into one of two archetypal identities of MISOR or MIPE. She may see the Divide and think it doesn't apply to her. She may be unaware that these forces are at work.

Sometimes in stories, a character in this part of the cycle is a child. This may be in the character's past, a part of her backstory. In the first quadrant, writers need to know what their character's life was like before she was forced into or chose her lane. For real-life women, they can look back at their own lives and see the time of their innocence. The lanes will become evident as we go through the discussions over the course of this book. In this diagram, the lanes women are forced into are marked by the dotted line and then a solid line. All women, whether in fiction or in real life, face this divide. The woman in the first quadrant is called undifferentiated and the time is called chimaeric because she has only a glimpse of the Divide—anything is possible. She doesn't live with the Divide as her everyday struggle. It is the chimaeric quadrant because she is pure potential. She believes she can be or do anything.

She is not whole. To be whole, you have to have awareness. That is why "undifferentiated" is the appropriate descriptor. She knows her potential, she belongs to her family or tribe, or she has some gift that she knows is there. She does not know how to use her gifts. She doesn't know that the place around her is safe (or unsafe). She doesn't yet know what choices the world will put in front of her.

I often see women in my therapy practice who want to skip from Quadrant I to Quadrant IV. They rightfully fear the underworld of the journey and the mystery they will encounter there. But no power can be acquired or goal achieved without traversing the unknown. There can be no self-sovereignty without confronting the restrictions of culture and family. There can be no form without mystery, no power without conflict, no success without awareness. And there can be no United Queen without there first being a Divided Woman.

Divide et Impera: Divide and Rule (Over)

In his most famous work on politics, *The Prince*, Niccolò Machiavelli spoke of the "Mathematical Sense," a strategy of war first made known by the Greek king Philip of Macedonia. Machiavelli called it divide et impera, better known to us in English as "divide and conquer." The words have become hollow after centuries of use, and we have become somewhat detached from their deepest and most nuanced meaning. In the current political climate, we see it in the division of people into factions, and our efforts to maintain our ties within groups based on excising members who do not meet standards of purity.

Divide and Conquer has become an easy trope. The original translation of divide et impera is not the simple "divide and conquer" that we have come to associate with political parties and factions at the PTA. No, the original meaning is a lot more sinister. The term means to separate or faction and then compel the divided parts by force to the point of their knowing no other command. A conquered people are threatened into fear for their lives. If you are talking about an individual, to be divided in this way means literally to split someone's psyche against itself. The impera part means that the person being divided doesn't own herself. She gives up her own sovereignty to the "rule" of someone else. The Divided Woman, then, is internally compelled by the person ruling over her. It means to make the woman doubt her own internal thoughts in favor of the culture or individual that tells her she is not allowed her own power. The person herself does not own her impera (her own will or drive). She is subject to whoever rules over her. As we learned in the previous section and will see play out as we traverse the Queen's Path, every woman is a Divided Woman.

Every woman's story begins with her moving from undifferentiated to divided. She is a little girl, and she may play with boys. She may climb trees, or play with dolls, or both. The undifferentiated period of a woman's life is defined by her being unaware of what is coming. She does not really understand that there is something on the horizon that will constrain her. She doesn't know that she will face a series of events that will divide her and force her into a lane of behaving a certain way for the majority of her life. The story of the Divided Woman has not been out in the open in a conscious way. Like most things in the lives of women, it is hidden in plain sight.

These masked parts of the story allow the belief to invade each woman's psyche that some of the story (especially the parts that are most painful) are within her control. But while her individual incarnation of the story is personal, the path it traverses is archetypal. Female characters are just as susceptible to this reality as real-life women. It doesn't mean that every character will be plagued by doubt. Women can be confident, villainous, or sociopathic too. But all women fall into the Divide. And the first critical aspect of the Divide is *hiding it*. Part of keeping women in darkness is making us believe that *we created* the Divide for ourselves. Some of these internal messages may be familiar:

- If I had been stronger, I would not have been abused.

- If I had stood up for myself, they wouldn't have treated me this way.

- If I just can find the time to work harder, I'll be able to catch up and show them my value.

- If I weren't a pushover, s/he wouldn't get away with this.

- If I were prettier, I wouldn't feel this way.

- If I were smarter, I wouldn't be in this mess.

- If I were _(insert adjective here)_, I would/wouldn't _(insert horrible feeling here)_.

And my favorite combo:

What's wrong with me? That other woman has perfect children, wears a size 2 and has a fantastic marriage, a gorgeous home, and beautiful car. She goes on vacations and has a great relationship with her mom and her husband. She has it all. Maybe if I try to do everything, I'll have it all too. Why can't I find the energy/motivation? I'm broken. Something is wrong with me. This is all my fault.

These statements are the tools of the divide et impera message. They are part of keeping women divided against ourselves. This is not to say that the message of divide et impera is one that is consciously passed down through the generations. No, this is an unconscious process that almost every social system buys into. It has been with us from the beginning of Western culture. You find the Divided Woman everywhere. She is Lilith and Eve in the Hebrew Bible. She is Demeter and Persephone in Greek mythology. She is Queen Elizabeth I and Mary Queen of Scots in Britain. She is Queen Elizabeth II and Diana, Princess of Wales, in modern history. What these stories tell us is that there are two, and only two, ways for women to be. You are either submissive or ostracized. This journey will take us down the winding staircase of the Divided Woman. As we take the deep dive, we will get more details about the Queen's Path, the pitfalls, the places we trip, and the other characters along the way.

The World of Invisible Forces and Mystery

Looking at Figure 1, you will see the hemispheres of the worlds. Above the horizon, the World of Visible Power and Form keeps us in the realm of what is seen. In it are the conscious acts and the beginnings of the changes women face as we move from innocent child to adolescent. Only once a woman has concluded her work beneath the horizon, in the World of Invisible Forces and Mystery, can the effects of her personal power emerge in the World of Visible Power and Form. Above the horizon lies the ability to see clearly. Below the horizon, everything is jumbled and messy. Below the horizon is the power of transformation. No one can become a Queen without slogging through mystery.

The lower quadrants, Quadrants II and III, make up the World of Invisible Forces and Mystery. These are the worlds where it isn't clear what is happening from the outside because the work is happening deep in the depths. All women experience these shifts, but most of us live unaware of their archetypal nature. These structures feel personal, and because they are personal, we feel as though we are responsible for some aspect of them.

What I have begun to understand through this work, however, is that while the way is archetypal, women interact with the Queen's Path on a personal level. We did not create the markers, divisions, challenges, and structures of the archetypal journey. We are traveling it, and it is working through us because it is a universal story that all women experience. Whether you are pursuing your own Queen's Path or you are a writer, it is critical to know which parts of the journey are archetypal. For an individual, the path doesn't *feel* archetypal; everything is personal. When we are able to make the unconscious parts of the story conscious, we free ourselves from the structural constraints that hold us captive. From the perspective of storytelling, the characters need to go through the trials along the path, just as real women do. The moment they leave the world that makes sense in the first quadrant, they are in the period of their lives where they are confronted with mystery. For real women, this period often feels like wandering in the darkness, where they are unsure how to make sense of what is happening and being frequently confronted with assertions that the Divide is their fault.

The Underworld: The World of Invisible Forces and Mystery

The individual woman cannot traverse from Quadrant I to Quadrant IV without going into the lower quadrants of the World of Invisible Forces and Mystery. It is in the lower half that she encounters all the unseen powers that will act on and through her in the journey toward sovereignty. The danger of the land below the horizon is that for thousands of years, women have been kept there. We have been subject to men's journeys and thus have occupied a kind of numinous space where we struggle to make sense of, and somehow also govern, the underworld. It is in the second quadrant that the final divide of the individual woman is complete, tearing her from her sister-self and turning those two halves against one another. This is called the Rendering, not in the sense of a created version of herself but more in the slaughterhouse meaning of the word. She is ripped apart. As she traverses the second quadrant, she starts to get a sense that there is something external about the journey. There is a structure keeping her in a lane, in a persona, constraining and defining her as sure as the broken toes of bound feet or the misshapen ribs of a lifetime in a corset.

As she leaves the second quadrant for the third, the woman "believes" that she is headed for salvation, when in truth she is about to face annihilation, death, or that particular ignobility of slavery, being erased. From the second to the third quadrant, death and rebirth chase her like a banshee. If the woman is lured into a "happily ever after" (HEA), then she metaphorically dies as an eternal girl. If she is shunned from her HEA, then she can metaphorically die in isolation as a power-hungry witch. In neither case is she free and in neither case is she happy and fulfilled. It is easy to see why women become associated with the underworld here. If she never gets to leave it, it becomes a place she haunts.

The third quadrant is traditionally where women's stories go to die. A woman plans her whole life around the day she gets married, only to be subsumed by that role thereafter. A woman who doesn't marry, who lives out her career ambitions, finds herself alone and longing, sometimes bitter, wishing for the HEA. What each of these women need to complete their journey into the fourth quadrant is Embodied Transcendence. This can be seen in movies like *The Color Purple,* where Celie finally gets to own her life. We see her *standing* on her own land, *embracing* her sister and her children, and surrounded by her family of choice. Transcendence is symbolized by a physical change in stories like *Maleficent,* when the title character regains the wings that were stolen from her. It is demonstrated in brilliant films and musicals like *Waitress*, where Jenna, the protagonist, realizes that she is powerful through the experience of labor and giving birth to her daughter, Lulu.

To return to the World of Visible Power and Form, she must take the Queen's Path and do the work of integration, which is the work of liberation. In the third quadrant (which is still in the quadrant of Invisible Forces and Mystery), the individual woman finds herself reflecting on her choices. If she doubles down on her role, whether it is as an eternal ever-pure maiden or the power-hungry witch, she will be lost to herself and her true power forever. She can return to the World of Visible Power and Form once she finds a way to integrate the Divided Woman. Once she does that work, transcendence leads her to her own personal sovereignty. Her own sovereignty and regency then will guide her in the world of power. She is no one's property; her story belongs to her.

Returning to Face the Light

If she faces her sister-self and sacrifices the idea of achieving perfection on either track, she has a chance to reclaim her other side and integrate both halves into a unified whole. When she does this, she has the power to ascend to a new role, one where she is untouchable by the divisive hands of the culture that separated her from her whole self. She is no longer interested in the tracks and the lanes. She sees them for what they were: a set of cultural chains forged to disempower her. In the fourth quadrant, her true purpose unfolds the sacred, embodied expression of her being. It is in this radical self-sovereignty that she finds her power, and in it we may call her a Queen, ascending to rule the domain of her true self.

Once the woman goes through the necessary trials of redeeming and integrating her sister-self, she then is free to drop all the expectations of roles and focus on her own impera. She is no longer divided, and no one can tell her what she should do, what her priorities are, or who she should give her words and work to. No, once she heals the Divided Woman, there are only a few steps left as she rises to claim her crown and rule her own domain.

Entering the World of the Divided Woman and the Queen

Every woman in the world embarks on this journey, whether we want to or not. Most of us never learn that there are steps beyond the "happily ever after" we were raised to expect. We compare ourselves to perfect versions of divided princesses and terrible witches, without ever recognizing that there is so much more to the story.

Almost every woman I meet struggles with a form of perfectionism that a therapist would determine is pathological. I have treated many men, and few of them suffer in the same way that women do when it comes to this expectation of perfection. The problem is not that women are more perfectionistic than men; it is *the way* that we are perfectionists. No matter which lane—MISOR or MIPE—we land in, we will always compare ourselves to a better, more idealized version of ourselves. No matter what we achieve in life, we will always look at other women as doing more and doing it better. Regardless of whether we are killing ourselves at the gym, studying at night school, and struggling to not lose our cool with our children, we will feel guilty if this isn't *effortless*. We will think something is wrong with us if we aren't effortlessly thin, beautiful, smart, or great parents. We never question that there is something wrong with us—of course there's something wrong with us! We have failed in our pursuit of perfection. It never occurs to us that we have no models of *imperfection*. It never crosses our minds that the way we think about the expectations of effortlessness is actually a symptom of the very thing that is tearing us to pieces.

In the next chapters, we will take a slow walk down the Queen's Path. Along the path, we will meet some familiar characters. The most important will be the Divided Woman. You will meet her next, and no doubt you will see yourself, the women in your life, or your characters more in one half than the other. You may also find that it isn't clear whether you should be in a single lane over another, and that is a good sign.

As we go through each chapter, I will introduce you to stories from my patients, history, literature, sacred texts, novels, movies, and popular culture that will demonstrate the qualities of the archetypal story I am endeavoring to explain. You will meet wicked witches, reluctant princesses, angry housewives, and bitter corporate executives. Throughout the journey, they will all share the path. Each character is either in the throes of the Divide or in the process of reuniting the broken pieces. There is no singular character who can emerge without first acknowledging the Queen's Path. Take a deep breath, let your hair down, kick off your glass slippers, and let's ease on down the Queen's Path.

QUADRANT I

The Chimaeric Period

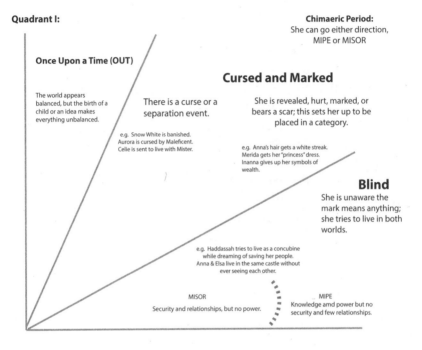

Quadrant I:

Chimaeric Period:
She can go either direction,
MIPE or MISOR

Once Upon a Time (OUT)

Cursed and Marked

The world appears balanced, but the birth of a child or an idea makes everything unbalanced.

There is a curse or a separation event.

She is revealed, hurt, marked, or bears a scar; this sets her up to be placed in a category.

e.g. Snow White is banished. Aurora is cursed by Maleficent. Celie is sent to live with Mister.

e.g. Anna's hair gets a white streak. Merida gets her "princess" dress. Inanna gives up her symbols of wealth.

Blind

She is unaware the mark means anything; she tries to live in both worlds.

e.g. Haddassah tries to live as a concubine while dreaming of saving her people. Anna & Elsa live in the same castle without ever seeing each other.

MISOR
Security and relationships, but no power.

MIPE
Knowledge amd power but no security and few relationships.

The first quadrant of the Queen's Path is the space of innocence transitioning to the Divided Woman. This is the place where, when we look backward, we can see all the pieces assembling for our own unique stroll through the archetypal realm. But when we're in it, we can barely make out the shapes of things that are working and lurking in this space. In workshops with patients, this is often the place that is the most difficult to look back at because it is the most romanticized. So many women I meet look at this archetypal time period and think that this is how life was supposed to be. The world is supposed to be always filled with innocence and possibility, always open and undifferentiated. Anything less is received as betrayal.

That is how the three major world religions treat this phase. This is the Garden of Eden, where everything was perfect and new. Innocence was the way of the world in this paradise. Even the premise, though, is a false one. The world is not the Garden. The first place is not the forever place. Everything moves, everything changes. A world without change is not a healthy one. Only dead things don't change. As a woman walks through this first set of steps on the Queen's Path, it is easy to get discouraged.

The first quadrant is challenging, the second is painful, and the third is brutal. Only the fourth quadrant holds the kind of life we want to achieve. The first and fourth quadrants are mirrors of one another. In the first quadrant, naïveté lurks in comparison to the fourth's knowledge. The first quadrant foreshadows separation to the fourth's unity.

The fourth quadrant gives us the life we long for. To get there, we have to traverse the other three quadrants. We can get there. We just have to keep putting one foot in front of the other on our very own individual yellow brick road.

CHAPTER 5

ONCE UPON
A TIME

Once upon a time, there was a princess who . . . almost every fairy tale you've read starts this way. Whether we're talking about Snow White, Cinderella, or *Legally Blonde,* we all know the Once Upon a Time moment when we see it. It's where the story begins, in innocence. The audience or reader is introduced to the girl. We get a glimpse into her world, and in that moment, we start the story with hope. The world's influences haven't touched her yet. We all have stories of this time. We remember playing with a puppy in the backyard or splashing in the kiddie pool. I remember dressing up in my grandmother's emerald-green ball gown, donning as much of her costume jewelry as I could fit on my body. I dug long white opera gloves out of her drawer. Despite my attire, she drove me to Tastee Donuts to buy a king cake. She handed me a crisp ten-dollar bill, and I bought the biggest king cake possible with that tidy sum. She didn't tell me she expected change!

In the Once Upon a Time, we don't see trouble. We feel invincible and free. Our lives don't seem defined. We believe in our power. Nothing has humbled us just yet. We notice hints at the possible negative influence of the world, but it hasn't quite touched us. It's there, and not there. Maybe it won't come. This period in a woman's history is often her childhood. But as we unwind the stories of our own path to sovereignty, those moments can just as easily mark any period of innocence: a new relationship, the first months of a new job, or the arrival of the first child. The period of Once Upon a Time (abbreviated as OUT) is one where a world of pure possibilities still feels real. How did you feel when you first set foot in a dance studio or on your college campus? Do you remember the sound the first time you clacked a pair of fancy shoes across a marble floor? Maybe it was the first encounter with someone you fell in love with—can you still feel your heart race? Or even now, perhaps memory brings back tears when, after nine months of waiting, you finally met your child?

In the OUT moment, we feel safe, like everything is right with the world. We see ourselves in the mirror on the first day of a new job and think, "I look good in this role!" Or holding the infant, we think, "I'm going to be the best mother." Or arriving on the college campus, we think, "Finally a place where I fit in." But there is another feature of the OUT moment. Risk haunts the periphery. Danger lurks at the edge. The monster at the threshold is usually one we are familiar with. Sometimes the danger is structural: sexism, racism, misogyny, or economics. But it can also be personal: our own trauma history, sexual assault, incest, or family tragedy. The monster at the edge can also take the form of something we're ashamed to admit, like disordered eating or criminal history in our family.

With the OUT moment, we can look back and trace the monsters lurking in the shadows. We couldn't see the threats when we were living the OUT moment, but in hindsight, we can make out their forms. They were lying in wait for us. We may have felt strong and invincible. We may have seen the world through the eyes of love. We likely ignored red flags. A 20-year-old woman gets on a plane to Los Angeles to follow her dreams of becoming an actor. A newly minted attorney joins her first firm as an associate. A young journalist is given a plum assignment at a prestigious newspaper. The world looks inviting. We feel we are becoming part of it in a meaningful way.

But the world always comes for the girl, because history and culture tell us that she will ultimately become a woman. Her presence is disruptive. She will change the world by her being. Just being a woman, she is a threat. The female body is disruptive for what it can do: Women are the channel of new life into the world. This power so antagonizes any civilization that the pure magnitude of it must be curbed. In most world religions, the power of life is reserved "for God alone." Giving women the power of life makes anyone else with power uncomfortable. Men, cultures, institutions, war—nothing compares to the power of making new life out of one's own body.

Men serve as the arbiters of death as soldiers, hunters, and judges. Men alone have had the exclusive right to determine who lives and who dies, until very recently in our history. By default, that means that it is men who are created in the "image" of God. If we were to balance the act of killing with its opposite, it would be "birth" not "life." Life is a state. Birth is an event. Death is both a state and an event. In recent years, there has been a movement for men to also be the arbiters of birth. But that is a topic for another time. I would highly recommend every woman read Merlin Stone's *When God Was a Woman*. In it, Stone, an art historian, looks back over the archaeological record and attempts to make sense of a historical record that produced thousands of female-shaped figurines that have survived in parts of the world where goddess cultures once flourished. She makes a powerful argument for there having been a role for women in the understanding of divinity long before the advent of the Hebrew scriptures.[1]

In most fairy tales, religious texts, and myths, the power of life cannot be trusted to women, and this is often demonstrated in the assumptions that fathers are the "natural" heads of households. Women need "a man." Children must have a father's presence to "come out okay." Men determine women's and children's fates. The primary responsibility of men in a patriarchal culture becomes control. In other words, culture must constrain women. The standards of propriety must hold her accountable for the possibility she possesses. Her body cannot be trusted to its own devices. The product of her body must belong to someone who can control death and life. She must be married to a protector, a warrior who will protect her life-giving power from anyone who would exploit it—including her. Oddly, in the culture that supports OUT, there is no immediate perceived threat from the warrior-protector. He is almost always expected to be a benevolent force, at least in the beginning.

What Happens in the OUT?

1. There is a disturbance in the force of life—a new woman is born—signaling that new life is possible (or there is a new job, new relationship, etc.).

2. A malevolent force is identified—in stories, usually in the form of another competing woman—or a dangerous man.

3. The vulnerable girl or woman is set on a path of desire—either her own or someone else's.

The subtext flows under all the Once Upon a Times. Whether a new job, new marriage, or new baby, newness is haunted with peril.

My MISOR Mom

Pam married Ricky. They were very much in love. She was stunningly beautiful. He was movie-star handsome. She was a good Catholic girl who had barely kissed a boy. He was only slightly more romantically experienced. He had been in love once before going into the Marine Corps. Now his tour was over, and he was free to do what he wished. He was ambitious and wanted a partner to help make his dreams of wealth and success come true. She wanted a husband who would take care of her and give her attractive children. The beautiful couple said their wedding vows on June 17, 1967.

Within the first year, the edges were fraying. Ricky drank. Pam was needy. She wanted someone to talk to. She quit her job without discussion after six months, placing the entire financial burden on him. She explained that she didn't think they needed to discuss it; they were married now. Her job was to be home and take care of the house and children. His job was to make the money and come home to her, where she would take care of him. He stopped coming home. He would go out with friends, and drink . . . and drink . . . and drink. He would come home reeking of alcohol and want to make love to her. She refused, disgusted. He stopped coming home.

These were my parents. They had a Once Upon a Time, and to this day, my father reflects that my mother was a "good wife." If only she'd have done x, y, or z, maybe he could have stayed. What happened to their idyllic dream life? They were caught in the Once Upon a Time, but neither could see the monsters hanging around the edges. My father had a tumultuous trauma history; my mother had led the life of a spoiled MISOR. If Pam had known the steps of the Queen's Path, maybe she would have been able to see what lurked in the shadows.

The Shadowlands

In psychology, the shadow is a metaphorical place where our unrecognized or unrequited realities are sent. It is a place of the unconscious, where the monsters dwell. The more you ignore the shadows and their inhabitants, the more powerful those shadow places become. If you grow up with parents who tell you that you shouldn't be too smart, then all your intellectual prowess will be banished to the shadowlands. If your culture, parents, or education tells you to reject weakness—then vulnerability is banished to the shadows. If your sexual desire is seen as an obstacle to heavenly acceptance, then off to the shadows it goes.

In the shadows is where we find our own demons. But be wary of them because these are often simply rejected parts of ourselves. It is the rejection that holds the demonic force, not the desire or longing. (That is not to say that there aren't evil behaviors, but that's not what we are discussing here.) And while we may look the other way so that we can avoid the inhabitants of the shadows, they are very close. We can see them clearly just by turning our eyes in their direction. We don't have to go far to find the place where our demons gain power and strength. What do you fear? Do you know the reasons? What isn't allowed in your life? When did that begin?

I once had a client, Jessica, who was a devout Christian. She read the Bible daily and was completely dedicated to her faith. She belonged to a conservative community and believed wholeheartedly that the patriarchal family model was the one ordained by God. There was a problem, though. Jessica was smart and beautiful and loved her work. She met Rich, a man of faith who attended church and had a thriving business. She knew he would take good care of her and any family they created together. They were married after a year of dating.

Jessica didn't want to give up her work; she was good at it. As a nurse, her job kept her in a position to be subordinate to doctors and more senior nurses. This fit with the position she was expected to hold. However she felt about her co-workers, Jessica knew she was doing good in the world. Rich wanted her to work less. He wanted her to be available for the family they both wanted to start. Jessica took a cue from her faith and agreed. He was the head of the house, and she would defer to his wishes. She would leave her job once they started a family, using her wages as savings toward future college funds until the first baby arrived.

It took two years, but baby number one arrived in July. By this time, they had a nice nest egg, and they felt comfortable with Jessica stepping back from her job. But something started to brew as their baby grew into toddlerhood. Rich was gone more. He blamed the economy. His business was starting to lose customers. He moved his office home to save money. The couple had a small guesthouse out back; he moved his office there and let his office staff go. Jessica could help with some of the office work one or two days per week.

The couple had not looked at what had been banished to the shadows in their Once Upon a Time. Jessica was ambitious, and she liked to be in control. Rich was terrified of his father's judgment, and his ambition was a function of that relationship. Jessica started to exert control in the home and in the business. Soon the couple had three children, and Jessica ran the house with an iron fist of schedules, chores, activities, and expectations. Rich started to let go of more of his patriarchal responsibilities. He stopped caring about his role in the business. Jessica was good at running the operations. She didn't give him a lot of credit for his work. Rich's father died, erasing the motivator for his ambition. Soon their life was in shambles.

Rich became addicted to opioids after a fall at a work site. Jessica pulled further and further away from him under the heavy pressures of their children and a business. She decided to go back to work in a hospital. At least she knew *she* was dependable, even if he proved not to be in the long run. The children acted out, frustrated by the pressures placed on them by their parents and their faith.

The shadow had infiltrated this family. Like most women, Jessica's Once Upon a Time began with possibility but was punctuated by the haunting possibilities banished to the shadowlands. What had she sent to the shadows? Can you guess by reading a little bit about her life? Jessica was smart and ambitious. She liked the power of her mind. She was pretty and worked hard to fit the description of a dutiful Christian wife. She deferred to her husband and wanted him to lead. But he wasn't great at leading—neither his business nor his family. Well, he wasn't good at making all the decisions and holding all the responsibility. This couple played by the book and expected things to just roll merrily along. By the time they came to therapy, things were a mess. Their oldest son had gone off to college and stopped talking to them. Their oldest daughter had been sexually assaulted at church, and their youngest daughter had developed an eating disorder. Why was God punishing them?

Whoa.

God wasn't punishing them. They were in the Divide and didn't see it. Worse, neither was willing to give up their view of the other. They struggled for years trying to find the language to speak to one another. The faith that first held them soon bound them. It took years of work with me and their religious community to make sense of their dilemma. They had to redefine everything. But Jessica continues to struggle with the idea of her own sovereignty.

Authority and Shadow

Authority is a mixed blessing. In a healthy person, or even a healthy family or organization, authority and responsibility line up with one another. There is an appropriate amount of authority given so that it aligns with responsibilities. In hierarchies, there is always more authority for the person one rung above. Ostensibly, this is because they have greater responsibility. But in a culture obsessed with power, this has become a different calculus. Instead of responsibility, it is power and authority that go hand in hand. Responsibility flows downhill while authority flows upward.

Haunted Shadows

Jessica and Rich were haunted. The monsters Jessica sent to the shadows were many: ambition, desire, anxiety, fear, sex, greed, independence, joy, and vulnerability, just to name a few. If you look at your own history, what was lurking at the edges of your own Once Upon a Time? Whether we are discussing the OUT of a romantic relationship, a career, or your own family of origin, it's important to see the OUT moment. What did you believe about the world then? What did you believe about yourself? If you could go back in time, could you find the monsters lurking at the edges? Write these down in your journal, and let's keep an eye on them as you traverse your path to sovereignty.

How to Look Out for Monsters

What have you banished to the shadows? What have you told yourself is no good? Or not desirable in being you? Have you banished ambition, anger, desire, sex, beauty, independence, dependence, intelligence, power, vulnerability, or strength? Where did they go? How did they get sent to the shadows? Or are there memories in the shadowlands? Have you locked away a terrible event, an accident, a rape, or an assault? Or perhaps you banish a behavior? Do you overspend, vomit up your food, starve yourself, or compulsively clean?

Exercise

Describe your Once Upon a Time. What do you idealize about it? Think back to a time in your life when you felt filled with possibilities. Can you make a list of the shadow objects (people, emotions, desires, ambitions) that you see now, but that were perhaps difficult to see in the moment?

Write about this time in your journal. If it helps, have a look at the next two brief sections and see if either helps you identify both the ideals and the shadow objects lurking in your own Once Upon a Time.

Once Upon a Time in Politics: Princess Diana and the House of Windsor

Diana Spencer was a beautiful English rose, ready to join the royal ranks of the Windsors. For months in 1981, her sandy-blonde hair and Bambi-esque eyes had been in every magazine. Diana's engagement to Prince Charles, heir to the British throne, brought new life to the press covering the royal family. Suddenly everyone in the world watched as Diana Spencer's photograph alongside a much older Charles (by 12 years) showed up everywhere, from tabloids like *The National Enquirer* to magazines like *People* and *Vogue*.

Diana's Once Upon a Time unfolded before a public hungry for a positive story. Throughout the late 1970s, the country fumbled through deindustrialization, strikes, labor problems, a trade deficit, and lagging public trust in the government and the monarchy. Punk band The Sex Pistols reflected the nihilism of the despairing youth of the late 1970s in their angry single, "God Save the Queen." Young people for a decade expressed the anger and rage of the "lost generation," growling and rebelling at the failure of the social welfare state to care for them. World War II wasn't that far away in history; the land and its people were still scarred by the costs of that war.

Their courtship plastered everywhere, the whirlwind romance of Charles and Diana took everyone by pleasant surprise. Here was a modern-day fairy tale. The beautiful Lady Spencer and the future king of Britain gave the world a sense that fairy tales could be real. Beauty and innocence could triumph over cynicism and excess. The OUT for Lady Spencer begins well before her introduction to the royal life. Her story follows the model of the Queen's Path, where she winds through multiple tracks as first a MISOR and then in rejecting the Crown's wishes (and therefore protection), endures becoming a MIPE. Her story ends in tragedy, which means she never truly got to sovereignty, though she made every effort to do so.

Before the tragedy of her life unfolded in front of a paparazzi hungry for images of her, Diana, with her beautiful face and lithe frame, reminded Britons of the image they held of themselves. She embodied the symbols they desperately craved: youth, beauty, innocence, wealth, and privilege. Britain, one of the smallest countries on Earth by landmass, dominated the seas and the land as a colonial power for hundreds of years. Her youth as the daughter of noble father and a mother who disappeared not only prepared her for an actual fairy-tale royal life but also created the exact conditions for her MISOR role.

Diana's mother abandoned her and her siblings when Diana was a child. This is a hallmark of the MISOR story. As a young aristocrat, Diana wasn't ambitious. When she officially met Charles, he could not help but feel smitten by her compassion for him. In every fairy tale, though, there is something lurking at the edge of the OUT. A threat looms at the edge of the enchantment. The specter haunting this royal couple took the form of Charles's first love, Camilla. Diana knew about her but was young and wanted to have faith in her royal suitor. Charles was also following a royal playbook. He had been instructed that Camilla was too problematic for the royal family. He had to choose a suitable wife whom the British public would like, not a divorcée that would remind his subjects of his family's struggles last time there was a king. His own grandfather, King George VI, had been forced onto the throne because of the abdication of his uncle, King Edward VIII, who had married American divorcée Wallis Simpson against the wishes of the royal family. Charles had to uphold the family honor, not repeat history. Diana was caught in the crossfire. She started out a dutiful MISOR to Camilla's MIPE. But it wouldn't take long for the dream to fade. We will follow Diana's story throughout the rest of book. Suffice it to say Diana's Once Upon a Time or OUT moment fits all the fairy-tale requirements. If you're a fan of history or a royal watcher, you know what happened, but perhaps the context of setting Diana on her own Queen's Path will help illuminate your own.

OUT in Entertainment

We all know this moment in the movies. It's when we are intro-duced to the characters and their environment. Once Upon a Time establishes the place and time of innocence. The characters don't know the dangers of the world. Power shows up as something un-controlled inside of her or in the world surrounding her. Once Upon a Time (OUT) in a woman's lived experience is usually a ro-manticized beginning. In a movie is it usually a short introduction.

Disney's *Frozen* first introduces the audience to Elsa and Anna as they build a snowman in the palace using Elsa's powers to cre-ate snow and freeze anything she points her magic toward. Anna entices her sister to use her magic, asking her, "Do you wanna build a snowman?" Magic is fun, innocent. The sisters aren't afraid of Elsa's power. But fun and games can't last forever, and Elsa struggles to keep up with Anna's antics. She hurts her sister by accident as she throws a jet of cold magic in her direction, trying to keep her sister safe.

In Patty Jenkins's 2017 *Wonder Woman*, Diana of Themyscira, a protected princess among the Amazons, is surrounded by the pow-erful tribe of warrior women led by her mother, Queen Hippolyta. Diana has great power that her mother doesn't want to encourage. But Diana cannot contain her fascination with, or talent for, the skills of battle. Her power soon shows itself as she trains with her aunt, the general, Antiope. If you've seen the film, you know that the real reason that Diana's mother wants to protect her is because she isn't an Amazon like the rest of the warriors at Themiscyra.

She's actually a goddess. Antiope and all the other Amazons have hidden this important fact from Diana. They believe that by hiding her they can keep her from her destiny.

We can't cover everything in this book, though you'll soon see that these patterns are recognizable. We will illuminate some popular films and television series and include them through the next several chapters. Feel free to take the outlines provided in each section and see if you can create a map or outline for your favorite movie, series, or book!

CHAPTER 6

CURSED AND MARKED

Women the world over describe their periods as "the curse." It would thus make sense to assume that this early part of the Queen's Path, Cursed and Marked is an archetypal reference to women, menarche, and the arrival of fertility for women. While there is likely a correlation on a symbolic level, it is far too simple an explanation. In stories from the Bible to *Barbie*, women are Cursed and Marked along the route to sovereignty. Colleen Hoover's book *Verity* opens with the main character being splattered by the blood of a stranger as he steps off the curb directly into the path of a truck. Anna in *Frozen* is hit with her sister's freezing magic, leaving her with a shock of white hair. Aurora in *Sleeping Beauty* is cursed to prick her finger on a spinning wheel and fall into a deep sleep. Malala Yousafzai is shot in the face for daring to speak aloud that she deserves an education.[1] In every story featuring a woman protagonist, you will find a curse and a mark.

We all have them.

One of the most memorable from my childhood was when my parents got my hair cut for the first time. I was six. I had loved the long, wavy curls that hung past my shoulders. Most of the time, my hair was in a ponytail pulled low at the center of my skull. Sometimes it hung in two ponytails just behind my ears. My mom, whose hair was even curlier than mine, had never learned to braid.

117

My options were limited: down and a mess, one or two ponytails, or in a tight, uncomfortable bun. The bun had only been suffered once for school picture day.

One Monday morning after a particularly raucous weekend of playing outdoors, swimming, and running around with the band of feral kids in our neighborhood, I fell asleep with pink bubblegum in my mouth. The next morning, I couldn't find the gum, but my parents found it when they went to brush my hair. My dad, angry that my hair was matted with twigs and pink sugar stickiness, trotted me down to his friend Nicky's salon and told him to cut it all off. Nicky obliged, and I was left with a terrible bowl cut. Figure skater Dorothy Hamill had just competed in the Olympics, and her signature haircut was all the rage. I was supposed to resemble her, but because of my curls, on me, the haircut looked awful. I cried for a month. The absent hair made me an outsider at school. The girls spent recess brushing and braiding each other's hair. Though I had only been invited a handful of times, I was now out for good. This moment is a minor one in my childhood. Indeed, most of us have both mild and significant curses and marks. They range from grief to sexual assault. My bad haircut was a cover for a much deeper wound. I was the surviving child.

There was no accident, no blame that could be laid. My aunt Molly had been in a difficult marriage and came to live with us for a little while. Her son, Shaun, my cousin, who was about a year younger than me, had been born with a congenital birth defect—a hole in his heart. He was a tiny baby. Surgery would have to wait until he was older, stronger. Her husband, a cruel man, blamed her. He was loud, abusive, and drank too much. About a year and a half after Shaun was born, my aunt and Shaun were living with us. My cousin was more like a brother to me. We slept in the same bed. We ate together, bathed together, and played together during the day. Our grandmother had professional pictures taken of us in matching outfits: navy blue with little strawberry appliqués. She had bought them in her travels. Shaun had a gentle face and bright ginger hair.

Molly got her own place, and we celebrated. My mom and dad organized a trip to Eight Flags for us kids and my father's sisters, with whom he was and remains incredibly close. Eight Flags was an amusement park designed for little kids about an hour and a half away in Biloxi, Mississippi. We'd been there many times; it was one of my favorite places. Every time the day passed in a weird hodge-podge of activities: a Wild West show, small and not very exciting rides like rollercoasters designed for little kids, and trained chickens and ducks that played tic-tac-toe and other games for a quarter. I always "fell in love" with the cowboys in the Wild West show. I was impressed by how they shot each other off the roofs of the faux Old West set and didn't appear to ever get hurt. It was the end of April, and my parents and aunts had decided that this weekend they'd take the kids for some fun, and the next weekend would be dedicated to a more adult outing at the New Orleans Jazz and Heritage Festival.

But the trip was interrupted. Shaun started to have some difficulty, and by one o'clock, he had fainted. At three years old, Shaun was a fragile child. He couldn't tolerate a lot. That day would be the last that he would enjoy anything. We piled in the car and rushed home. He was in and out of consciousness. The adults took him to the emergency room. Shaun had not fainted. He had suffered a stroke. His blood was clotting, and no one could tell my aunt why. They gave him a bed in the hospital and said they would operate. His little heart couldn't tolerate life like this. My grandmother had collected me at the hospital so the adults could manage. Hours later, they came and returned me to Shaun's bedside so that I could see him before his surgery.

No one told me that this would likely be the last time I would see Shaun. They brought me into a barely lit room that he shared with another child in the hospital. They stood over his bed telling him how much they loved him. I played with the other child, jealous, not understanding what was happening. My father picked me up and instructed me to give Shaun a kiss good-bye. We had to leave and let the doctors do their work. I kissed his ginger head and was taken home.

Shaun died.

My survivor's guilt started the moment that my mother tried to explain it to me. I felt incredible shame that I hadn't given him my full attention in the hospital room. I felt guilt that I lived, and he had not. I couldn't bear knowing that I was going to school, and he never would. I felt shame that my mother still had *her* child (me) and at six months pregnant, had another on the way. They didn't let me go to the funeral. My family never recovered from losing Shaun. Though my father and his sisters had endured a childhood of terrible abuse and neglect, they had bonded and were all determined to do better, be better. Losing Shaun was a shattering blow. The world opened up and swallowed any hope my family had cultivated. We were all left in the ruins to make sense of the loss. It showed my parents and my aunts that maybe they weren't in control of their destinies after all.

In the 1970s in New Orleans, it wasn't usual to send children to grief counseling. In my Catholic family, it wasn't normal to speak of the dead or to ask a lot of questions. I would try to talk to my mother about Shaun, and she would just try to get me to be a little kid. But Shaun was all I thought about. His death haunted me throughout my life until I reached my 20s and finally got therapy. I felt shame to have been the one still here. While I knew my aunt Molly loved me, I reminded her of her son, and it stoked a fire of deep sadness in her. My father never recovered from losing Shaun. Even though Shaun was his nephew, my father grieved as though he had lost a son. When my brother, Richard, was born several months later, my father wouldn't let himself get too close. He became distant and cold, treating my mother very badly.

My curse was being the surviving child. My mark was weirdness. I didn't know how to talk to other children. I turned five a little over a month after Shaun died. I became existential. My mother sent me to summer camp to help socialize me before school started. But I didn't have the energy to engage with the girls in my class. By the time I got into the classroom in the morning, the girls would already be playing together. Usually it was with dolls, like Barbie and Skipper. I would sit off on my own with a box of tissues and a spool of thread. I would make my own dolls by fashioning the tissue into little human forms and tying the arms, legs, head, and so on with the thread. I used my lunch box as the house. I would make the dolls, which took most of the free time before camp started, and then I'd pose them inside the lunch box house. By then, the day would begin and we'd be making macaroni necklaces and finger painting. After a few days, my mother asked me about the tissues in my lunch box. When I explained, I saw the alarm in her face. She didn't know what to say or do. Her kid was strange, and *different* wasn't really in my mom's vocabulary.

My curse was "surviving child." My mark was "weirdo" but there was also "sad," "quiet," and "existential." There were another two that came out of this experience: "fat" and "smart." I wasn't a chubby child, but I was solid and muscular. I was strong, played outside, and wasn't afraid to eat. I was tall, had enormous feet, and could use my body for cartwheels and pull-ups that upset my mom's sensibilities of what girls were supposed to be. Meanwhile, my dad had taught me to read by sitting on his lap and reading the newspaper aloud while he drank his coffee. I could read on my own before I turned three years old. Smart would become both curse and mark that would follow me throughout my life. It covered strange. Smart started innocently but morphed into something very different in the face of grief. Smart became my cover. Smart was safe. Someone would see me, and I didn't have to explain. Sad made me strange. Smart was acceptable. Depressed was something to avoid. Smart made grown-ups pay attention.

Almost any new endeavor will follow the Queen's Path. There will be a new curse and mark each time. Surely you have several of these stories. Perhaps it was a professional embarrassment—a dig at your expense at a dinner or meeting. One of my most memorable was being called "the girl director" working on a commercial. Or there was the time I walked into a meeting of engineers, and someone started singing a *Sesame Street* song: "One of these things is not like the other . . . " Another time, I had spent months planning a high-end research retreat, and the director singled me out for "making these great copies" while the new guy who'd been there four days was praised for the financial acumen he was *going to* bring to the center. Or maybe it was being singled out by another woman as being "too pretty" to be accepted among the other Ph.D.'s. She congratulated *me* when we hired a very attractive woman who also wore makeup saying, "Now you'll have someone to talk to." Being cursed and marked is sadly one way we know we are on the path and headed for the Divide. In this stage, the Divide hasn't hit us yet in its full force. But we can feel it coming. Once we are cursed and bear the resulting mark, we can rest assured there is a complex process underway.

The curse and mark can be distinct from one another, or they can be combined. I have seen many clients who reported that their curse was sexual abuse, rape, or incest. The mark was invisible to anyone around them. They bore a shame that isolated them in jaw-locked silence. Tell the secret and your whole world might fall apart before your eyes. As children, they suffered the physical pain and humiliation of being a sexual object. Worse, most felt that their parents betrayed them for their own protection. This put those clients in the unenviable position of having had sexual experiences that made them feel ashamed combined with abandonment by parents who should have protected them. Incest or child abuse is the curse; abandonment is the mark.

The curse I hear most from my women clients is sexual assault. Even though we are in the safety of a closed therapy office dedicated wholly to their healing, women still struggle to let this curse be uttered. I can't count how many clients believe that they had a role to play in becoming victims of sexual violence. They either blame themselves for trusting the person or take responsibility for some behavior, like getting drunk. They overshadow the responsibility of the perpetrator with stories of their own stupidity, innocence, or ignorance. Listening to their stories underscores the Divide for me. Women are responsible for our own victimization. We bear "the curse of Eve." We are made to feel that no matter what befalls us, we are marked simply by being women. To receive the mark along the path is to be reminded of that role. But for us as sojourners along the Queen's Path, we can look to the curse and mark as important signposts along our route to sovereignty.

Malala's Mark

On October 9, 2012, Malala Yousafzai was on the crowded school bus on her way to the Khushal School her father had founded years before. Malala describes herself as a bookish girl who loved to learn.

She recounts the day of her shooting as being mostly the same as others. The girls had exams, so their day was starting a little later than usual. As the bus rounded the corner toward a military checkpoint, a man in Western clothes wearing a ball cap approached. Another man had flagged the bus down, and the girls on the bus assumed the man in the Western clothes was a journalist. Malala's father was an outspoken critic of the Taliban, and Malala had been forthright in her assertion that as much as any boy her age, she too deserved to be educated. She had been public, outspoken, and forthcoming with everyone from journalists to government officials, and not just local ones.[2]

The man with the ball cap climbed into the bus, asking which one of them was Malala. Still under the impression he was a journalist, Malala raised her hand. Her friends filled the gaps in her memory, as Malala doesn't remember much after this point. She reported that upon learning her name, the man produced a Colt .45 and shot her point-blank in the face. Two other girls on the bus were injured when the man continued firing his weapon after Malala slumped over unconscious. Malala and the other girls were taken to the hospital. Malala was ultimately taken to a hospital in England where she had several surgeries to save her life.[3]

Malala was cursed long before she was marked by the gunshot of a Taliban member trying to make a name for himself by murdering a child. Malala's father owned a school that taught girls and had spoken to Western journalists about what was happening as the Taliban began to encroach into the Swat Valley of Pakistan. When she was 11 years old, Malala was writing a daily blog under a pseudonym for a newspaper in Karachi. She was the subject of a *New York Times* documentary called *Class Dismissed in Swat Valley*. Malala was a known spokesperson for girls' education, even at age 12. She gave interviews and was well-known at home and in journalistic circles. By the time she reached age 14, Malala had prizes and schools named for her. This made her parents a bit anxious, as in Pashtun culture, (like many others) naming as an honor is typically reserved for the dead. The Taliban targeted Malala, calling her disgraceful for spreading "secularism." Her curse was intelligence and outspokenness; her mark was given to her by a Talib with a Colt .45.

A Mark to Remove a Mark

Despite widespread condemnation, female genital mutilation (FGM) continues to be performed in many parts of the world, primarily in Africa, the Middle East, and Asia. The practice is considered a violation of the human rights of women and girls. These practices have been carried out on more than 200 million women and girls who are alive today. More than 3 million girls and women are at risk each year. The procedures include but aren't limited to removing certain parts of the female genitalia (often the clitoris and/or the labia) and combining this with sewing either the inner or outer labia together, leaving only a small opening for bodily functions not related to intercourse.[4] The idea is that women should not be encouraged in their sexual desire. For decades, the World Health Organization has stood against these practices and made efforts to educate communities, traditional leaders and healers, and families that FGM is not necessary and may in many cases lead to profound health problems.

The Face of Bossypants

In her memoir, *Bossypants*, Tina Fey describes the scar she received as a five-year-old. A man attacked her in the front yard of her house while she was playing. He just walked up to her and slashed her in the face. She reported that as she grew older, she didn't think much about the scar. Being put in front of a camera on a regular basis forced her to consider what role it had played in her life. She describes in her book that she was able to see it more as an indicator of how mature, compassionate, or downright idiotic people around her could be. She noted that as a child, the scar should have made her self-conscious. Instead, the scar wound up giving her an inflated sense of herself. Family members, neighbors, and friends of the family often felt that they had to make up for her experience and would lavish her with extra candy or larger gifts. Fey reflected in writing her book that it wasn't until she was writing that very memoir that it occurred to her that she mistook the attention and increased generosity as reflections of her worth, when they were more likely symbols of adults' sense of guilt and shame.[5]

The scar or mark doesn't always have to be something we can see. Sometimes, like mine, it is the loss of someone dear, a parent, sibling, or even a beloved pet. We are marked by grief, scarred by loss. The mark or scar can be something we are taught by culture or religion is "bad," like being gay or trans. It can be longing for something that is unavailable to us because of our gender, race, ethnicity, or social class, like a particular skill, talent, or profession.

Hiding the Mark from Ourselves

Angela had been my client for about two years. She had come in originally to discuss her anxiety over a career change that she felt her family would never understand. She lived hundreds of miles away from them. Her father had been diagnosed with cancer, and her mother spent most of her time taking care of him and their ranch in New Mexico. Her family had sent her to college to become an engineer. Angela worked in aerospace and loved to hike, run, and take her dogs on adventures.

Angela's dad worked as an engineer too. And while he loved to talk about his work, building and designing engines and machinery, Angela hated being an engineer. She found it boring. She had fought hard to be the top of her class. Her parents were very proud of her. She had never done anything to let them down. She thought they were wonderful. As her father's illness progressed, Angela's life started to crack. She loved her dad and didn't want to be an engineer anymore. Worse, what she really wanted was to be a painter. She had painted her whole life, taken classes at college, and continued afterward. She was both talented and skilled. She had never shown her paintings to her parents. And she had never introduced them to anyone she had ever dated, because Angela only dated women.

For the entirety of her 38 years, Angela had lived the role that her parents had created for her. She did the job that made her father proud and gave them something to talk about, even if she hated the work. She pretended that men weren't interested in an engineer, that she was too mannish for most of them. Her mother cooed that she was too smart. Her father thought the men were too weak for her. She needed someone even stronger than she was. The truth was that Angela had lied about almost everything in her life. She knew she liked girls from the time she was seven years old. She was good at math but didn't enjoy it. She had notebooks filled with drawings, art, sketches, and poetry that dated back to middle school. While most children shared their creativity with their parents, Angela had not shown any of her paintings or drawings to them, not since grade school. They didn't know their daughter at all.

To Angela, being gay was a curse and being creative was a mark of that curse. She didn't want her parents to place her in that category. She believed that it would destroy her relationship with them. As we dug into her childhood, she examined memories that exposed a subtle homophobia from her parents. She feared that they wouldn't understand and would reject her. Though she made a good living for herself in her work and saved money, she feared being alone and penniless—a symbolic interpretation of being orphaned. She felt that she should be the dutiful daughter and, as best as she could, do what was expected of her. And what was expected was that she live a small life, save money, get married, have children, and live near her parents so she could help out as they got older. But here was the moment; they were older. She didn't live close. She couldn't live close. And the real reason for her coming into therapy was the way she had walked through her life with the scar hidden under layers of obligations executed or lied about perfectly. She thought she was there to figure out how to become a full-time artist, but the truth was that artist was the smallest problematic role in her life. Her whole life had been determined by her curse and hiding her resulting mark.

Exercise

Can you identify your curse and mark? You likely have more than one. What are the most consequential ones? How have you related to them? Do you hide them? Which ones have created the most problems?

Spend a few pages in your journal reflecting on the curse and mark that have had the most influence on your life, how they have manifested, and what consequences came as a result.

CHAPTER 7

BLIND

Our hopeful Queen is starting to feel the pressure build. She is early in her journey. The ground is moving under her feet. She is on her way to the Divide. It's not that she is choosing this route. It is coming toward her because it comes for every woman. In this part of the journey, she thinks that her experience is unique. She believes that the feeling she has of not fitting in is hers to bear alone. She believes other women and girls are effortlessly thin, happy, popular, successful, or satisfied. She doesn't see that every woman around her has been cast into the same trap and that every woman she knows is navigating it in silence. Every single one of them feels alone and isolated. She doesn't realize that the woman next to her is assailed by the same awful truth: I am not okay, and no one sees or has noticed. I am alone. And worse, I am solely responsible.

In the first version of this research, this section was called "In the Blind." I chose this language because it seemed to fit the experience of what I was trying to describe. The way the myths and stories unfolded showed me characters who were unable to see one another, either through choice or treachery. It seemed to me that it was like being behind a structure that didn't allow you to see very far and that protected you from being seen. As I investigated modern stories, I also saw that this could be a form of willful blindness. A character is so focused on revenge that she doesn't see she is becoming a monster. Sometimes it is someone so hurt that they cannot see past their pain. Or, in contrast, it is someone so overcome with love or joy that they don't see the terrible things looming on the horizon.

As I refined the research, I dropped the "In the" and just relied on "Blind" because it seemed to be a more appropriate descriptor. Does the heroine see what's coming? Is she blinded by her ambition? Is she focused only a goal, like marriage or getting pregnant, blind to everything else? Does she think if she plays small, she can outwit fate or the curse? Does she willfully look away at the treachery unfolding around her? Does she tell herself happy stories or revel in good memories as a way of blocking out her suffering? Or like Diana of Themiscyra in *Wonder Woman*, is the truth kept from her? All these count as blind on this step of the Queen's Path.

The experience of blindness is both outward and inward. It comes in stories like the tale of Cassandra who was cursed to see the future only to have no one believe her. Blindness describes the stories of children suffering sexual abuse whose parents, teachers, or caregivers don't see it or who are too scared to look. Blindness describes the wife who trusts that her husband's constant absence couldn't possibly be infidelity, despite all the signs. Blindness describes the woman who thinks she won't be affected by the tide of sexism she faces in school, college, or work. Does she see the presumed inequality that launches her into the world? An individual woman is blind to the structural reality that all women face and that most are afraid to name. Being "Blind" at this stage is the place just before the Divide comes up and grabs her. It's where she pauses for a moment, expecting that everything will be okay. Except it won't. It can't.

The world starts coming at her a thousand miles per hour. What is happening around her? Why is she having this experience? She tells herself that she can absolutely be the one to change things. She won't be affected. She can be the first woman president. She believes that misogyny is a sordid tale from history. We don't need feminism anymore, she says openly. Women have won the rights to fair pay, fair work, and equal opportunity. Is she wrong to feel angry at her partner for not helping with childcare? What is she doing in her workplace that encourages that guy in the next cubicle to consistently act inappropriately? Did she make a mistake in her paperwork that caused her to be disqualified from a bonus during her maternity leave? Who does she believe when her friend is raped by a co-worker at a party? How does she navigate when her professor or boss propositions her? What about the moment she realizes that because so many women entered her profession, it no longer pays as well? How does she make sense of the fact that her world seems to have gotten smaller when she had children? If she admits that she isn't fulfilled by (marriage/motherhood/career/education), does that make her a bad (wife/mother/professional/student)?

I'm getting a little bit ahead of myself. Blind represents the moment in the journey when we all believe we aren't going to be affected by an old pattern or pretend that the pattern we don't want to acknowledge is real, even if we experience it. Or we think that the pattern is gone, or that it doesn't or shouldn't exist. I am free. I am not subject to anyone else's will. I don't have to accept sexual innuendo. No one is telling me what to do. Aren't they, though? And what happens when you don't accept it when you turn your face away? The Divide is what happens. And at this step on the Queen's Path, the Divide hasn't quite taken over, but it is clear on the horizon. It is the next step.

The girl or woman thinks she can avoid its effects. She is blind to the fact that no matter what she does, it is inescapable. Even me, the researcher who discovered this pattern . . . I am uncomfortable writing this. My own inner voice says what you're probably thinking: "Not me!" Or even, "What a bunch of bullshit. I'm not blind." I fear the backlash of describing this step. No one wants to believe that they are blind to something important. And yet, every time I dig deeply into an individual woman's journey or look at the myths, stories, movies, and fairy tales . . . there is Blind ironically staring me in the face.

This is not a personal statement. Blind is a step on the path and a structure of the Divide itself. Like a magician's act, we are distracted and told constantly that a new fact or awareness isn't important or is a one-off. Looking for the places we are blind or have been entreated to turn a blind eye *is* the point of this step on the journey. This is where we, as women learn to *accept* blindness. The experience of blindness does another magic trick, though. Accepting blindness means that, by default, we are individually responsible. If I bought a car that had a five-star rating and was injured in a car accident, well, then, it's obviously my fault. I should have done more research. Except, I'm blind to the fact that the car's safety rating wasn't tested on people with my body type. If I befriend a male co-worker who routinely makes sexist remarks that I dismiss as just stupid guy talk and then he rapes me in the pantry at the restaurant I work in, I will worry that I did something to encourage him. (Both of those are real stories from clients.)

When we turn our eyes away from the people and systems that endanger, hurt, or ignore us, we are in the step called Blind. When we compare ourselves with other people without comparing the circumstances as well as the outcomes, we are also giving in to Blind. When we compare ourselves with men of equal status, education, experience, and capability, we are Blind. The danger of Blind is that we can wind up in very real peril. We can find ourselves bullied or scapegoated. We can have unrealistic expectations that constantly manifest as doing more, taking on more responsibility. We can walk into situations where the risks might have been evident if we hadn't followed our "girl" training that tells us to be nice to everyone, usually at our own expense.

To his credit, my father had told me from a young age not to let anyone tell me I couldn't do something because I was a girl. As a child and teenager, this was patently ridiculous to me. Why would being female keep me from anything? I was just as smart, if not smarter, than the boys in my school. I was strong and capable. When I was young, it seemed like a ridiculous thing to have to encourage. I didn't have a college fund or parents who could pay for things. Indeed, my parents didn't care if I went to college at all. I always had a burning desire to be educated. So, when it was time to go to college, I pushed and failed. I would enroll in school, work two jobs, and around week 10 or 11 of the semester, my body or spirit would collapse under the pressure. I would get sick or depressed. I could usually do about a year at a time, then I would have to take a break. And I would feel like a failure. My peers from high school weren't dropping out. My stepsister was able to keep going and thrive. What was wrong with *me*?

I neglected the obvious fact: My stepsister had a very wealthy parent, and it wasn't the one we shared. My parents didn't value education and didn't see any point in setting aside money for it. My high school peers had scholarships or wealthy parents. My last year of high school, I had a scholarship to a Catholic school arranged for me by my grandmother, who had finished school at eighth grade but who had pull with the archdiocese of New Orleans because of her decades of service. I was blind. I was blind to the effect of money (or lack thereof) on my life. I believed that I should be able to leap through all the hoops and pay for college and get straight A's because I was capable.

It wasn't until I was married and finishing my Ph.D. that I realized what had kept me starting and stopping all those years wasn't a lack of willpower but a lack of financial and structural support. College was easy once I wasn't working two jobs. I probably could have done it had I not needed financial aid, but to qualify for financial aid, you have to be a full-time student. Minimum full-time student status meant taking at least three science classes or four liberal arts or humanities classes. When you work two jobs, that's a lot to manage. Of course I quit. Of course my body got sick. I was blind to the structural issues, lost in a set of "shoulds" that told me I was weak and lazy if I didn't just live my life on three or four hours of sleep every night. I was blind to the reality of the situation, until I wasn't in it anymore.

The Girl Game

Growing up in the Southern United States, I became familiar with a behavior I call "the Girl Game." The professional women in Louisiana were the most amazing experts at it. I remember sitting in a meeting with a group of women from a local business group who had come to meet with the leadership of several LSU departments. They were planning an event, and for the first half hour, the male department heads and professors had shared their opinions and plans. Most of what they offered wasn't possible with our budget, and a lot of it was self-congratulatory dribble. But the ladies with the big, coiffed hair; thick lipstick; and tailored suits didn't bat an eye. They took notes, complemented the men, and made sure the coffee service was stocked.

After about 40 minutes, the guys were running out of steam, and some of them were getting bored. A woman in a bright-pink suit who had organized the meeting brought it to a close. She offered, "You guys go ahead, and I'll get all this finished up. Let me just make sure I've got all the notes and everything." She stood up, and everyone followed. I started to gather my things to go. When the last man was out of the room, and I was crossing the floor, I noticed none of the women were packed up. I stood there for a moment, and the pink suit lady said, "Okay, we've got 15 minutes to decide what we're actually going to do. Let's hurry." The real meeting had begun.

The Girl Game is played when women don't have any obvious power, so they wield their power surreptitiously, offering flattery and deference as a way to engage. The pink-suit lady wound up taking the ideas and coming up with an entirely different plan, and the guys were none the wiser because she gave them the credit. The Girl Game is often a useful manipulation, but there is no guarantee that you're going to get any credit for your work. The Girl Game is a skill game, like chess. It's one that I am in awe of and absolutely lack the skill to play. The MISOR is often most gifted in this realm. For MIPEs like me, we watch and seethe.

Like most women, I was blind to the Divide. The culture that places women in the Divide makes our humanity invisible. We are kept effectively if not intentionally blind to the processes and structures that devalue our humanity in favor of our subjectivity. This has become so pervasive that we barely question it. Women see it as just "men are helpless" or "boys will be boys," or "that's just the way things are." As opposed to seeing these as systems of behavior that are reproduced in our culture by our own behaviors and participation. Cultural blindness is the norm. Like Neo waking up in the matrix having never used his eyes, we are often surprised by how much we have been bending under the structures that keep us subordinate. Indeed, this stage of the Queen's Path is painful because the systems are so pervasive that we don't have clear tools to illuminate them. Invisibility protects the systems even as it keeps women's labor, effort, suffering, and struggles from appearing serious or real. Blindness puts an individual woman's experience into the bizarre no-man's-land of being 100 percent her fault and responsibility and 75 percent unreal. Thus, if she has a problem, it's her fault, but it's probably not a real problem anyway.

What Is a Witch?

Blindness can take on the form of obfuscation and diversion. The witch trials that lasted nearly 500 years are a great example. The economies of Europe were undergoing unprecedented transformation during those centuries. The land-based feudal systems were becoming obsolete. These systems had kept the peasants loyal to the nobility who owned the land. The peasants lived on and worked the land for hundreds of years, swearing fealty to the landowners. The peasants worked the land and in return were guaranteed protection and a portion of the resources they cultivated. As invasions increased, wars ravaged Europe. Liquid capital became a requirement for the defense of property. Armies had to be paid with cash money. This put strain on both the peasants and the landed nobility. The group that benefited the most were those who already lived in between them: the merchant class.[1]

Until the beginnings of cash economies, being a merchant was not considered a desirable position in society. It meant you weren't "noble." A merchant was neither endowed by the lord or king with a specific duty or purpose, nor were they, like a serf or land tenant, loyal to any noble family. Their loyalty could be bought. This made them suspicious in the eyes of much of society. But with the shift in the economies of Europe, the land itself became collateral for cash raised to defend those territories. And the landed nobility soon found themselves reliant on the merchant class. This upset the power structures a great deal. The wealth that was generated from the shifting economy didn't naturally flow in traditional ways. Merchants had smaller families than the landed nobility. And to further complicate matters, the ongoing centuries of war reduced the numbers of available marriageable men. Men were called to war, both peasant and noble alike. Thus, the dominant forces at home were women who didn't have men around to keep them focused on domestic roles. In addition, women entered the merchant class out of necessity. Merchant businesses transferred to women when husbands and fathers died in battle or from diseases like plague that were running rampant through the populations of cities.

A system of inheritance that favored first-born sons had been exercised for hundreds of years and was based on land-based economies. Land and those who lived on it required protection from marauders or those who would simply take over and occupy land not their own. The threats in a system of land inheritance are different than those based on one exchanging money. When resources like land and water are taken by force, the protection of lords with swords is reasonable. When the heritable property is a business that requires shipping, trade, and cash, protection can be bought. Protection becomes built into the price of acquiring or trading in goods. Under these different circumstances, the rules of primogeniture naturally can't hold as much meaning. A woman can hand over a half-pound bag of gold as easily as a man. And more importantly, this shift completely upends the expectations in families. Who should inherit a 1,500-acre farm if the oldest son is off battling for God and country in Jerusalem? Is it the first-born son? Or his wife or sister, who has collected the rents and made sure the wool and wheat got to market to pay for the son's crusade?

Before we move into the witch hunts specifically, let's talk a little about how rumors work. While it may seem ancillary to the discussion, rumor is a powerful force. In small communities, rumor is a regulating power. Shame keeps people in line, behaving according to community standards. However, rumors proliferate in communities where there is insufficient reliable information. The *reliable* part is important. If there aren't enough trusted sources, or if the trusted sources are themselves part of the problem, then rumors are the preferred communication. It relieves tension in the community when group members talk through and speculate on the causes and consequences of their collective problems. The witch hunts weaponized rumor during the Middle Ages and Renaissance.[2]

The social systems of the time were breaking down. Nobles who had land but no cash suddenly found themselves in the position of having to constantly fight to protect their property holdings.

Invasions throughout Europe by warring families caused great upheaval. Soon, there were ongoing wars from the top down—smaller kingdoms falling to larger ones. Power consolidating at the top, wealth flowing upward to those who could afford to hire armies, either for defense or offense. The powers that held the most sway were the kingdoms who claimed divine right to govern and the church who sanctified those claims with the endorsement of God's messenger on Earth, the pope.

Why is all this important? Because it gives context to both the content and manner of the blindness and distortions that created the opportunity for the witch trials to flourish. The population was strapped for cash, and the systems of authority that had protected people for decades were no longer functioning in ways that could be considered reliable. So, in the absence of trusted information that soothes people's fears and anxieties, rumors flourish.[3] A supernatural response is the only one that makes sense, because the authorities can no longer hold the center. Their influence and power are not enough to change the situation. Whether this inability is because of their own capacity or will isn't important. What matters is that the supernatural solution addresses the problem effectively and allows the community to organize around a common enemy. This takes pressure off the ineffective authority and organizes the community in a way that their effort, will, and fear can be managed and put to work.

Unmarried women are a problem in any gender-ordered society. The circumstances aren't that important. Whether she was never married because no suitable suitors showed up or widowed because her husband went to war or because her father died from the plague before he could arrange a marriage doesn't matter. What matters is that you have a woman who has no legal power or authority in society, a dependent being forced into the circumstance of having to pay for and manage her own livelihood and that of the rest of her household. In the absence of an effective welfare system, what can be done? You either create a system to care for widows and orphans or get rid of them. But how do you make people believe it's okay to get rid of them? You demonize them; you take their humanity away from them. In a nutshell, that is what happened between

1200 and 1800 all over Europe and in parts of the American colonies, like Salem, Massachusetts.

The psychological aspects and nuances are obviously complicated. No one sat around a big medieval banquet table and said, "You know what? There's just too many women; let's kill them." No, that's not what happened. What happens in these circumstances is that the community feels the anxiety from some event, a pandemic, a significant death, an invader. And the response from the authorities is ineffective. The people feel that God must be punishing them or the devil is afoot. Then the community goes looking for the source—this takes the pressure off whoever is in charge because they can join the community. "Let's find the problem together!" The idea of "evil" is easy because the source isn't obvious. The people can then direct their effort to finding the source of the problem, and the problem is never a thing that is spread throughout the group. When a terrible curse plagues a group, social psychology has shown that the problem cannot also be the source. For example, the problem of men not coming home from war cannot be because the cause is unjust or the system has failed us. It must be that my people or family is cursed. It cannot be random or quixotic. Instead, a unique source and reason must be found.

The search for some reason other than the obvious is what causes cultural blindness. This unconscious process is happening because to source the problem in the at-risk community, the people who are already suffering, or the authority that has failed is too painful. It is incomprehensible to think that the pain the community feels might be caused by the people and institutions who are suffering from the pain. Time and time again, this is what social psychologists find when they study witch hunts, regardless of the century or environment. The system that was destroyed by war and geopolitical shifts in power released the pressure by targeting women under the guise of hunting demons and witches. In the time where contracts were first being developed as a structural norm for trade, the pact of selling one's soul to the devil was a reminder that trade and commerce have legal structures. And what better way to educate someone about the importance and permeability of contracts than to suggest a supernatural bond between two people signing a deal?

Medieval society was built on waging war for power and expanding territories to bring money and resources back to the communities that sent men to fight as soldiers. Unable to answer for the loss of blood and treasure to the decimated communities, the authorities of the time blamed demons and witches. And the only people to blame at home were the women left behind. The culture created an invisible threat embodied by the devil. His target? Women who would not submit. This obfuscated the real threats that plagued people: economic change, debt, war, poverty, pandemic, migration, and political upheaval. Ultimately the devil is responsible for them too. So fighting the devil at home is almost as good as fighting the devil on the battlefield. And in return, we get a benefit. Women are silenced. They don't compete with men for resources. They learn their place. This distraction campaign to blind women to their circumstances was very successful. When there's a woman you don't like or that seems conniving, we still call her a witch. In doing so, we obfuscate any power dynamics that might influence the behavior we see. We fall into line with power and authority and degrade the "witch" for thinking she's more important than the status quo.

But the witch isn't the only one who is blind. The MISOR is blinded too. The MIPE is often cast as a witch and made to believe that she is wholly responsible, that her fate is her fault. The MISOR is told that failure is not possible. If she does what is expected of her, she'll be fine. And if she's not fine, then she broke a rule she wasn't aware of. If she just does what she's told, she'll be rewarded. The MISOR is blind to the possibility that the Divide will also come for her. Being deferential and demure will not save her. The MISOR's blindness is not folly. She believes wholeheartedly in her goodness and acts on it. She is not vying for power or control. Roles don't bother her; in fact she likes them. These rules set up structures that are easy for her to understand. She can live her life according to the patterns imposed by authority because she truly believes that the authority she seeks has virtue and will protect her.

Legally Blonde and Blind

Elle Woods is the most popular girl in the Delta Nu sorority. After being dumped by her boyfriend, Warner Huntington III, Elle decides that the only way to maintain her relationship to Warner is to follow him to Harvard Law School. In applying to Harvard Law, Elle is completely blind to the reality of her situation. She doesn't see that she won't be accepted. It doesn't occur to her that she will be treated poorly or that she will be shunned by the more serious students of the incoming first-year law school class. Elle's blindness is demonstrated as she moves into Wyeth House, the Harvard Law School dorm, and when she shows up for her first few days on campus. She doesn't notice all the people staring at her when she moves into her dorm. Further, when she's attending the first-day events, a mixer, an orientation, Elle is overdressed for the occasion. She also misreads the vibe at the orientation, behaving in her typical MISOR way, being cheerful and engaging people in conversation, which none of them expect or appreciate. She is blind to the social expectations. When everyone around her is boasting about their intellectual achievements, she chimes in with her social successes, like being elected homecoming queen. She's a MISOR, and she's relating.

Her blindness continues to define her time at Harvard as she tries to make friends and connections. She shows up to the library to try and connect with her ex-boyfriend's study group. She brings snacks, hoping to relate and be of service, in true MISOR fashion. She is rebuked and made fun of, and finally her detractors openly tell her what they think of her. While this hurts her, it isn't enough to end her blindness. Elle is just sad and disoriented. She doesn't know what to do in response. She only knows how to be a MISOR and try to relate and connect. She finally crosses from the Blind step into the second quadrant after she is invited as a joke to a party being thrown by her ex's new flame, Vivien. Walking through the halls of Wyeth House, Vivien is inviting everyone she encounters to a party she is hosting. Elle hears the word *party* before she sees who is making the invitations. Seeing Elle's eagerness for something familiar like a party, Vivien invites Elle to her "costume" party, a lie intended to embarrass her rival. Elle arrives at Vivien's party in a scanty bunny costume. She is embarrassed but plays it off as a choice. Typical MISOR, she is going to get along. She doesn't get past her blindness until Warner mocks her for thinking she's smart enough to be considered for a competitive internship in a prestigious law firm where their professor is a partner. Warner tells her point-blank, "Oh, honey, you're not smart enough." It is finally at this moment the spell of Elle's blindness is broken. She realizes that he doesn't see her. Her accomplishments are not seen as equivalent to his, even though ostensibly hers are greater. Warner was waitlisted to get into Harvard and his father had to make a call, while Elle was admitted on her own merits. In this moment she says, "I'm never going to be good enough for you." She leaves the party and goes directly to the Harvard bookstore in her bunny costume and buys a colorful laptop. She is no longer blind.

Exercise

Looking back on an important time in your life, can you see where there was movement or intrigue that you ignored? In line with your curse or mark, is there a particular form of blindness that accompanied or followed?

QUADRANT II

Into the World of Invisible Forces and Mystery

Quadrant II:

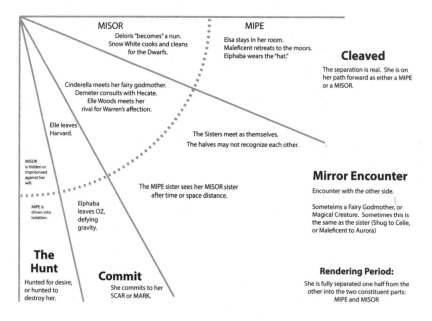

We are now crossing from the World of Visible Power and Form into the World of Invisible Forces and Mystery. This is a consequential change. For the next two quadrants, the woman is going to have a harrowing experience. It will reach its climax at the Hunt, and without recognition and integration, could keep the woman in a tortured state indefinitely. In the second quadrant, each woman finds herself thrust into the track of either the MISOR or the MIPE. She will try to make sense of this role, even as she denies that the forces acting on her are archetypal. She may keep making decisions to try and break free, only to continue to find herself stuck in the purgatory of the second quadrant, replaying it over and over again.

CHAPTER 8

RENDERED

I always cry when I see it. For me it is one of the most painful scenes in cinematic history. In Steven Spielberg's 1985 adaptation of *The Color Purple*, sisters Nettie and Celie are violently separated from one another by Celie's abusive husband, Albert. In the previous scene, Albert, whom Celie only ever calls "Mister," has tried to seduce Nettie as she walks to school. Nettie successfully thwarts his advance and runs home to her sister. But Albert's pride will not allow the sisters to stay together, so he kicks Nettie out. Though the two women hold on to each other tightly, he forcefully separates them over and over again. First, he pulls them apart as they embrace each other tightly on the front porch. He picks Nettie up, and Celie holds on to her sister's hands as Mister drags her around the property. Not letting go, Celie falls and gets dragged down the stairs, her arms and hands holding tight to Nettie. At one point, Mister drops Nettie, and the sisters run to the pole of a grapevine. Nettie holds tightly onto the pole, and Celie shields her sister with her own body to protect her, wrapping her body around from behind. But Mister punches down on their fingers with his much larger fists. When he finally succeeds in picking Nettie up again, he throws her face-first into the dirt outside the gate to the house. She quickly gets up and desperately reaches back to try and grab hold of her sister, Celie. Mister stands between them. When he raises a fist to backhand Nettie, she backs away and screams "Why?" through agonized tears.

This scene is the first one I think of when I consider this step along the Queen's Path. It is the most illustrative of the experience of the Rendering that I have come across in film. The Rendering step is monumental. Not only has the woman set foot into the space where she will find herself cleaved in two, but she is also leaving the familiar World of Visible Power and Form for the World of Invisible Forces and Mystery. She is entering the underworld. In this part of the journey, the world will not make sense. She is in the place where her power is drained, cleaved by the experience of the Divide. In this transition, the woman is set on her path to be either a MISOR or a MIPE. She will be focused on her track by external forces, regardless of whether or not she wants that track. She will start to feel herself longing. The longing can be for any combination of MISOR and MIPE attributes. She may long for power, relationship, belonging, or to express her gifts. The Divide has come, and she will struggle either to belong to a family or a group or to her own goals and desires. The gravitational forces of culture will feel disorienting and unreal.

What are we reacting to? Women the world over, regardless of culture, feel the internal and external pressures to be either a pretty, effortless princess who takes care of everyone else or a self-determined woman who gets labeled "difficult" for having ambition and desire. Women know instinctively, but not explicitly, that they are being affected by the pulleys and wheels of a vast engine that pervades their world and affects their daily experience. The machine has become so ubiquitous as to have become invisible. The machine that divides women against themselves is built into the fabric of everyday life. It is sometimes called "patriarchy," as though it is simply the role of father-led families that causes this abusive system. That word, while descriptive, is too flat. The experience of the Rendering can better be likened to a factory, an enormous, far-reaching set of Rube Goldberg machines that connect, disconnect, and interconnect seamlessly in response to fissures or transgressions as needed.

In each situation, a new instrument pushes women to conform. Their purpose is to divide an individual woman away from her own will so that it is easier for her to strive toward the cultural ideals of femininity. Most of the time, these ideals include being quiet, passive, small, and attractive. The systems of this infrastructure ultimately colonize her inner world. When she strays, an inner mechanism corrects her. Her desires, dreams, ambitions, fears, limits, and ideals will be determined by external forces that have taken up residence within her being. These inner forces will complicate her choices, causing internal conflict that can present on a continuum from mild to debilitating.

How do you turn a living being brimming with life and exuberance into a passive observer? How do you contain her joy, passion, ambition, or beauty? You make it distasteful for her to be outspoken. You punish her for being "too much." You admonish her to "be ladylike." You mock women who don't conform. You make examples of women who break the rules. Systems punish women for the near-impossible task of failing to police the behavior of those with more physical, cultural, or political power, usually powerful men. En masse you teach them that there are different expectations for women and men. Ideally, women are obedient and silent, while men are strong and brave.

What is the machine made of? The mechanisms are complex, consisting of sections that cut, strain, and crush. The implements that make up the conveyor belts, filters, and sharp dicing sections exist to divide a woman's inner voice from her embodied existence. She should watch her weight so that she is always seen as "desirable." She should mind her manners so that she is never offensive. She should be smart so that she isn't caught off guard. She should be cunning so that she can deflect unwanted predatory attention. She should be modest so that she doesn't draw the "wrong" kind of attention to herself. She should always be mindful that to progress, she will need to be liked above all else. As a result, she must learn the subtle art of applying only the most minimal amount of pressure. She must become an expert in reading others' intentions. She will need to be creative and subtle so that it never appears that she is being pushy or mean-spirited. She should, she must, she should, she must . . . that is the key point here. She always "should" consider everything and everyone else first. In other words, her will, her body, her intelligence, and her being are not "for" her. They are always in service to someone or something outside of her first.

If you doubt me, just think about how many times you yourself may have disliked a woman who was "too loud." Maybe you or someone near you may have said that a woman was "asking for it" if she dressed scantily. Or maybe you have looked at a "bossy" woman and called her a "bitch" or "manly." Were you taught that she was compromising her femininity? You have certainly heard these things around you, perhaps spoken by those close to you— whether family members, co-workers, or friends.

This shows up in predictable ways. In the most conservative view, a woman is a handmaiden to patriarchy first, a mother second, and an individual last. Her role is first, then her biology, and then her authenticity. As a result, she is pushed through expectations, ideals, slurs, and unconscious biases. She jumps through cultural hoops to attain an impossible ideal. The sinister purpose of the hoop-jumping is to distract her from broader cultural and social tides that don't, and won't, include her. These mechanisms exist and are perpetuated with brutality. Though they are created from powerful systems and beliefs, they are reproduced and enforced mostly unconsciously.

The instruments in the machine include subtle and brutal forces. Subtle forces include (but aren't limited to) coercion, comparison, status, idealization, gaslighting, and shaming. Brutal forces are a bit more obvious, with physical violence and rape at the top of the list and threats of violence, silencing, covering, and public condemnation following. The process of introducing these systems is hardly subtle. Most women remember the moment they learned (usually the hard way) that the rules for women were different.

These systems create in each woman a lens that can take on a light tinge or a deep wash of internalized sexism. They become a worldview held on to by mothers, aunts, neighbors, and grandmothers, subsequently passed down to girls and women in parallel, simultaneous systems of control. We feel their vice-grip in competition for resources, in everything from jobs to attention and partners. Whether women accept these structures or resist them will determine the rest of their lives. To accept the structures even tacitly is to keep faith with cultural bonds, and in truth there is hardly a place on Earth where this can be avoided. To resist these rules, to point out their nature and the way they entangle women, is also part of the system. For in doing so, your self-definition is created by either being inside or outside of the structure. Like most structures, the invisible walls that guide our steps don't get our attention until we bump up against them. Our ire is saved for the individual insult, the jealous lover, or the rapist. But it is the invisible walls of the structure that create and empower those forces. There is a path out of the internal system, even if we cannot yet dismantle the external one. Its ultimate destination outcome is sovereignty, complete ownership of oneself.

Deferring Your Self

In her book *Girlhood*, Melissa Febos frequently describes scenes from the Divide. In researching the sex lives of young women, Febos describes a phenomenon that I have seen in my own younger patients. When these young women were asked to rate their satisfaction with their sexual experiences, the women bypassed their experiences and instead reported on how satisfied they believed their partners were. With my patients, it looks like this:

Therapist: Are you sexually active?

Young Woman: Yes.

Therapist: How would you describe your sex life? Do you feel satisfied with the amount of sexual pleasure you experience?

Young Woman: My boyfriend says that I'm great in bed. We do stuff all the time.

Therapist: You do stuff?

Young Woman: Yeah, it's okay. He enjoys it.

Therapist: What do you like about it?

Young Woman: I mean, he likes it. He gives me attention. I guess that's the part I like.

Therapist: So, without wanting to be rude, do you have an orgasm?

Young Woman: (Gets uncomfortable) I mean . . . no . . . but he always does.

In the study Febos examined, young men of the same age group answered not about their partners but about their own satisfaction.[1] Febos realized a similar pattern had emerged in her life during a particularly controlling relationship. When friends and family would inquire after her well-being, she would respond about how she believed her partner felt about her in that moment. Febos goes on to discuss how consent becomes muddied in these circumstances. That the implied consent offered by a woman who fears for her life in the presence of a larger, more powerful person, usually a man, is often the only power she has. Implied consent is a way to stave off a more violent and unpredictable exchange. Saying, or implying, yes is a way to maintain one's sense of control in the face of danger.

I hear it anytime a woman describes a separation from herself. It is present when she describes an incomprehensible yearning for an undefined aspect of her identity. It shows up when a filmmaker shows us an all-too-relatable trauma that pits a woman against herself. The Divide appears when women discuss feeling "torn" by their decisions around motherhood, career, creativity, money, or responsibilities. The Divide holds a very binary idea of who women can be. We are either ideal or are excised. Both categories are traps . . . and dependent on one another. The MISOR's value comes from her outright acceptance of the role of dependent. The MIPE's value comes from her knowledge that she is not dependent on anyone. As a result, any time she wants the things associated with the MISOR, she butts up against a protective force of both the MISORs holding the line and an internal critic that reminds her that she doesn't fit. Until now, our culture hasn't named it, but we all know this force. If you read any narrative where women are the focus, you will find these powers in action.

While we haven't had reliable ways to describe the Divide, I see it at work in the creativity of many women. Whether discussing Melissa Febos's work or that of other writers like Jessica Valenti, Elizabeth Lesser, Colleen Hoover, or Jess Zimmerman or of filmmakers like Sarah Polley, Céline Sciamma, Gina Price-Bythewood, or Patty Jenkins, just to name a handful, the Divide is always present.

One of my favorites of these is the work of Céline Sciamma. In two of her recent films, *Portrait of a Lady on Fire* and *Petite Maman*, we see the two characters representing the Divide. In *Portrait of a Lady on Fire*, the painter Marianne represents the MIPE. She has a profession. She is not married and not interested in becoming anyone's spouse. Meanwhile, her subject, Heloise, is a noble woman who has struggled to find a suitable partner. Her mother has hired several portrait artists to create a painting that would make Heloise appealing to suitors. But Heloise has sabotaged every painter's efforts. When Marianne shows up, the two embark on an amorous affair. A beautiful and very different portrait results. Both women are transformed as a consequence.

In *Petite Maman*, eight-year-old Nelly is surprised to find a little girl named Marion living in the woods. Nelly's maternal grandmother has died, and she and her family are there cleaning out her house. Nelly's mom becomes so overwhelmed by the loss of her mother and the idea of cleaning out the house that she leaves her husband and daughter to complete the task. As the movie unfolds, we see that Nelly is frequently disoriented walking in the woods. She stumbles upon Marion building a fort out of sticks among the pine trees. When the girls eventually make it to Marion's house, it appears remarkably familiar to Nelly. It has a similar layout, but some of the furnishings and décor are different. Soon, we learn that eight-year-old Marion is Nelly's mom, and, magically, while Marion the adult has been gone, her childhood self has been at home with Nelly. Marion can't face her childhood self, but the relationship of her own inner child with her daughter is healing.

Sciamma's films are a self-described examination of the idea of "the gaze," both the idea from art history and the idea of the "male gaze."[2] In art, the gaze is a concept that asks us to examine both how art is observed and who is doing the observation.[3] In film theory, the idea of the male gaze explains that women are represented in film and television for the pleasure of "men."[4] You will find the same type of filmmaking associated with the male gaze placed on anyone who is deemed inferior in culture. I would argue that what feminists term the *male gaze* in film is about the subjects of the film being conquered more than it is about men specifically. Whoever is empowered in conquest is who the gaze is for. This becomes important because women can also align with the powers of conquest. The alignment is more dangerous. Women who abuse other women or who help men do it are not unique. They engage in the hegemonic systems of power because it benefits them. They shallowly believe that if they can remove enough layers between them and the power that oppresses, then they'll be free. It is never that simple, and almost always turns back on the women taking the side of the oppressor.

The Rendering step places a woman on the path that will define her behavior, her aspirations, and what she conceals about herself. A MISOR will hide any personal ambitions. A MIPE will stifle her desire for children. The MISOR will long to fit in, long for her sacrifices to have meaning. She'll hurry up her courtship in hopes that marriage and children will help her feel more fulfilled, more in line with her purpose. If only she had a loving husband, obedient children, a beautiful home, then her life would be perfect. A MIPE will long to belong, believing that if only she were richer, more beautiful, more successful, more . . . something . . . then everything would be better. The Divide keeps these aspects separated archetypally. Each woman believes that if she could just fulfill an ideal, then her life would *work*.

This step follows Blind because in Blind, the woman can't see the power that is about to be usurped in the Rendering. Her inherent power for fulfilling her desires, for becoming herself, for bringing new life in any form, from creativity to children, will be redirected to the Divide. All that power has to go somewhere, and it goes into the splitting of her psyche into one of the two paths that will define her for the next phase of her life. In the Hero's Journey, there is no correlation to this step. The hero never has to worry about unequal power in the same way. He never has to navigate the questions of marriageability, sex, or virginity. While he also will have to find his power, there is no step that says, "you can't" because of your sex or gender.

The MISOR holds our culture's archetypal ideas about what it means to be a woman. The MIPE holds our culture's shame. When a woman cannot live up to the MISOR ideals, she is automatically cast into the class of the MIPE. Our culture has structured itself around this idea. This is why we blame rape victims. This is why women who are assaulted don't go to the police. It is not only because we won't be believed but also because if we acknowledge this estrangement from the ideal, it changes the category or track that we get to occupy. Denying authority in this manner is an act of defiance, a refusal to be categorized by cultural demands. It doesn't always succeed. The Divide comes for us all, whether we defy it or not. Indeed, defying it also is a risk that easily puts women on the MIPE track.

Teenage MIPE

When I was a teenager, there was a boy who spent his whole summer trying to seduce me. Matthew had met me at my job and asked for my number. We went out a few times, to dinner or a movie. He came from a wealthy family and drove a fancy sports car. He had just graduated from high school. I had just completed 10th grade and turned 16 that summer. This was his summer between high school and college. It was exciting to be pursued by someone who was college-bound. It made me feel special. I felt pretty, sexy, and desirable, though I ultimately didn't really understand what those things meant at 16. I just knew that being desired was a good thing.

He pushed hard for me to have sex with him. I refused. I wasn't ready. I wasn't against sex, but he wasn't the person I wanted for my first experience. He broke it off with me. I was hurt but not devastated, which confirmed my decision. As people started to connect and hang out in preparation for school to be back in session, rumors started to spread. Matthew had told people that I had indeed had sex with him. Amid the rumors, I learned that while he was pursuing me, he had a serious girlfriend who had spent the summer in Europe. I told anyone who confronted me with the rumor that he was a liar. I had refused him, and this was his punishment. But no one wanted to believe that Matthew with the fancy car and shiny blond curls was a liar. It was much more attractive to believe that their golden boy had earned another notch on his belt. So I chose the MIPE route. When people didn't believe me, I told them he had a teeny tiny dick. If they were going to believe a lie, then I'd have a part in creating it. I got laughs but no redemption.

I had already been on the path of the MIPE since well before high school. I was sensitive and smart. I was also confident and grew into a woman's body in the summer between seventh and eighth grades. I awkwardly tried to fit all the weird expectations put on me. My mother was the quintessential MISOR. She was dutiful. She cooked and cleaned. She also took abuse, first emotional abuse from my father, and after their divorce, physical abuse from her second husband. I knew that I didn't want any kind of treatment like that in my life. I would not be like her. I floundered in middle school to fit in. It was impossible. I was the butt of jokes, the girl who got bullied by the mean girls. I had breasts and a mop of frizzy hair in seventh grade. When most of the other girls were in Mary Janes and still looked like children, I wore a ladies size 7 shoe, was 5'4" and could fill out a bathing suit like a swimsuit model. In high school, I started to pay attention to how to wear clothes and makeup. I took up a disciplined workout routine. I figured out how to manage my curls. By tenth grade, I had gone from awkward ugly duckling to promising swan. But the experience with Matthew turned my temporary victory rotten. I was angry, and soon I was trading my preppy Lacoste polos for black spikes and leather. MIPE fit me better.

Teen MISORs and MIPEs Today

I have a handful of clients who are young women. Some of them I have been seeing for years, since they attended middle or high school, and now they are in their 20s. I have had the privilege of watching them grow over the years. They do the work of therapy, but the young women who have been in therapy for a long time especially struggle with what it means to have a dialogue with their psyche. The biggest pressures are coming from outside of them. I am almost always undone by the ways these young women have absorbed the devaluing messages of our culture. I have one client, Marcy, who sent her father a scathing series of e-mails one night in her first year of college. In these long, feverish messages, Marcy begged him to explain to her what happened in their relationship. What had happened in her childhood that made her feel that without male attention she was nothing? Had he not spent enough time with her? Had he not seen her as equal to her brothers? She was so far into the Blind that she couldn't see that it was a cultural experience. She assumed it was personal. It must be about her relationship to her own father.

When Marcy came into the consulting room that week, she was adrift and terrified. She led with the e-mails to her father, sent late one night after a night of unceremonious sex with someone she barely knew. She felt compelled to do anything for the approval of this young man with whom she shared only the briefest of encounters. She didn't want him or aspire to love him. But she couldn't bear his rejection either. So she gave her body over to a loveless act to avoid experiencing the anguish of rejection. The Divide expresses itself in more than just sexual encounters. It shows up in experiences with other women, parents, teachers, ministers. Anywhere there is power and authority, there will also be the Divide.

Marcy's experience is not unique. Almost every one of my female clients describes a version of needing attention or approval to feel real in the world. The younger they are, the more this experience is part of their day-to-day life. The Divide has always been with us, but the age of social media has made the effects even more obvious and pernicious. A colleague and I were just discussing how, in our generation, the images that affected us were characters on television and in film. We longed to look like the supermodels that graced magazine covers. While we experienced bullying, and sometimes it was horrific, we never had the constant onslaught provided by mobile phones and social media.

The Tools of Rendering

One of the critical tools of the Divide is the experience of separating authority from responsibility. As women grow from girlhood into womanhood, they experience greater responsibilities and fewer areas where they have authority. This will often look like having less autonomy than their male peers. But lack of autonomy is not the greatest threat. Autonomy can be addressed. The mechanism for granting autonomy is responsibility. The more responsibility you have, the greater autonomy you can earn. Autonomy and authority are not the same thing. A teenager earns the right to drive by following rules—she gains greater autonomy by demonstrating that she can act with responsibility. However, the responsibility rarely equals the ability to make decisions that impact others or that might make her appear insubordinate. Authority is the right to make decisions for yourself, and sometimes others. Autonomy is the freedom to move about of your own free will. As women grow from teenagers to young adults, they are likely to have more autonomy and responsibility, and less authority.

Authority flows upward to institutions, parents, and . . . boys and men. Teenage boys are given deferential treatment, a practice run at authority. They are asked their opinions more than their female peers. They are encouraged to tackle hard subjects, like math and science—subjects that often require that they cultivate and defend their opinions. They are taught to compete. Authority is the reward for winning in competition.

It is a well-researched fact that girls and boys have equal interest in science and mathematics until approximately eight years of age. What happens in this time frame? It is when girls begin to be groomed for their roles as women. Research has shown that girls are entreated toward "softer" disciplines like reading, art, and social studies beginning at this age.[5] Girls begin to internalize their expectations of being softer, likable, pretty, and desirable. Recent research shows that girls as young as six begin to have negative ideas about their bodies. Before middle school, girls are beginning to internalize the idea that they must diet and watch their weight so that they can be seen as attractive. They know that to get along in our culture, they must "look the part." Even before they acquire the language to describe this phenomenon, they are living it out.

The psychology that informs these experiences is not a personal one. The experiences of women and girls are easily discerned in their own lived experience. However, their experiences as members of a group with specific and confining cultural expectations, women, informs how they think about themselves and the world they inhabit. We see how social psychology intersects with personal psychology. As women, we are reluctant to map our personal onto the cultural. We want to believe that we are given an even playing field with our peers. We want to believe in the meritocracy. But the meritocracy has different steps for women. The experience of most women (and minorities) in any merit-based system is that they have to work harder and ignore more bad behavior than their peers.

Before you call me a woke culture warrior and throw this book across the room, stay with me for a bit. If you believe that the system is fair, then ask yourself how fair it is. What does fair look like? Does fair mean that men and women do the same work for the same pay? Does it mean that women and men share tasks equally at home? Where there are divisions of labor based on sex, is there parity? In a household where the man works and the woman stays home, does she have equal access to finances? To decisions? Does she have the capacity to spend her time or her money as she chooses? Or are there distinctions based on gender roles? I'm all for traditional divisions of labor if the couple has agreed to a set of rules that keeps things fair and considerate of both parties' needs. But a system built for submission is going to make it easy for that submission to be baked into both the day-to-day experiences and the ultimate outcomes.

Rendering happens when a woman finds herself following invisible rules to fulfill a vaguely defined and yet somehow precisely expected role. For the most part, she'll only be half aware of the system at work. She'll see it in the behavior of her mother, her sisters, her aunts, her friends, and her teachers. She'll bump up against it as she tries to build a unique identity for herself. Whether the characteristics of that identity are celebrated will ultimately be determined by which track of the Divide she walks. The Rendering is one of the most painful steps along the Queen's Path. How women internalize the cleft that emerges within them as a result is often the telltale sign of how she will navigate the complexities in this journey. If she feels strongly that her best self emerges in MISOR ideals, then she may have an easier time. There is danger, though, as she is also likely to struggle with her banished sister-self.

Any hint of the part of her that would be considered MIPE will be relegated to the underworld of the unconscious. As a result, those unlived aspects of her will be despised and feared.

Similarly, the MIPE woman who hears the call of identity and wants to "be someone" also has a debt to the unconscious. Like the MISOR, she cuts out the parts of her that might not be acceptable. The MIPE may long for connection, but her ability to submit is lacking. She may revolt against any form of submission for fear of her sublimated MISOR. Like a princess in a tower or dungeon, the MIPE's "feminine" side is pushed away. In this way, the MIPE too experiences an unrealized life. The world of nurturing and care feels like a chain. The manacles of domesticity send the MIPE into a fear-tinged expectation that to become a wife or mother means death.

In their purest forms, the MISOR and MIPE archetypes represent the extremes. There are women who live out the black-and-white versions, but there are far more who live in a vertigo-inducing tightrope walk between the two. The Divide shows up, pushing an agenda and forcing women into one of two tracks. It starts early. Most women encounter the Divide as early as six years old. The majority face the first challenges of the Divide just before the beginning of puberty. Being placed on a track isn't a choice. A woman who has the misfortune to be placed on the MIPE track early will often think that if she could just be a "better" version of a girl or woman, then she'd be fine. If she could just master the MISOR gifts, then her life would work. If she were thin, quiet, and could submit, she would be happy. She'd be accepted. Her life would make sense. But this is just the Divide talking.

The Tools in the Dividing Machine

Money and Resources

Most women are taught that men are a resource. Men are taught that their primary role is as a provider. In the Industrial Revolution, wages were paid to men. As a result, the title "breadwinner" has been associated with the person earning the money. From the 18th and into the mid-20th centuries, those wages were expected to provide for a family, not an individual man. Though this was only the case for about 100 years in the West, our culture treats this idea as a sacred contract. Being a "provider" gives a man his authority over the women in his life. A "good" woman was connected to a man, either his wife or daughter usually. She stayed home, and he provided for her and any children. Even though there has always been a class of women who worked outside the home, women are trained from early on, even now, to see this as part of the complex calculus of their lives. To attract a good provider for yourself and your children is upheld in many circles as a womanly virtue rather than a dehumanizing attribute that reduces both men and women to functions.

Women learn early that marriage and relationships are monetary exchanges. Dating is like a trial run to find out if the two people are compatible partners. In the West, this partnership is often focused on the man having a woman in his life who supports him emotionally and who contributes to his status. The woman provides sex and emotional support in exchange for financial resources and "safe" status in a world where men are predatory. Being married makes her less likely to be a target. Women don't discuss these issues so bluntly. We are given unconscious direction that directs our behavior, even if we aren't being clear about what those behaviors create.

Idealization and Comparison

Women compare ourselves with other women all the time. Competition is preferred over acceptance, especially in the United States, where cultural myths of rugged individualism permeate every aspect of our lives. As a tool of the Rendering process, idealization keeps us constantly striving. No woman can ever live up to the ideals of a culture that is constantly moving the goalposts. We compare ourselves with movie stars, models, social media influencers, our neighbors, our friends, our mothers, our sisters, comic book vixens, porn stars, and HGTV home makeover celebrities . . .

the list could go on and on. If there's another woman within 10 feet of me, I guarantee most of us engage in a comparison on some level. Is she prettier than me? Does she have a nicer house? Are her kids more obedient? Does she have more education? Does she work out more?

Beauty

We know about the standards of beauty. We are so familiar with this that I feel kind of ridiculous writing about it, as though it's some secret that women don't know. While some of what I write about illuminates invisible forces, the beauty standard is something women openly discuss. In our culture, we expect women to make efforts toward being pretty. To be pretty is to be desired. Being attractive is currency for women. For men, being attractive is a bonus. Rendering uses beauty as a way of separating women into either the MIPE or MISOR category.

Some of the best examples of this tool come from films. The 1990 film *Pretty Woman* is one of the best. In a pivotal set of scenes in the film, the main character, Vivian, played by Julia Roberts, tries to buy "acceptable" clothes on Beverly Hills' Rodeo Drive. The women in one of the shops are rude to her, refusing to wait on her based on her "trashy" appearance. Later, she shows up in stylish designer clothes, her hair beautifully coiffed. She fits their standard of beauty. As the same rude shopgirl tries to wait on her, Vivian confronts her about her prior treatment. There's a lot to critique in this film, but for the most part, everyone feels vindicated when Vivian dresses down the salesgirl who humiliated her.

Another wonderful, if painful, example is from the 1999 film *Never Been Kissed*. In a flashback, Josie Geller relives her humiliation when the boy she likes arrives to pick her up for the prom. Josie is dressed in a metallic pink dress that is absolutely dreadful. Her hair is in a side ponytail, and her braces clearly dominate her smile. As the audience, we are hopeful but know something isn't right. The boy arrives in a limousine, standing up in the sunroof. Josie is so excited. We see it in her face: she's the luckiest girl in the world.

Billy is there to pick her up—finally she's noticed. But Billy has a secret. There's a pretty, popular girl waiting in the limo. She rises to join him, standing so they are up through the sunroof, and they both throw eggs, hitting Josie. Then they laugh and drive off. She is so humiliated, she runs away from her own house, not daring to go back inside and face her parents.

We are very familiar with this tool. Think of some of your own experiences. Were you ever shamed or bullied for how you looked? What resulted? My women clients frequently discuss the costs, expectations, and desires for beauty in their experience of the Divide. Sometimes the most painful perpetrator of these standards isn't partners or husbands but mothers. For many this feels like a betrayal. Why would my mother not love me for who I am rather than what I look like? Our mothers are some of our first teachers in the Rendering. They pass the system down to us.

Body and Body Type

While you could argue that body type is in the category of beauty, it warrants its own category for many reasons. Much of our self-loathing plays out on or because of the body. It is also the *place* women are taught from a very young age to deny ourselves. As a result, many women become disoriented when discussing the body. How can you own your identity when you are taught to deny the place of identity formation? How can you feel confident when you are taught that the very foundation of your material existence is "wrong"? Women are taught to override our physical instincts in favor of not rocking the boat or making others uncomfortable. This is especially true when discussing unwanted touch but also extends to conditions like pain, fear, or hunger. Women are trained to feel that our bodies are not our own. Our bodies are *for* others, not for ourselves. Whether we are discussing sex, domesticity, beauty, athletics, or pregnancy, the female body is a means to many ends, almost all of them to do with someone else's power.

For a woman to be seen as valuable, she must first fit the bodily expectations placed on her. She will be expected to care about her body's attractiveness to others. To be a MISOR, this is a requirement. Not caring or not being able to meet the standards will automatically place a woman in the MIPE category. But achieving an acceptable appearance won't save the MIPE from being rejected. The body must also be small, receiving, capable, accepting, thin, lithe . . . basically not intimidating. The body should advertise availability and fertility. If a woman's breasts are too small or her waist too wide, she will consider herself falling short. If she has bigger hips and thighs, she will consider her frame unattractive. If she is overweight, not only will she beat herself up but she'll be also treated like a negative object, a nonperson whose opinions, fears, complaints, and intelligence are of zero consequence.

Able bodies are also part of the Divide. Any woman whose body has a disability or different range of abilities is considered a MIPE as well. Any woman who needs the assistance of a wheelchair is invisibilized. Oddly enough, though women are expected to be dependent, women who need assistance are often shunned directly into the MIPE track. A blind woman, a deaf woman, a paralyzed woman—they will always be MIPEs. Sometimes if they work hard to occupy the MISOR track, they can live ignoring their disability. This may require behaving as though the disability made them braver or that they overcame some big obstacle despite it. Either way, it's another way to keep the body in the forefront of how we think of women and how the body is often used to divide us.

Finally, there is fertility. I have a handful of specialties, and one of them is working with clients who struggle with chronic illness. Fear and pain live with these patients as constant companions. Therapy is very different for these people than it is for others. It is impossible to give these folks empty platitudes about "trying" or "getting better." Living with the real possibility and likelihood that they may not get better is a requirement for psychological health. One of the most difficult issues comes up for women who, for any number of health reasons, may have lost their fertility. It is striking how often these women ask themselves, "Am I a real woman?" Why would a woman who lost her uterus to an accident or cancer be less of a woman than her neighbor who has five children? But that is one of the ways that the rendering machine divides us. It tells us that we are functions first and people second, if we're lucky.

Understanding that the body is the first place of denial is critical to understanding how women's lives are systematically impacted by all the ways that rendering diminishes us. The ultimate goal of traversing the Queen's Path is for an individual woman to reclaim *herself* as the terrain of her sovereignty. Her body doesn't belong to culture, a man, an expectation, or an ideal. She stands in her body and claims it (and all the accomplishments she has done in her body) for herself.

Likability

One of the greatest surprises for me in the last 20 years has been the treatment of women politicians. It really shouldn't have been a surprise. The visceral reactions that people have had to Hillary Clinton, Alexandria Ocasio-Cortez, Sarah Palin, Lauren Boebert, Marjorie Taylor Greene, and other women who seek or hold public office illustrate the importance of the likability tool in the rendering machine. Sarah Palin first came on the scene of national politics as John McCain's running mate in 2008. She was the governor of Alaska, was physically attractive, and had four children. If conservatism was going to invite a woman into the halls of power, Palin represented the ideal candidate.

Pretty soon, though, there were cracks in her candidacy, not because she didn't look the part or have legitimate conservative bona fides. I'm going to be generous and say that Sarah Palin wasn't prepared, and she didn't care to be prepared. I'm reluctant to write that what I actually believe is that Sarah Palin is not a very intelligent person. She has skated through her life on her ability to live up to our cultural MISOR ideals throughout her career. She appeals to men and has been rewarded for it. This is attractive to both men and women. Women who idealize the MISOR want to be like her and find her presence comforting—someone like them is in power. Men like her because she doesn't threaten them. She hunts, she has kids, she wears snug but high-collared suits, and she wears her hair up in a bun. She doesn't claim to know a lot. I didn't like her as a candidate first because of her conservative policy positions. But the more she talked and tried to defend her views, I disliked her because I thought she was stupid and made women look bad.

Conservatives liked Sarah Palin. She filled the MISOR ideals to a T. Compare how they liked Sarah Palin with how much they then and even now continue to despise Hillary Clinton and other women like her. You find similar animosity toward representatives Ilhan Omar and Alexandra Ocasio-Cortez. Women in positions of political leadership have to contend with the catch-22 of needing to be seen as competent, capable, and strong to compete with men in the political arena. But this is confounded by the fact that what is attractive in a man is often despised in women. And attractiveness as a candidate gets quickly conflated with the kind of attractiveness women are typically expected to embody in everyday life.

Looking at women politicians can tell us a great deal about likability as a tool of rendering women into either the MIPE or MISOR categories. One of the core traits of the MISOR is that she has a family, man, or other protector. Women are expected to be deferential to authority. Whether we are talking about the police, the state, a husband, or government, a woman who challenges authority is not likable. And likable for women is required for belonging. The MIPE is disliked because she dares to confront authority. She challenges the status quo. She asks tough questions. A likable woman is one who waits her turn to speak. She doesn't rock the boat. She is always upbeat. She takes care of other people. She will conform to any standard set before her to be liked. Being liked is central to the equation of her well-being. When it isn't, she's out of the MISOR club.

Women often come late to understanding likability. Well, maybe it's just the MIPEs who arrive late at understanding it. It is a useful tool in the rendering weapon list because its parameters change easily. Likability is amorphous—it isn't easily defined and doesn't need definition. It easily relies on "gut feeling" or, my favorite, "vibes." Going back to the discussion of witches, the reference of "vibes" gives me the creeps. People who refuse to examine parts of their lives that make them uncomfortable often give me the "vibes" comment. This is true whether we're talking about women or other issues that require introspection.

The reality is that something is happening for people at the psychological level. They have pushed an idea, experience, or fear into the unconscious. The niggling feeling that they have is an indicator that something painful needs to be examined. But instead, the conscious mind takes the niggling as the thing itself, and voila, that "vibe" is born. It goes something like this: "I get a weird, yucky feeling when I see Hillary Clinton, and because I get the dislike feeling (or worse), I presume that it is because she is a terrible person. I don't use it as a thread to pull at my preferences or assumptions." When people say that a woman is unlikable, what I usually hear is that she makes them uncomfortable. They don't know why, and usually don't care to find out. Now, that isn't to say that there aren't good reasons to trust your gut when you dislike someone. But if it's someone you don't actually know personally, then you might want to ask yourself what's happening in your psyche and do a little digging.

A Quick Note on Nice

Right next to Likable on the tool shelf of Rendering you'll find Nice. This word deserves its own book to be sure, and several writers have taken on that task. The idea of being nice is one that haunts me. It is the container that holds almost all the ideas I am discussing in this chapter. Depending on whom you're talking to, *nice* can simultaneously mean to be quiet, passive, demure, unobtrusive, allowing, generous, kind, affectionate, submissive, pleasing, agreeable, and many more adjectives that make women smaller. To me, *nice* is dangerous. The admonition to "be nice" teaches women to cover up their feelings with a form of politesse that negates their experience, desires, and comfort in favor of maintaining the status quo.

Violence

It wouldn't be possible to talk about the tools of Rendering and the Divide without discussing violence. Women are much more likely than men to be the victims of domestic and intimate partner violence. Domestic violence is a broad term and can include violence and abuse of children or parents, while intimate partner violence typically reflects a relationship between lovers, couples, or sexual partners. Intimate partner violence is particularly dangerous for younger women. The World Health Organization has authored multiple studies on the impact of intimate partner violence on women's mental health. They have found consistently that intimate partner violence has a progressively negative impact on the mental health of women, and their children.[6]

It seems obvious that violence would make the list of tools of the Divide, but it is sometimes omitted in feminist examinations, not because it isn't real but rather because it is disproportionately represented as affecting poor women, uneducated women, and immigrant women. That's not to say that other women aren't affected by intimate partner or domestic violence—quite the contrary. Intimate partner violence is universal, regardless of income or social class. Where there are cultural norms for any form of domination, there you will also find intimate partner violence. It's just that well-to-do, educated women are less likely to admit to being victims of intimate partner violence than their less-well-off counterparts.

Violence is a particularly effective tool in splitting someone from their deepest self. Intimate partner violence experienced over a long time will contribute to lower self-awareness, lower self-esteem, and greater disconnection both from others and from oneself. In addition, abused people are conditioned to hypervigilance. They often will maintain peace at any cost, including sublimating their own identity. The fear of violence can lead them to anxiety associated with an uncontrolled environment. As a result of trying to mitigate feelings of anxiety, a woman who fears for her safety will easily take on behaviors that she hopes will reduce her victimization. She will be deferential, quiet, obedient, and agreeable, all attributes associated with the MISOR. What's worse the MISOR who can't live the MIPE life will just take the abuse. Her reasons could be diverse. Perhaps she hasn't gained the skills to live independently. Or maybe she doesn't know *how* to leave. It could be that she has cultural reasons. Perhaps she is isolated and doesn't have the social, cultural, or financial means to seek independence.

The threat of violence will ensure compliance. Mostly this is done by making someone so frightened of the possibility of violence that they will comply before a slap or punch is connected. As such, violence becomes an internalized structure. In the 1960s and 1970s, psychologist Martin Seligman and his colleagues at the University of Pennsylvania conducted experiments on dogs to assess how the animals would respond to aversive conditions. They placed the dogs in cages that were sometimes electrified, with the opportunity to jump out of the enclosure. But in a second step of the experiment, the animals weren't given a way out. They couldn't leave the situation. The dogs didn't have any warning, and there were no signs of when the cages would carry an electrical charge. In the second step, the dogs didn't move. They became terrified and avoided any movement even when the cages weren't electrified. When the experiment was over, the dogs wouldn't leave their kennels out of fear. Seligman and his colleagues called this phenomenon *learned helplessness*.[7] It describes the experience of what happens when someone is in a terrible situation and has no perceived exit.

Modesty

Women have been held responsible for men's desire for millennia. Evidently, the power women have over men's sexual desire is so strong that by merely showing an ankle or a bit of cleavage, a woman can trap a man's soul. When you read about men's desire and the modesty rules and religious laws that exist as a result, you'd think that women's bodies were the source of all evil. Indeed, that is what most religions teach.

You need only read the scriptures of any tradition to find admonitions that women cover themselves and behave modestly. This is sometimes described as a protection for men, but more often it is prescribed as a protection for the soul of the woman herself. She is encouraged to cover herself, keep her voice low, and to act deferential out of fear. Should she engage in the sins of vanity, immodesty, outspokenness, or a similar transgression like having an opinion, she is warned in almost all religious texts that she is thus unpleasing to the Lord. Excuse me while I take a break from typing to go break something in anger, or maybe it would be easier to vomit in disgust.

Modesty rules exist to regulate women's bodies. Even in the present, this still materializes in the strangest ways. In 2023 the Missouri state legislature enacted a rule requiring that women dress modestly, that they cover their arms and shoulders. The rule was introduced by a Republican woman, State Representative Anne Kelly. There were no new rules introduced to police the dress code for their male colleagues.[8] Similarly, in many school districts in the United States, school dress codes for girls and boys are quite different, with girls receiving more attention and more punitive action for breaking the rules than their male counterparts. In recent years, schools have banned shorts, skirts, yoga pants, and leggings for girls. The explanation for most of these restrictions is that the clothes are too sexually suggestive. One school in Kentucky said explicitly that the restrictions were in place to make the learning environment less distracting for boys! So just to recap, teenage girls are being told in school that their role as women in the classroom is to comport themselves in such a way that it doesn't distract the boys from their educational goals.[9] Meanwhile, no one is telling the boys that they have any responsibility to the girls to help ensure that these young women achieve their educational goals.

Final Thoughts

This step of the Queen's Path is one of the most important. It determines almost everything that happens afterward. It is marked by a systematic transition from the world of the undifferentiated girl to one of the regulated woman. In this step, the girl or woman is given her track to walk on the Queen's Path. She will be either a compliant MISOR or the ostracized MIPE. How she behaves and how other people respond to her will be determined by which one of these tracks she is set on. While it is easy to revile one or both of these roles, it is critical to remind ourselves that they are both traps. They are instruments of a culture and society that strives (whether consciously or unconsciously) to keep women invisible and submissive.

The track we are on doesn't change the steps that follow. It only affects the nuances of how the world engages with us and how we respond. For example, as we move into other steps on the Queen's Path, it can feel that the treatment of the MISOR and MIPE are very different, but as I'll show, the outcome is the same. Although the MISOR and MIPE's experiences look somewhat different from each other in the moment, the thing to keep an eye on is the outcome. In the Abjection step, which is coming up in the next few chapters, the MISOR gets her Happily Ever After, while the MIPE might be killed in self-defense. The importance of this step for both is that their identities are obliterated. It is the outcome that is the same, not the means to it. Seeing these as unifying principles is critical to seeing the trap of the Divide. In being rendered into either the MISOR or MIPE category, women are taught that their experiences are different; therefore, not all women experience discrimination. This false premise keeps women striving for an ideal, arguing over which version of domination is worse rather than seeing that the whole thing is a system of control over women, regardless of how well or poorly we fit the expectations placed on us.

CHAPTER 9

THE MIRROR

Snow White's stepmother famously had a magic mirror. She and the mirror had a deep relationship. When she needed reassurance, an ego boost, or a daily affirmation, the Evil Queen (we don't know her actual name) would ask, "Mirror, Mirror on the wall, who's the fairest of them all?" And every day, the mirror would reassure Step-mom that she was in fact the most beautiful woman in the land. It wasn't until her husband died and she had responsibility for her stepdaughter that Evil Queen started to worry about the relation-ship with her mirror. The older Snow White grew, the more she approached womanhood, the more insecure Evil Queen became. Rather than develop a deeper understanding of herself, Evil Queen decided that beauty, youth, and innocence were the enemy. So, nat-urally, Snow White had to die. Evil Queen doesn't want to do the dirty work, so she hired a hunter to do it for her. He chased Snow White through the Enchanted Forest. When he captured her, he couldn't kill her. Instead, he slaughtered a boar and substituted its heart, bringing it to Evil Queen as proof that the deed was done. Youth, beauty, and innocence are no more. But the secret, of course, is that the Huntsman protected Snow White . . . even after he chased her almost to her death.

What a fucked-up story on so many levels. Where do we start? Do we discuss the "normalcy" of the Huntsman chasing Snow White down, only to let her go? Do we talk about the representation that what matters most for women is their beauty, innocence, and youth? Do we discuss how the Evil Queen doesn't even get a name?

How about questioning why it is that in the world she inhabits, her power is only in her beauty, and she is imperiled after the death of her husband. I could ask a thousand more questions just interrogating the premise of *Snow White* before we even get into the details of the story itself . . . there is, of course, the domesticity of Snow White caring for seven dwarfs in the woods, and the glass coffin, and true love's kiss . . . et cetera. Right now, we're on the Queen's Path, so let's talk about the mirror moment and how it relates to the Divide and the experience of being rendered or cleaved.

Snow White wasn't in real peril until becoming a young woman. Evil Queen doesn't want anything to do with her once she becomes competition. If we focus on the mirror, we find multiple layers of meaning in this symbolism:

1. We believe that mirrors always tell the truth.

2. Aging can make women evil and undesirable.

3. Having a relationship with your mirror (i.e., vanity) is dangerous.

4. A mirror will drive us to all kinds of behaviors.

5. Seeing and being seen is critical to our well-being.

6. People seek mirrors outside of ourselves to model ourselves on.

7. When the mirror fails us, we are capable of terrible things.

Some of these messages are contrary to the healthy ways psychologists think about mirroring. The fact that women are instructed to avoid mirrors is telling in and of itself. It shouldn't be that we elevate mirrors to the point of obsession, but everyone needs appropriate mirrors in life. Therapists learn about mirrors early in our training. One of the most important aspects of predicting whether someone can regulate their emotions on their own is to know how well they were mirrored as a child. When therapists talk about mirroring, we are usually describing the experience that mothers and infants engage in together as part of developmental psychology. Mom holds infant. Mom smiles at infant. Infant recognizes the facial expression and reproduces it. This delights Mom, who keeps it going. Mom and baby go back and forth, doing this for a while. Most of what children learn first in life begins with the mirroring process.[1]

Healthy mirroring continues for parents and children throughout their lives. If I am an infant and I'm crying and no one comes to my aid, or worse, someone yells at me or hits me when I cry, then I have no mirror to learn first what the behavior even is, much less how to regulate the emotion behind the tears. I also learn that emotions are generally not safe, because whenever I feel something, there is no one there to help me understand or soothe the ground of being that feeling occupies. Many of my clients struggle with not having had enough positive mirroring. In Western culture, we have had a long history of believing that it is better to force children to toughen up from an early age. We have children sleep in their own beds, alone in their own bedrooms, from a very young age. We look down on moms who breastfeed longer than a few months. We let kids "cry it out" in their beds. We isolate children, sending them to "time out" to reflect on their behavior rather than help them regulate their own emotions through soothing or mirroring. This school of thought proliferated during the 19th century. It aligned with the experiences of the Industrial Revolution. People moved to the cities for work in droves and no longer lived in extended families. When the world is more difficult, parents feel the need to make tougher children. But a lack of mirroring doesn't make kids strong; it makes them fearful and rigid.

If we don't get enough positive mirroring in our young lives, there are two possibilities: either we will instinctively seek out someone or something to provide it for us, or we will do anything in our power to avoid the negative feelings that show up around emotions, even positive ones. Most people use a strategy that combines the two in some way. Most people enter therapy because their once-adaptive ways of avoiding negative feelings have stopped working, or, in the case of addictions, work too well at numbing. All people need validation. All people need emotional regulation. All people need joy. All of us also need safety in self-expression.

If a person had negative mirroring, trauma, or shaming or was neglected, any mirroring can feel threatening, invasive, or create a sense of anxiety. They may blunt that with shopping, video games, sex, drugs, or alcohol. It is also where we find behavioral addictions like anorexia and bulimia. When mirroring goes wrong, the behaviors that result can be dangerous, even life-threatening. Anorexia, for example, is a behavioral response to mirroring gone wrong. The person who struggles to nourish themselves usually does so out of a complex behavioral pattern that both idealizes a passive, effortless vision of self and simultaneously has a fundamental need to prove to an early caregiver that they can out-control them, that they don't need the caregiver. Mirroring is one of our most fundamental needs throughout our lives. And if we don't have sufficient mirroring as children, we struggle to find appropriate mirrors throughout our lives.

When a person who has had only negative mirroring tries to create positive mirrors on their own, at first they find fun house mirrors, warped and out of balance. For some, mirroring will be overwhelming, and for others, normal mirroring will be too little. As the person learns to identify their own needs, the mirroring will become more aligned with their nature. Personal work like therapy, art, spiritual practice, journaling, or contemplative reflection will bring the fun house mirror more into line with reality. One of the first steps is simply to acknowledge the need for mirroring and connection.

If I were doing therapy with Evil Queen and she told me about her unhealthy relationship with her mirror, I'd ask her who in her life had been her primary caregiver and what that relationship was like. I'd be very curious about whether anyone saw her as an individual when she was young. I'd want to know who in her life "saw" her and how. I'd also want to know who had stood in for the mirror in her life. Did she have a good relationship with her mom? Her grandmother? Was there a beloved aunt or an abusive older sister in the picture? In whose model did she "see" herself?

The final area where I'd want to understand Evil Queen was what opportunities she had to see herself through someone else's eyes. Was she only valued for her beauty? Was her intelligence channeled into pure cunning to win at the game of husband-catching? What was that like for her? Was it wholly negative? Or self-serving? When she was young, had she been a damsel locked in a tower? Had she been taught that being protected by a man or family was the only way to be safe? What happened in her life to make her rely solely on her magic mirror to provide her with information about herself and her standing in the world?

My guess would be that she didn't have too much positive mirroring. I would presume that my client, Evil Queen, had a mother who made her feel that beauty was her greatest gift and her only source of power. I would guess that she had been relatively isolated, perhaps with only her mother as a model. I would examine whether or not she was led to believe that she was worthless if she didn't have children. Maybe she couldn't? Or maybe she struggled with the complexity of what it would take for her to be a mother? The world undoubtedly reinforced the double standards of the Divide for her. When we talk about the mirror in this step of the Queen's Path, we're looking for the ways that a woman has seen herself and her sister-self (MIPE or MISOR) in the world. What have the models been? Who has shown up to help her? Who has she sought out to help understand herself better?

Mirrors can also be used like Perseus hunting Medusa. He could not look at her, so he used the mirror to look around corners. When he finally confronted her, he used the mirror to horrify the Gorgon herself. When she saw her own reflection, she was turned to stone. Afterward, the goddess Athena wore the Gorgon's head on her armor in battle as a means of scaring off anyone who would come near her. The mirror can also be a way of losing ourselves in our desires. Like Narcissus, we can become obsessed with our own reflection, losing ourselves in its magic, never seeing reality. Or from the same myth, we may lose ourselves longing for someone who only sees themselves and like Echo become a voice in the wind, with no substance left to hold us to Earth.

MISOR MIRROR MOM

It took me a long time to realize that I longed for powerful women in my life. I loved my mother dearly and desperately wanted approval from her that never came. She was proud of the things in my life I had accomplished. But those things had been done in spite of her. My mother had always looked down on my desires and ambitions. She saw them as "too much." She understood my longing for achievement as a referendum on the life she lived. Though I couldn't see it at the time, she was absolutely correct. I was terrified of living her life. Any achievements had been accomplished with mostly her derision and little help or encouragement. I didn't realize until I was older and a seasoned therapist that my own mother issues had directed my life for a very long time. Since I was a little girl, I looked at my mom like she was a beautiful but old-fashioned doll. I saw her as weak and a victim. My relationship with her was very complicated. I knew my mom wasn't at all nice to me. She struggled with her own anger. Looking at her as a mirror, I only saw someone who hated her life and felt sorry for herself.

I looked for other women role models. I found plenty. I almost always wound up choosing someone who appeared strong, but who, like my mother, had a lot of wounds and few tools to do the self-repair necessary to avoid hurting me. I chose women friends and mentors who built me up so they could tear me down over and over. It wasn't until I was in graduate school that I started to realize that this pattern was an unconscious constellation that I kept reenacting. I wanted my mother to mirror me. I longed for her to "bless" my becoming a MIPE to her MISOR.

Carl Jung is credited with saying, "If you do not endeavor to make the unconscious conscious, it will rule your life and you will call it fate."[2] Freud was a little more blunt. He called it "repetition compulsion." What he meant was that we all have an unconscious need to repair patterns in the unconscious that are broken or maladaptive. And so we unconsciously engage ourselves in relationships that give us the opportunity to repair the original wound. When psychotherapists talk about a "family constellation," this is part of what we mean. We all put ourselves in situations that feel familiar enough to us. This familiarity is a psychological one that makes us feel relatively comfortable—whether the situation is fraught or not, we know what to do and how to respond. This can be subtle and nuanced, like always putting yourself in situations to be an interlocutor or translator. It can also be incendiary, like being the person who receives the blows (real or emotional) to protect children or loved ones, because you do it so well. It depends on the person and their original mirror(s).

When my client, Evil Queen, looks in the mirror, she sees herself as "less than" Snow White. Her beautiful stepdaughter becomes the object that lies just on the other side of the glass. What the Evil Queen sees is what she doesn't have and can't become—or so she thinks. The part of us cut away in the Rendering inhabits a projection somewhere in the unconscious.

When thinking about how this shows up in stories, it is relatively easy to see. In *Legally Blonde*, Elle Woods gets dragged to the nail salon by her girlfriends to cheer her up after her breakup with preppy heartthrob Warner Huntington III. While waiting her turn, she sees a news article that inspires her to apply to Harvard Law School. The MISOR didn't need a mirror until she experienced Cleaved. And so, she sets her sights on being a "law student" in the hopes of getting her boyfriend back.

Celie in *The Color Purple* befriends Shug Avery, the only woman her husband has ever loved. She doesn't do this out of self-preservation but connection, and she doesn't know it, but this relationship will transform her. Cassie in *Promising Young Woman* identifies with her dead friend, Nina. Cassie's life has become hollow after realizing how unfair the world is to women, the point driven home by the abuse and death of her friend. The mirror tells her who she has to be. In every case, when we embrace the mirror, women are transformed.

Consider how we've landed at this place on the Queen's Path. We have left the World of Visible Power and Form and crossed into the World of Invisible Forces and Mystery. We are in the world where things are deeper than they appear. Everything has more meaning than we can see at first glance. We have been cursed and marked.

And we walked blindly into the experience of being divided, cut in two. We only are allowed to carry one aspect of our identity forward, no matter what we might want for ourselves. At this stage, the self that has been cut from us lives like a ghost in the unconscious. She haunts the places we don't get to inhabit. She lives like a disembodied soul. Whether we long for her or banish her, the outcome for us is the same. She sets the tone of our own personal underworld, our unconscious.

This banished self is the secret mirror. What parts of ourselves have we driven into the underworld? Is it our joy? Our sadness? Is it our intelligence? Beauty? Sexuality? Innocence? Only you can know. But a hint can come in the way you think of looking in the mirror. What do you look for? What do you reject? Who are you hoping to see in the reflection?

For me, the shadowlands of the unconscious have always been haunted by my mother. I measured everything about myself unconsciously against how much or how little I was like her. Was I pretty like she was? Was I smarter than her? Did I have more options? Was I more adventurous? Less afraid? Was I more independent? It took me a long time to realize that the specter haunting my unconscious was her. She is the MISOR to my MIPE. My MIPE self was created like a relief sculpture. Where my MIPE ends, her MISOR begins. Everything I find strength in is something that I learned by *not* doing what she had done. Every place I feel weak is where I avoided what she lived through. I scanned every strength and foible for any comportment even a little bit close to her in personality or appearance.

My personal mirror is a negative one. But it doesn't have to be. A mirror in this step can also be someone positive, like a mentor or teacher. For Cinderella, it is her Fairy Godmother. Cinderella's complete lack of power and resources are mirrored by the Fairy Godmother's otherworldly all-encompassing magic. For *Frozen's* Elsa, her sister-self, Anna, is the opposite of her in some ways. But as the story unfolds, we learn that Anna is more complement than opposing force. Where Elsa is anxious, Anna is carefree. Where Elsa is cold and afraid, Anna is warm and welcoming. Where Anna longs for interaction, Elsa keeps to herself. When they work together, they save each other. When they ignore each other, or try to isolate, all is lost. As you examine this step, ask yourself about the complements to your own personality. Do you long for something that you believe someone else has easily? What are the complements and/or opposites that show up for you? If you stand before your own magic mirror, what do you long to see? How do you design a complementary reflection rather than a competitive one?

I have a client named Ruby who is a twin. Sometimes in utero, twins develop something called "twin syndrome," where one twin gets the resources and the other twin struggles. Ruby was the healthy twin. Her sister, Gemma, was the one who struggled when they were infants. Twins are already smaller at birth than single babies. Ruby weighed just over five pounds; Gemma weighed just under four pounds. As a result, Gemma was in the hospital for the first few weeks of her life, while Ruby got to go home. This obviously caused a strain on their parents and their older brothers. When they were infants, Ruby was always seeking her sister's presence and was a noisy, scared baby. When Gemma finally came home, she was much smaller than her sister, and the parents feared putting them in the same crib. Both cried constantly the first year of their lives. As they got older, Gemma developed at a slower rate than her sister. She was shorter and more frail. She had terrible anxiety. Ruby became more confident and outgoing. Gemma had developed her own mental health challenges. Most were related to her early medical trauma. She struggled to soothe her own anxiety. In childhood, she developed behavioral addictions like trichotillomania, pulling her eyebrows out, and in high school, she struggled with bulimia. Because they were the same age and were in all their classes together, Ruby and Gemma were inseparable most of their lives. Ruby felt that it was her responsibility to take care of her sister. When they got to the end of middle school, Ruby's protection of Gemma intensified. This was an adaptive skill for an anxious teenager whose own sense of safety depended on seeing her twin safe and healthy. In young adulthood, this complex of feeling became more challenging for 23-year-old Ruby, who felt constant anxiety around her relationship to Gemma and about her sister's well-being.

In her early 20s and at college, Ruby began to resent her sister. She moved out on her own and had her own apartment. Gemma left college and moved home with their parents. Ruby was constantly trying to encourage Gemma to move out and have her own place, but Gemma felt comfortable at home with Mom and Dad. After graduation, Ruby got her first job in the entertainment business and was enjoying the fast pace of the work. Gemma was working at a local coffee shop and doing some singer-songwriter gigs at open mic nights around Los Angeles. Ruby was resentful and struggling to contain it, even though Gemma wasn't asking for any help or attention. Ruby's mirror was shifting, and she didn't know what to do about it.

At 25, Gemma and Ruby were in a terrible car accident, and Gemma was killed. Ruby had been the passenger. Obviously losing a sibling in young adulthood is traumatic. But Ruby's grief was more complex. Her sister had truly been the container for all Ruby's unconscious mirror needs. Before the accident, Ruby never let herself feel sad; she was supposed to always be there for Gemma. Ruby couldn't ever be sick or miss a day of work or school; she was the healthy one. Ruby wasn't allowed to feel sorry for herself or be sad about anything. It was Gemma who had health problems from lungs and kidneys that hadn't developed robustly. Ruby also felt terrible survivor's guilt for having felt any negative feelings toward or about her sister's status in her career or life.

It took a long time for Ruby to allow the idea that her anxiety wasn't only the grief of losing her sister and the trauma of her car accident. She had lost the mirror that had given her life meaning. What was she supposed to do if the measuring stick she had used for the last 28 years wasn't there? The mirror wasn't just broken— it was gone. She kept going to it, as though the frame of the looking glass were standing there without a mirror in it. Ruby regularly stood before the empty frame looking for her sister-self. And then after three years of working through grief, out it came: "I shouldn't be happy. I can't be happy." I listened as it all came pouring out. She felt responsible for the accident. Why hadn't she been the one driving? She almost always drove. But she was tired, and they had been out Christmas shopping. Gemma offered to drive, and on the rare occasion that Ruby didn't take the lead, Gemma was killed. The driver that hit them had been intoxicated on multiple substances. Had Ruby been driving, she would have likely been killed. But that didn't matter. Ruby could only see that she had failed her twin. And now not only did she feel grief, guilt, and shame, she also didn't have a place to rebuild. She shouldn't rebuild. If there was no Gemma, then there was no Ruby. How could she stand before a mirror and see nothing? The reflection was empty. It was disorienting and anxiety producing. Ruby had always managed her life by comparing herself to Gemma. It didn't matter if Gemma did better or worse. It didn't matter that Gemma had not put expectations on Ruby in adulthood. The structure of meaning in Ruby's life had come from building around Gemma. Without it, the scaffolding was in constant threat of failing completely. Ruby had to find a new mirror.

Ruby did eventually create a new mirror for herself. It was a very challenging process. She had to first allow a new image of herself to exist. To do so, she had to painstakingly examine and sift through all the broken and scattered pieces that she had never let herself consider because they "belonged" to Gemma. The mirror is the place we go to look for the discarded pieces of ourselves. Some people call this "the shadow." For women on the journey toward sovereignty, the mirror is related to, but much more than, the unconscious place we send our rejected pieces. For women, the mirror can become both positive and negative embodiment. We build our lives based on the mirror. We long for the welcoming that the mirror is meant to offer. We yearn for our hearts to be quelled with the satisfaction of embracing the sister-self. Where have you invited or created mirrors for yourself? Do you compare yourself to mothers, sisters, or friends? What would a mirror of your own unique sister-self look like?

Mirrors in Scripture

Biblical scholars generally agree that the first chapter in the book of Genesis was written by a different author and at a different time than the second chapter, which was likely written hundreds of years later. The first and the second chapters both tell versions of the creation story, but in the first chapter, the author says that God created people, "male and female we created them." The second chapter is the one that goes into detail about Adam being created first and naming all the animals. It's also in the second chapter when we get the story of Adam and Eve.[3] The Jewish scholars who wrote later interpretations of the Torah compiled a detailed examination of the rules, laws, and mythology that informs Judaism's history, and its interpretation over the last several centuries. This collection is called the Gemara. These secondary sources of Judaism's mystics and scholars wrote that the first chapter describes a world that includes Adam but not Eve. But Adam wasn't alone; he had a first wife whose name was Lilith.

According to the Talmud, Lilith was created from the earth of Eden, the same as Adam. She was created in the same moment. She was given the same divine *ruach*, or breath. Despite their having been created equally, when Adam wanted to have sex, he wanted to dominate Lilith. She wanted some say in their intimate life. He wanted her to submit to him, literally to lay beneath him. She wanted to be on top and control the act herself. Rather than be submissive to Adam, Lilith opted to leave paradise. She wouldn't be less than him. Paradise isn't heaven if you're less than your partner.

The second chapter of Genesis goes into the familiar story most of us know. Eve was created from Adam's rib so that she would always be part of him. This came about because Adam complained to God about how lonely he was. God's point of view was that it "wasn't good for the man to be alone." So God created a "companion and helpmeet" for him. That way, she would always be connected to Adam. God took a part of him that was simultaneously close to his heart, connected to his breath, a part that would move and support the rest of his body, the rib. In other words, she was designed for submission.

Eve is not a mirror to Adam but rather a mirror to Lilith. Eve is the complement to the characteristics described about Adam's original spouse. Where Lilith is bold, Eve is submissive. Where Lilith affirms her own will, Eve's origins presume her submission to Adam. Where Lilith would rather live independently than submit,

Eve is dependent on Adam and on God. As a result of Lilith's desire to own herself, she is portrayed as a demon in the rest of the midrash. Over millennia, her reputation shifted from an independent woman to that of a child-eating demoness. Sounds like the kind of story that narcissistic exes spread about their former partners.

I Feel Pretty

One of my favorite examples of the Mirror Encounter is in the 2018 film *I Feel Pretty* starring Amy Schumer. In this film, the lead character, Renée, played by Schumer, is an insecure but aspiring beauty writer who manages part of a website for a high-fashion cosmetics company called Lily LeClaire. Renée longs to live in the rarefied world of the beautiful women she writes about. Renée is in a high-energy spin class when she has an accident and suffers a minor head injury. One of the beautiful women who works there escorts her to the locker room to help her. When Renée sees her own reflection in the mirror, her vision of her external self is completely transformed. She sees herself as her idealized version, the sister-self she has always wanted to present to the world.

It is the mirror that makes the difference. If we examine the mirror with the previous quadrant's step of Blind, there is a connection. Where Renée is blind to her actual appearance, she is enchanted with the woman she sees in the mirror. Spoiler alert: Ultimately Renée gets everything she ever wanted—the job, the prestige, the man—only to find out that she was never any different on the outside. In the end, her journey to sovereignty ends with her reuniting and making peace between the divided pieces of herself— the person she idealized in the mirror and the real person she had always been.

The Magic Mirror in the Forest

In my practice, when my clients get to a place in therapy where they are actively reflecting on their journey but haven't yet figured out the next phase, I engage them in this visualization exercise. I have found that it helps clients to see themselves with a little bit of distance. The exercise also helps clients to consider their journeys as something archetypal rather than idiosyncratic. This distinction about the archetypal versus individual experience is important. The danger of an overly individual point of view tends to advance the idea that all the aspects of one's life are within the control of that person. By contrast, an overly archetypal view risks removing individual responsibility in favor of cultural or social forces. This can lead to either an overly pessimistic or idealistic point of view. The truth requires a weaving of both the individual and archetypal. When we place our individual experience within the archetypal frame, we can illuminate the ways that our own personal stories align or don't with the archetypal ones. For most people, this is done via religion, but it is not the only nor the most powerful of these models. For women in particular, we have been subjected to archetypal stories where we are not central to the story itself. In every major world religion, men hold the center position in the story. Their journey, their sacrifices, their tribulations are told through the archetypal lens. And in culture, men easily see themselves in those archetypal roles. But women often struggle to do the same. Taking small steps on the archetypal journey can help recenter women's experience as central to the telling of stories.

Imagine you have traversed a perilous forbidden forest. You fought your way through the enchanted forest. You learned how to make traps for monsters so you could escape. You learned how to defeat predators who wanted to devour you. You learned how to navigate the narrow paths to arrive at beautiful vistas. You know where the trolls live. You've avoided the dragon's lair. You learned which plants and fungi were edible versus poisonous. You've learned how to cut a path and fashion weapons. You have learned how to traverse streams and rivers. You've climbed trees and befriended animals. Your journey through the forest has been perilous; in it you have done very difficult things. But you have learned how to survive, maybe even built a life of meaning. You have gained knowledge of the terrain. And now you're leaving the forest. You have finally succeeded in the original goal. You've survived. And now you stand with a wall of high trees at your back—looking out at a clearing—a feat that may have taken years to achieve.

As you stand there, admiring the beauty of the clearing and its green grass, you notice that you cannot step forward. Some invisible force keeps you from moving ahead. You take a moment to look around and get a lay of this new terrain. Is there anything in the distance? What do you see? What time of year is it? Are there flowers? Animals? A castle? When you pull your attention back to the clearing, you notice something glinting in the sunlight just a few steps off to your right. It is parallel to where you stand, and you easily walk along the line of trees toward it. It is a beautiful gilded mirror. As you look at its frame, you begin to notice something incredible. Built into the ornate, twisting metal are scenes and symbols from your life! This is your very own magic mirror. The important battles and discoveries of your time in the forest are all laid out in the mirror's décor. It's quite a sight to behold, encrusted with jewels and hand-painted scenes, it's a magnificent creative accomplishment.

As you pull your attention away from the spectacular frame, you catch a glimpse of yourself in the reflection. You are not the same person who started the journey. Who looks back at you from the glass? Do you recognize her? Does she appear battle worn from her time in the Enchanted Forest? Standing there, you begin to align the scars and exhaustion with the story emblazoned in the frame of the mirror. The battles, achievements, and jewels look beautiful, but the reality of lived experience looks a bit different. You can stay in this place as long as you need to, looking at your reflection, looking at the story. You also may notice that by looking in the mirror, you can see the Enchanted Forest behind you. It gives meaning and depth to the stories. Stay as long as you need.

When you are ready to move forward, you stand up and look around. You realize that the mirror is a gateway. It is the way to move beyond the Enchanted Forest. But there are no hinges—there is nothing that moves. As you consider whether or not you want to sit at the edge or move ahead to the next chapter, you realize that the only way into the clearing is to break the mirror. Gathering your strength, and with any tool you choose—a magic wand, a brick, your feet—you break the mirror. As soon as you do, the force field is gone. You are free to move forward. But there is no more mirror. There is no beautiful story to look at. There is no reflection to tell you you're not ready or not good enough. There's just you. As you get ready to set foot into the clearing, you notice the broken pieces of the gilded frame. You can take whichever pieces you like, but you can't take them all. You only can take what fits in your pockets. Be careful, for some of these have sharp edges. They will always need to be handled with care.

The Tools of the Mirror Encounter

Looking in the mirror is more than just seeing a reflection. Part of this step of the journey along the Queen's Path is to look beyond the reflection and see how you have developed in relationship to either an unattainable ideal or a rejected person or aspect of self. Ultimately the definition of the "other" in the mirror will most likely be a sister-self defined by whether or not you align more with the MISOR or MIPE archetype. It will also depend on how you see yourself with regards to other people. What do you allow yourself? Are you hypercritical of yourself or others? How do you think women are supposed to "be" in the world? All these will impact how you move forward with your reflection in the Mirror Encounter.

The mirror as a tool opens a door. Think about all the ways that we can use a mirror. You can use it in the ways that we use mirrors on a car—to look behind us or beside us. If we use a mirror this way, looking behind us, we see the past as a flattened road. Perhaps we look back at the path we have traveled to arrive at this point. Maybe we look at the mirror to check and see what has followed us. What specters lurk there in the history of our reflection? If we check mirrors to the side of us, who is next to us? Who accompanies us on the journey? Who might be competing with us? Who are we trying to outrun? If the mirror is directly in front of us, is it impeding our path? Are we blocked by our expectations of ourselves or others? Like the mirror in the forest, are we standing before it before moving on to the next phase?

The MISOR's Mirror

Who does the MISOR see in the mirror? Normally she will see the version of herself that everyone else wants her to be. She may try to live up to MISOR ideals. If she is succeeding, she'll see a projection of cultural ideals. However, she only needs to fall short by a tiny bit, and soon the reflection will look like all her worst shadow attributes. The MIPE sister-self will come alive before her very eyes. A MISOR who denies her sexuality will have unresolved frustrations; she might even harbor a secret sex life that no one ever learns about. A MISOR who feels pressured to be beautiful and thin may binge and purge when she's alone. Looking for the sister-self is almost always painful, for the MISOR has banished the side of herself that longs for power, that wants to make decisions.

The MIPE's Mirror

The MIPE looks in the mirror and sees all the ways she can't compete. She longs to be pretty, shiny, desired. She longs to belong. Her sister-self will look like all the ways that she believes the beautiful girls live. She'll long to be prettier, thinner, better. She'll long to be popular, or have better clothes, or a fashionable job. She may succeed at these, but even if she does, she will always feel like an imposter. The MIPE's mirror is the one who is unfulfilled, and she blames it on her status as an outcast. If only she were thin enough, pretty enough, charming enough . . . you get the idea . . . the MIPE's sister-self is the girl she doesn't trust and secretly longs to be.

Exercise

Mirrors can be difficult for people, especially women. We long to be accepted by others, often as a means to accepting ourselves. But the mirror moment is about looking for the mirror and finding meaning in it. Perhaps we find the meaning in what we compare ourselves to, as I did with my mother. Or perhaps the mirror helps us discover the deeper self we long for, like Renée in *I Feel Pretty*. If you can, sit in front of a mirror for about 10 minutes. As you do, notice how you feel. What do you notice? Are you uncomfortable? Does it hurt to look? What are you afraid of seeing? These aspects say a lot about the mirror you long for. That reflection has all the aspects you wish for. Can you do the work of finding them? Make a list of them, and then as slowly as is necessary write about each one and what it means to you.

CHAPTER 10

COMMIT

The moment on the Queen's Path when the woman "commits" is a dangerous one. It symbolizes the acknowledgment of the curse and its resulting mark. A curse is more than a wound. The curse is something that sticks around, that acts as an organizing principle in our lives. Whatever happens to us, the curse lives on, inhabiting the life of the woman, directing her fate from the depths of the psyche. The curse will become a sort of unconscious North Star, reorienting and reorganizing her behavior, renewing the commitment to her curse. She may think she's pushing away from the curse, but in truth, it's still organizing her behavior, even if she's opposing it. If her parents tell her she's lazy and she spends her life proving she's not by overworking, or if she gives in out of depression by being a couch potato, the curse is still organizing her life. If an early caregiver or first love tells her that she'd be beautiful if she were thinner, whether she becomes a marathon runner or morbidly obese, the curse is still organizing her life. This commitment to her curse and mark is the thing that will keep her divided. Importantly, this isn't her last opportunity to lift the curse. In stories, this symbolic commitment will usually happen early in the story, and maybe only once. A real-life woman will revisit the commit moment over and over again. When someone is stuck in this circuit, she will often make every effort to *submit* her way out of pain, conflict, or sadness. The way to know if this is happening to you is a simple test: Are you conflating submitting with committing?

Committing to Disembodiment

As I've mentioned, my parents were both beautiful people. My maternal grandmother, Norma, was so pretty that she was asked more than once to come out to Hollywood to be a "movie star" in the 1930s. My paternal grandmother, Edna, was pretty and sophisticated. She had gone to college, which was quite unusual in the 1930s. She had lived in New York and spent the first two years of her marriage to my grandfather living in a villa in Italy. The members of my family cared about appearances. When I was a tween and started to struggle with what it meant to have a woman's body, everyone took turns commenting on how that process was unfolding. Comments came in about my size, my figure, my frizzy hair, my skin, but no one was more critical than my father. He critiqued every blemish, every stray hair, every inch of fat. I didn't know what to do. Sometimes I would exercise; other times starve. Starting at age 12, I tried to figure it out on my own. It didn't matter how hard I tried, my efforts were almost always met with shame about my expanding hips and thighs and the breasts that seemed determined to catch up with the rest of me. The only words my father could find were, "You're getting fat."

One day I asked my father, "Why do you criticize me all the time? Why is it so important to you that I'm skinny?" We were in the car, driving across a long bridge on the outskirts of New Orleans. I'll never forget his response or looking past him at the water, not knowing what to do. His response to my question was, "You have to be skinny . . . so you can be beautiful . . . so I can love you." Those words have been tattooed on my little 12-year-old heart since that moment. I can still hear them now, his voice searching a little in the response, trying to say something that didn't sound "mean" but that he believed would motivate me.

And did it ever.

That was the first day that anorexia got hold of me. Fat was one of my first scars, and that moment switched my brain into commitment to it. At first, not eating was a challenge. But it soon became a point of pride. By the time I was 15, I had changed the patterns in my brain that created rewards. Eating made me sick. I desperately wanted to be a bulimic instead of an anorexic, but no matter how hard I tried, I couldn't make myself throw up. There were many moments in the high school bathroom crying in the stall as a result.

Every time I would think about getting better, something would happen—a fight with my mom or an instance of being ignored by my father—and I would be right back, recommitting, submitting to the curse, "You're fat, Stacey." One bad feeling and I would find a new way to play with hunger, like drinking water with vinegar or wearing a waist-training corset. I'd submit to anorexia, to the role of pretty, thin, and fragile, trying desperately to make myself small enough to fit in. By the end of high school, this pattern was deeply entrenched. I was good at it.

At 19, I had taken up modeling and was enjoying some minor success. I had auditioned for a local benefit runway show being sponsored by *Vogue* magazine; I hadn't gotten it, and I presumed it was because I wasn't thin enough. A few weeks later, my agent called me and asked me to fill in at the last minute because the girl who had gotten the job had called in sick. I knew the model I was replacing; she was a little taller than I was and, in my mind, much thinner. The show was the next day. The other model had already done the fitting for the clothes. I was sure I wouldn't be able to wear them; she was so much smaller than I was. My agent told me that they would rip the seams, if necessary. They were that desperate.

The next morning when I arrived, they put me in makeup first. Nervous, I kept quiet. The director of the show was a handsome man with beautiful blond hair. He told me he was grateful I was able to step in and led me from the makeup area to my makeshift fitting room, basically a set of curtains. Each outfit had a Polaroid photo of the girl I'd replaced wearing the fully styled outfit, including accessories. It was a summer show, with open-toed shoes, silk scarves, hats, and sunglasses. The first look was beautiful. I will never forget it: a pair of silver silk pants and a white, wide-knit sleeveless sweater with a long gold chain, sunglasses, and beautiful clear and gold sandals. I checked the size of the silver pants: size 4. I thought to myself, "They're definitely going to have to rip these seams." I put my left leg in first, then my right, I pulled them up around my waist and buttoned them, then reached for the top. As I did, the pants fell to my feet in a shimmery pool. I pulled them up, assuming they had come unbuttoned. But they fell immediately to the ground, still fastened. I started to hyperventilate out of sheer panic. The stylist came in and saw me. She grabbed the knit top and a handful of straight pins. Soon she was pulling the fabric of the silver pants tightly from behind, then pinning them to me while tears streamed down my face. I was terribly confused. The world didn't make sense. She put the sweater over my head, smoothed my hair and placed my feet in the sandals. The director placed sunglasses over my eyes while tears ran down my face. The director was panicked by my behavior. He kept saying, "Just walk" over and over, practically yelling in my ear. He put me in the lineup and pushed me onto the runway with another harsh, "Just walk!" When I had made my pass with the first look, the stylist and the director grabbed me and dressed me in the next look and then the next. I don't remember anything except my panic, and the stylist pinning the clothes on, occasionally hitting skin. I could register that it hurt but couldn't feel the pain. There were bright lights focused on the runway, so it wasn't easy for me to see the audience. "Just walk!" was burned into my consciousness. The directive focused me, and I compartmentalized as best I could, another skill that would follow me for a long time.

When the show was over, I was exhausted and confused. Across the dressing room, two other models were chatting. It took me a minute to understand what they were talking about. A dark-haired beauty with a 1930s-style bob was explaining something to a redhead with luxurious waves that fell below her shoulders. She explained that she didn't know how long she could keep working, but here she was in her sixth month, and no one could tell yet. I didn't get it at first and then it hit me. She was pregnant and proud of the fact that she'd successfully hidden her pregnancy for as long as she had. Between my own inability to judge how thin I'd become and hearing the other models discuss their own body issues, I was sick.

This event showed me that I couldn't trust what I saw in the mirror. The fear of my distorted vision wasn't enough to cure me of my anorexia—that would take another 10 years of therapy. But it was the first time I saw my commitment to the scar and the mark.

Even decades before unveiling the framework of the Queen's Path, I understood how I'd doubled down on my scar over and over again. Whenever I felt powerless, longing, or just hungry, I would find new methods, support for, or motivations that took me to the tool that had always worked: starvation. This particular tool of the Divide takes a woman's ability to commit and to surrender and perverts it. She becomes smaller, fitting the expectations, and still somehow has the sense that she has absolute control. She has absolute power over her hunger and her ability to sate it.

No one had been able to help me make sense of my body after all the myriad traumas that played out on my physical being. Years into treating my anorexia with therapy, I suffered an ovarian rupture and nearly died. The hospital was a brutal reminder that committing to my physical body was fraught with danger. The emergency room experience ran the gamut from physical pain that left me unconscious to assault by one of the surgical residents. Then there was the reality of having nearly bled to death. I had come very close to death. My usual go-to of psychotherapy didn't help. My relationship, while loving and supportive, couldn't touch the experience of feeling like I had a new door to the underworld that no one else could see. I felt like I was still cut open, bits of me escaping, evaporating like ether into the atmosphere. My body felt separate from those events, as though it was lying to me and everyone else about what had happened. I felt like I was getting smaller, but my body decided to balance that out by getting bigger.

My body rebelled. I gained 70 pounds within four months post-surgery. No one could explain what was causing my body to pack on the pounds. Doctors tested me for every form of cancer possible: adrenal, thyroid, ovarian, pituitary. When no tumors appeared on scans and images, they blamed me. I heard the most insensitive comments. "You must be eating candy when no one's looking. You must be lying. No one gains this much weight this fast without a clear cause." I was eating a little, to get my strength back. I had, after all, lost four pints of blood without receiving any donor blood in surgery. I wasn't starving, but I also wasn't binging on pizza and chocolate. Here I was again, more trauma and no one reflecting my experience back to me. The people I relied on to help me were instead doubting and invisibilizing what I was living. With an additional 70 pounds on my once-anorexic and more recently athletic frame, my body became unrecognizable to me. And in turn, I became unrecognizable to myself. My face was full and round. My lips were smaller. My breasts seemed enormous. I always considered my body a strange shape: straight hips, curvy breasts, my waist the same circumference as my hips. Suddenly I was all round face, big boobs, and tummy. So much tummy.

These days, we know now that weight both from a psychological and physiological perspective is often a protective measure. And the weight around the belly is often a direct result of stress and cortisol coursing through the body.[1] But back in the late 1990s, this was all a mystery. My doctors blamed me for my body's behavior. I had always had issues with my physical embodiment—body dysmorphia and anorexia had not budged easily; they required daily attention. The experience of the traumas that had happened in the hospital and the added insult of gaining a mysterious 70 pounds expanded my own Divide.

Because there was no scar, my body hid the truth from me and the world. Ten years later, I had a new scar from an elective plastic surgery to deal with the weight I had gained because of that first emergency. It completed my body's journey in a way I hadn't expected. I had decided on liposuction and a tummy tuck after years of abusing and trying to "fix" my body. This is a drastic elective surgery. The recovery is intense, with drains implanted to help the body process the fluid building up in the belly. You can't stand upright for 5 to 10 days. Once I could see myself in the mirror standing upright, I stared at the new scar. Sometimes I would just gaze at it for long periods of time. I smiled at it. I thanked it. I wrote poems about it. It was as though I hadn't had a tummy tuck at all, but a surgery to cut out the remnants of that experience and leave a scar that finally told the truth about my life. It finally felt like my body was in line with my history. You could say my scar finally matched my mark.

My journey of committing to my curses and marks has been, like most women's, challenging and filled with successes and failures. As a teenager, I committed to the curse of "fat." Though in hindsight I can objectively look at photographs and know that I was far from being overweight then, my curse and mark had stigmatized me enough that I found flaws in any errant centimeter of flesh. By engaging in a long-lived love affair with anorexia, I told myself both unconsciously and consciously that I was taking control of my life. What is food if not the way of maintaining your living, breathing body? I committed to a relationship with my body that I believed would give me control. I hoped that this commitment to my appearance would once and for all settle any need to prove that I was good enough. I would be pretty enough. I could tame the wild thing in me that no one seemed to like and that everyone seemed to punish me for. Except that's not how it worked. Committing to being thin did nothing more than bring predators to my door. I made a brittle mansion for my divided self to live in. And what's more I was a 24/7 servant to its every critique, fleeting thought, or passing fancy. And this mansion was a shiny beacon to men who could detect the fragility in my rigidity.

At first, control was scary and challenging. Would I give into temptation? Could I keep myself from eating something I longed for? Sometimes it was difficult to keep hunger away, but soon it started to feel good. When I became a therapist, I learned that the expression of pleasure receptors in the brain switches over time when someone engages in anorexic behavior. In a healthy person, eating food releases dopamine in the brain, rewarding them for nourishing themselves. In anorexia, this shifts. The brain starts to use dopamine as a reward for exercising control and denying the delicious (or necessary) food. A normal person gets dopamine when they eat, and an anorexic gets dopamine when they don't.[2]

The scars we are denied, given, or earn are a form of currency. They give us proof of our curses. They act as evidence of the journey. No one tells you something "didn't happen" when you have a scar to mark the experience. Along the Queen's Path, the curse from the first quadrant almost always is accompanied by a scar of some kind. Like mine, they don't always line up in the timeline of events. But scars and life events have a way of intertwining. Sometimes what we receive isn't exactly a scar. It starts as a mark, a psychic brand that goes along with some expectation or pronouncement.

In my clients, I have heard of many heart-wrenching marks given mostly by parents and caregivers. Sometimes by spouses and lovers. In childhood, sometimes these come from teachers and other children. Professionally they often come like knives in the back from mentors, bosses, and peers.

Most women will have familiar ones. They've been used against us to keep us checking ourselves: fat, skinny, ugly, tall, short, clumsy, plain, dumb . . . those are the most blatant, the simplest. There are others, often used as a very sharp weapon: stupid, dramatic, lazy, emotional, too much, boring, spoiled, slutty, anxious, needy—these show up a lot. And then there are those that are instant banishment to the MIPE track: witch, whore, smart, magical, cruel, bad, ridiculous, nothing, hateful, brilliant, ambitious, gifted, haughty, uppity, bitch. The clients who share stories of these marks often tell the story of a deep, severing cut that came with the mark. These deep cuts aren't singular events. They are enacted again and again by parents, caregivers, friends, teachers, lovers, partners, and children. The mark remains because of what it meant in the moment it was given, and how it still remains, tied to that original wound or curse. If we don't find the source, we will organize our entire lives around one or more curses and their requisite scars.

The Reluctant but Committed Star

I have a client named Sarah. I don't think I've ever seen a more beautiful woman in my life. She has deep-blue eyes, dark hair, a beautiful complexion, and a naturally lithe frame. For the longest time, I watched Sarah enter and exit my consulting room with poise, grace, and no sense of vanity whatsoever. I thought that her looks gave her confidence. She had been a dancer and was very accomplished in this domain. When she walked into a room, people noticed her. She had come to Los Angeles to be an actor, choosing to forgo dance because longevity as a dancer is just one injury away from an already short career.

We were discussing a project that she was being considered for, a television series that would have paid her well for at least a year.

There was a series order already, which was unusual at the time—having not "proofed" a pilot for advertisers. The competition was between her and another actress. She wasn't sure of who the other person was, but she had some ideas. Sarah spent an entire session comparing herself to an imaginary person whom she believed an equally anonymous person in a position of power might be comparing her to. It made my head hurt trying to follow her. She went through everything, talent, training, and then came the remarks about her looks and grace. Sarah started talking about how her eyes were too close together, her hairline was all wrong, and she was too tall. I couldn't get a word in edgewise to counter her self-critical list of flaws. In that one session, she had a laundry list of shortcomings so long that I couldn't keep track; further, there wasn't an objective reality on that list that I would have considered in a thousand years.

I asked Sarah where these thoughts came from. Whose voice was in her head contradicting what anyone making an objective observation would see? All I saw was a beautiful, nearly flawless woman standing before me. Sarah stared past me from the sofa. I was taken for a minute with her quiet. I asked what was happening and where her mind had gone when she heard my question. She responded that she had never considered the voice in her head was not her own. But now that we were talking about it, the tone of the voice sounded eerily like that of her mother, though other folks had contributed—her older brother, sometimes her father.

These formative voices told Sarah that she was plain. They added to this diminishing comment that she was also clumsy and mannish in her gait and mannerisms. Her mother was constantly telling her how to walk with her knees slightly bent and her butt tucked ever so slightly under. Her mother told her how to wash her face, fix her clothes, straighten her hair, do sit-ups, and moisturize, moisturize, moisturize! What I first believed looking at Sarah was that her poise, skin, figure, and grace represented a natural state for her. But they weren't. They were a performance that reinforced the voice of an internal commentator, the critic who lived to win Sarah's mother's approval. And if she couldn't receive her approval, at the very least Sarah didn't want to receive her mother's ire.

The initiating moment that created Sarah's commit moment had already happened long ago in the past. What I was seeing was a remnant of that moment. When Sarah's mother expected her daughter to become a perfect, beautiful MISOR, Sarah committed to "plain" by accepting her mom's critique and acting on it. She committed to doing whatever she could to banish "plain" to feel that she had some control over her life. She committed to being a beautiful, lithe, and graceful version of herself—the one her mother wanted her to live out. Her mother's judgment created the curse of plain and the mark of ungraceful. Sarah did everything she could to not be what her mother accused her of. Whether she had gone the way of the MISOR and tried to fit the ideal or the way of the MIPE and embraced the characteristics of plain, Sarah's life would have still been organized by the curse and the mark.

This part of the journey is called Commit because a woman decides to dedicate herself to something—usually to the curse or the mark. At this stage, it's kind of like she looks around and realizes that the curse is the organizing principle of her existence. If she's a MISOR, she's going to organize her MISOR characteristics around that curse, maybe trying to avoid it. If she's a MIPE, she is more likely to say "hell yeah" to the burden of the curse and the mark, saying to herself, "If I'm going to do the time, I might as well do the crime." For some women, this will be trying to prove that they can live with the curse and mark. Others will try to elevate it, or maybe prove they're bigger than it.

For me, my curse was the surviving child, and my mark was weird or strange. But with that came others. Out of weird came smart. In elementary school and junior high, smart soon got aligned with fat and ugly, though objectively neither of these were true at the time. The multiple times I have wound my way through the Queen's Path at different stages of my life, I have worn weird, strange, smart, fat, and ugly as badges of honor. I have pierced multiple parts of my body, shaved my head, and intentionally worn startling or bizarre clothes, all to commit to a mark I could not describe. I could only feel it and translate those feelings into behavior. During my teenage years and into my 20s, I also committed in the opposite direction driven by the *fear* of fat and ugly to dangerous behaviors like anorexia and compulsive exercise. Committing to the mark will look different for every woman. The behaviors can be subtle or blatant. They can support the dictates of the curse or be dedicated to pushing it away. Either way, the curse is defining what the woman is doing, orienting, and orchestrating all her behavior toward that end. The curse doesn't get "removed" until the third quadrant, if it's going to be dealt with at all. Everything at the commit stage is behavior being defined by the curse that made the Divide possible and rendered the woman into a MISOR or MIPE.

The MISOR's Commit

Most MISORs will commit to being the prettiest, best, most perfect versions of themselves that they can muster. They'll embrace the role of "good girl," "good wife," or "ideal mother." They believe that if they can just be perfect, then everything will be okay. If they value beauty and a beautiful body, then anorexia, bulimia, or another dangerous behavior might take over. If the MISOR's marriage is the core of her identity, then she'll double down on being a dutiful wife, trying hard to live up to the ideal wife by being attentive to her husband or family, even at her own expense. She may come forward with a secret and risk falling into the MIPE track. She may get therapy or recommit to her faith. If she's struggling at her job, she'll try to be of greater service. The hallmark of this part of the path is that the commitment she makes is to the very thing that will keep her divided.

In 1985's *The Color Purple*, Celie commits to her role as a MISOR when she tells her stepson Harpo to beat his wife, Sophia, to get her under control. In *Barbie*, Barbie commits to stereotypical (MISOR) Barbie even as she is confronted by a rift in the space–time continuum described to her by the shamanistic Weird Barbie. Even when Mattel threatens to "put her back in the box," she is compliant up until the very last moment. When the MISOR gets to the Commit step, she knows something is wrong, but she's trying to make it right by being prettier, smaller, and/or more compliant. Of course, all these behaviors are the very thing that sent her to one track or another to start with, but she won't consider another way because the authority outside of her says this is the way to be. At this stage of the Queen's Path, that doesn't work. If she stays "in the box," she'll still confront her own personal state of Abjection down the road.

The MIPE's Commit

At the Commit step on the Queen's Path, a MIPE might quit her job and try to start her own company or go back to school for a new career. She might try to be what her mom has always wanted her to be and take up a new course of study or commit to getting married. A MIPE who's always been on the outside might try to find a way toward what she perceives to be the MISOR path. She might try to fit into traditional beauty expectations. She might lose or gain weight. She might have plastic surgery. A MIPE who commits to her mark might find herself becoming fascinated with astrology or some other spiritual domain that is outside of "traditional" authority. She might begin to experiment with her own creative voice, taking up writing or painting.

The MIPE might suddenly become interested in things that make her more of an outsider or nonconforming. She might shave her head. Or she might take up a martial art. She might move across the country or suddenly decide she's going to medical school. The MIPE who is faced with the Commit step thinks that she can think or perform her way out of the messy second quadrant. She can outsmart it. She can run faster, do more, and more, and more. She doesn't see that the harder she works, the more she's digging down into the Commit step, investing in it. She truly believes that if she just works harder at being smart, or talented, or skilled, then she'll be rewarded for her efforts. Someone will see her. But it's a trap. The MIPE is the same as she ever was, outside, different; she doesn't belong. The harder she tries, the more of an outsider she is. This isn't because her efforts aren't good, or that she isn't smart; it's because of the MIPE track. The MIPE thinks that performing is the key to being on the inside, but it's not. The key to being on the inside is submission, which is something that the MIPE quite frankly sucks at. Further, as the MISOR can tell you, submission has its own problems, like never being seen as smart enough or only having responsibility and never authority.

The MISOR holds the ideals, while the MIPE is the catchall for not meeting them. The MIPE has already been on the outside; as a result, the borderlands are already known to her. In stories, this might show up as the threat or taint of having been an outsider. For real women, they know too much. They've seen what the world does to MIPEs, and they can't unsee it or pretend it's not real. Committing to the mark isn't necessarily bad, but it does always fall short. It is not enough to accept how the world would define you. To successfully navigate the Queen's Path all the way to sovereignty, you must ultimately define yourself. But that's coming in the next few chapters.

Princess Di Becomes a MIPE

When we look back at the life of Princess Diana, we can see her on the Queen's Path circling this area twice. At first, she tries to fit in as a MISOR. She goes to the balls; she wears the gowns. She marries Prince Charles, and within the year, the fertile, dutiful wife gives him a son. A little while later, a second son. Diana has upheld her MISOR role; she has provided the future king of England with an heir and, as the saying goes, a spare. But for all of Diana's efforts, she soon became unhappy. She tried to live up to the MISOR role, but once her husband had left his marriage vows behind, Diana no longer felt the need to live up to the MISOR ideal. She committed to the MIPE role that the royal family cast her in. And she did it remarkably well. Diana went to places that the royal family abhorred, from AIDS wards in Africa to New York appearances with Mother Teresa. Diana flew in the face of the royal family's wishes. In doing so, she raised eyebrows and remarkably earned the title of the People's Princess, an outcast from the royal cloisters, whom the people of the world adored. To read about Diana's life, you quickly learn that this wasn't an intentional jump. She didn't sit down one day and say that she wanted to thumb her nose at her royal in-laws. She did what she felt called to do, and that made all the difference.

Exercise

Write about how you have committed to your scar and/or your mark. What attitudes and behaviors have been organized to make them make sense? How have they shaped your life? Notice the places where these scars have organized things in your world. It might be useful to go back and think more deeply about the scars and marks by reflecting on the previous section, the mirror moment. What have you rejected in the mirror? What have you embraced? Use these as a starting point. It may mean you add to the list of scars and marks from the last section, and that is okay! Don't be afraid of what you find. Down here in the shadowy land of the second quadrant, there are likely dark places and surprises.

CHAPTER 11

THE HUNT

When I was first codifying the discovery of the Queen's Path, I found this part one of the most distressing. In every instance, a woman finds herself either chasing something or being chased. Snow White is chased by the Huntsman through the woods; his goal is to kill her and cut out her heart at the bidding of the Evil Queen. Elle Woods is hunting Warner Huntington III all the way to Harvard Law School. Wonder Woman is hunting Aries, the god of war, as he plots to throw the world into chaos. Julia Roberts, playing characters from Vivian the prostitute in *Pretty Woman*, to Alice Sutton in *Conspiracy Theory*, to *Sleeping with the Enemy*'s tortured wife, Sara, is chased by a man. His goal is to love her, convince her, or control her.

In my own clients, I have seen women chasing goals as simple and mundane as getting a job and rising in complexity to getting pregnant at 40 or creating a multimillion-dollar company. I have supported and counseled women in complex, abusive relationships, and women whose husbands feel that it is their right to control them in everything from a job to the colors of the clothes they wear. Being in the Hunt feels like possession—either you yourself are possessed by an idea or goal or you are being treated like an object to be possessed.

In a story, the Hunt is symbolic on the Queen's Path. It drives part of the plot or acts as an internal motivator for the character, but in real life, the Hunt is a catalyst for change, and there is very real peril at the edges or on the other side. On the Queen's Path map, the

Hunt is the threshold between the second quadrant and the third. As such it has a liminal quality about it. There is something other-worldly here. It is not a place of normal gravity or consequences. Everything in this space feels important, radical, dangerous, heavy, or tinged with magic.

The first iteration of this map had the Hunt not as a pie piece in a quadrant but as a force symbolized by an arrow that connected the second and third quadrants. As I shared the map with friends, clients, and focus groups, the arrow confused people. Was it a step? Did it have a beginning and an end? Does it move around? Because it was so confusing, I opted to make it simpler and place it where it has the most impact. But the Hunt in the life of a real person is not a singular event. It is an organizing principle. If the Curse organizes what motivates a woman in her life, then the Hunt is how she acts it out with other people.

When a woman is at the transformational end of the Hunt, meaning the point where change is eminent, she may feel dysregulated, out of her body, or like she is going crazy. The world feels like it doesn't make any sense. People will tell her she's wrong, out of it, or not okay. If you're in this stage and feel this way, it is an important indicator. Being in the Hunt and feeling disoriented or crazy means that you are nearing the threshold. Figure out what you need to complete the transformation and either commit to it or run from it. As we move into the third quadrant, I'll explain that there are dangerous outcomes, ones that may imperil your safety or even your life, so proceed with caution. Transformation can be as beautiful as the ugly duckling realizing she's a swan, or it can mean transforming into a new state, like banishment or even death.

If she is a MISOR, she may be hunted like a beautiful animal, a trophy for someone to have as a conquest or a spouse. Perhaps she is an abused partner, unable to claw her way free. If she is a MIPE, she may be hunted to subdue or break her—to make an example of her or to force her to submit to authority. Think of Malala Yousafszi on the bus being shot by terrorists, Oprah Winfrey being sued by cattle ranchers in Texas, or Britney Spears being held captive by her family and management team. These are all versions of the Hunt (as is Britney's pursuit of justice for herself as well!). While the Hunt appears on the map at a particular place on the Queen's Path, it is not limited to that space. The Hunt can begin anywhere, but its outcome always culminates as we transition from the second to the third quadrant.

Women are socialized in our culture to believe that being pursued is a good thing. To be sought after is supposed to be a positive experience that makes us feel desired. But the reality is that the pursuit often takes on a hue of domination. To submit to the desire of another can mean we are defined by their vision, longing, or control. And yet we produce and reproduce the stories of women being pursued by men or longing for a "Prince Charming" to show up to give us our Happily Ever After. The problem with Prince Charming is that he too is not a whole human being. He is only partially himself, caught in a world of expectations that diminish him down to a function. Taking on the responsibility for the Happily Ever After will make both partners miserable.

The hunt in this stage of the Queen's Path is taking the woman down into the darkest part of the unconscious. She is leaving the quadrant of the Rendering, where she has been cleaved into parts. Going into the next phase, she has no choice but to drag that rendered self into the quadrant of the Depths. No one can help her here, and she finds herself in a most perilous pursuit. Either she is engaging in a dangerous chase, or she is being pursued as though she were a wild animal or a coveted object.

Psychotherapy Examples

I have a client named Jenny. Jenny is a first-generation American with two siblings; she's the middle child. She has an older brother and a younger sister. Her sister, Faith, was born when Jenny was just five years old. Her mother and father were undocumented and worked constantly to provide for their family. So the kids were often alone by themselves. Her older brother, Jamie, was tasked with watching his two baby sisters, but care of baby Faith most often fell on Jenny, even at the young age of five. As the family grew older, Faith and Jenny were inseparable. Jenny took Faith to school, helped with homework, and cooked meals. She made sure Faith bathed for school, brushed her teeth, and went to bed on time.

But as the trio of kids got older, cracks started to appear in this caregiving structure. Jamie went out and partied with friends in high school, and then college. Their parents split up after years of stress and domestic violence. Their newly single mom had retreated into her friends and work relationships. Their father kept working himself into the ground, even though he was no longer living with his family. Jenny alone was trying to be the glue that gave coherence to family life, especially that of her baby sister, whom she had raised practically alone. Jenny's own life revolved around housework, and her own and her sister's school and sports schedules.

When Faith started to show signs of a serious mental illness, her other family members shrugged it off. Faith was fine; she was just "going through something," maybe teen angst. But Faith's condition worsened, with auditory hallucinations and delusions that went far beyond the usual teen drama. The only person paying close attention was Jenny. By 22, Jenny was making appointments for her 17-year-old sister with psychiatrists, therapists, and sometimes in-patient treatment in hospitals. Jamie had gone to college, graduated, and moved out, and was angry at the world. Their mom was angry and frustrated without a partner. Their dad was working multiple jobs to contribute and to give meaning to his own life. Jenny dreamed of college and independence but didn't think it was possible for her. She had too many responsibilities, especially around Faith and her care.

Jenny was engaged in a pursuit to help her sister. She chased her sister's care like a goal that could be achieved. Faith could be healed, and Jenny could make it happen. Jenny attempted multiple times to go to college, and almost always had to drop out midterm or near the end because her sister would have a crisis that required an in-patient hospital stay. Jenny was trying to simultaneously pursue her dream of higher education *and* take care of her sister like she had always done. Except her sister's care got much more complicated. Faith could only be treated; she would never be cured. And Jenny didn't have the tools or the financial wherewithal to completely take care of Faith. Soon Jenny's mental health started to decline as her sister's illness progressed, and Jenny ran out of internal and external resources. She became intensely depressed. Her romantic relationship with someone her mother liked, but with whom Jenny felt little connection was flailing. Jenny came into therapy confused, trying to figure out what she was doing wrong!

The answer was that there was *nothing* wrong with what she was doing. She was caught in the grip of the Divide. The Hunt had her chasing an unattainable goal. Jenny believed that she could and should take care of her sister while pursuing the goals that were important to her. She was pursued by a romantic relationship that would have placed her on the MISOR track, trying to live up to a Happily Ever After that she had not defined for herself.

How do you know if you're caught in the Hunt? You won't feel like a full person. You'll feel like a function, with the expectations of a machine. It might be that you have a routine that makes everything make sense. Your Hunt could be that you are dedicated to keeping yourself attractive for external attention. Your Hunt could look like pursuing relationship or marriage. It could be being pursued by a man or work. The Hunt can be short-lived or it can last your entire adulthood. But to feel that you have no choice but to soldier on with only the will of achievement, or pursuit, or beauty is a sure indication that you are in the Hunt. An important thing to remember is that this part of the journey can start anywhere in the first or second quadrants, but when it ends, it will end in the third quadrant. Nothing ends in the Hunt, but it can end on just the other side of it.

If you are observing someone in the Hunt, whether yourself, a girlfriend, or a relative, you'll know because the person in the Hunt is not a complex person anymore; she *is* a goal. If you are telling the story of your life, then ask yourself where the Hunt began for you. If a woman's curse is "not enough," her Hunt will focus on being seen or being accepted. If her curse is beauty, she may endure the Hunt of pursuit by others. If her curse is believing she is stupid, then her Hunt could be for education or acceptance. The Hunt is the most confusing step in the Queen's Path. How do I know what is my pursuit versus something outside of me? How do I balance those aspects of my life that have been given to me via culture or family versus the ones that I define for myself? The answer eventually lies in the body in the third quadrant. We must learn to make peace with the body so that it can be a reliable guide. But we don't get to experience that right away. Most of us must go through the steps on the Queen's Path before we can learn *how* to trust the body. That step will come as part of the next and most dangerous third quadrant. However the curses and marks present themselves, they are about to drive the woman on the Queen's Path into the face of her worst fears as she crosses into the third quadrant, the Depths.

Exercise

What have you pursued? Or what or who has pursued you? Has it felt like an obsession? Did it feel good? Did it ever frighten you? I want to ask you to do something that feels like movement around this step. Identify the players in your own personal Hunt. Next, draw an image, write a poem, or dance a dance that expresses what this experience has been like. Here's an example of a poem from my own journal on this topic:

To the Cabin

I don't feel her breath

Though she is shouting at me

So close I can see the pores on her cheeks

I want to stand before her candy house

To see for myself the gumdrop finials

The gingerbread walls

She tells me it's the path to my house

I refuse

I am happy to jump into the oven

She says I'm too old

There's only one option

I can take her place

But I run instead

Pursued by the hunter

He wants me for himself

Next a wolf wearing a suit

He sleeps with his mother at night

Afraid of the witch in the woods

But the branches grab

Vines pull me in

I become a tree

Staring up at the stars

My feet grow into roots

It's the only way off the path

I hear the old woman calling my name

But my leaves and twigs speak with the wind

And send her to find another

The Hunter looks for me, knife drawn

He rests on the trunk, ignorant

The wolf sniffs the roots, leaves his mark

I remember the look, the scent

My voice is a pitch of the wind, running from
one tree to the next

The warning sounds

I am free, but can only move to turn

Lest I become a meal, a piece of meat, or a sacrifice

I'll stay

Rooted and grow

QUADRANT III

The Depths of Danger

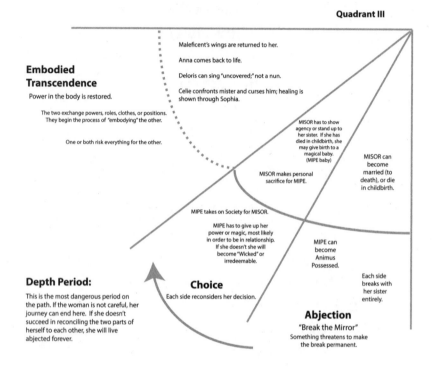

Quadrant III

Embodied Transcendence
Power in the body is restored.

Maleficent's wings are returned to her.

Anna comes back to life.

Deloris can sing "uncovered;" not a nun.

Celie confronts mister and curses him; healing is shown through Sophia.

The two exchange powers, roles, clothes, or positions. They begin the process of "embodying" the other.

One or both risk everything for the other.

MISOR has to show agency or stand up to her sister. If she has died in childbirth, she may give birth to a magical baby. (MIPE baby)

MISOR can become married (to death), or die in childbirth.

MISOR makes personal sacrifice for MIPE.

MIPE takes on Society for MISOR.

MIPE has to give up her power or magic, most likely in order to be in relationship. If she doesn't she will become "Wicked" or irredeemable.

MIPE can become Animus Possessed.

Each side breaks with her sister entirely.

Depth Period:
This is the most dangerous period on the path. If the woman is not careful, her journey can end here. If she doesn't succeed in reconciling the two parts of herself to each other, she will live abjected forever.

Choice
Each side reconsiders her decision.

Abjection
"Break the Mirror"
Something threatens to make the break permanent.

As a reminder, in the third quadrant, we are still in the lower hemisphere. The second and third quadrants are part of the World of Invisible Forces and Mystery. You can consider the lower hemisphere akin to the underworld or the unconscious. Of the parts of this world, we face the most danger in the third quadrant. As we spend time in this space, please consider that it is the darkest place on the Queen's Path. The Hunt drives us here in pain and fear. When we get to the first step in this quadrant, Abjection, it is the darkness of the soul, the depths of pain, the emptying of hope. This place doesn't provide joy or resolution. Abjection can kill a woman. This is the place where the story can end. In any story, whether a real woman's narrative, a novel, or script, motion and action are most important here. There are several risks in this quadrant. Getting lost here can keep a woman trapped forever. She can die in childbirth or become a lost MISOR in a Happily Ever After (HEA). She can die as a result of animus possession. She can be chased to death being pursued, whether she is a MISOR or MIPE. If she survives Abjection, she'll have another opportunity to be destroyed in Choice.

In Choice, the pressure is a little lower, but she's not out of the woods yet. In this step on the path, the concept of Choice asks the woman to sort through the discarded pieces of her being scarred, divided, and rendered. This work can send her back into Abjection or even back to the second quadrant into the Hunt. What we look for in Choice is to sort through the parts of ourselves that we cut off from our identities. We can liken it to a sister-self, the ostracized version of us composed of our disavowed parts. In films and other narratives, this is often portrayed by a sister or sisterlike character or reflection. The protagonist must save her sister-self or liberate her. There is no version of getting through Choice without realigning the discarded pieces. For real women, the choice is often challenging. Though to everyone else it might appear obvious, for the woman in the Depths, there are difficulties. She has just been hunted and abjected; she isn't seeing clearly. That's why she has to look at everything carefully.

If she makes it through Choice, pulling the important pieces back to herself, then she can move to Embodied Transcendence. It is in this step that the protagonist finds her power in her female body. In reuniting her discarded pieces, she is united in her deepest self. The embodiment step is what makes the queenly ascent in the fourth quadrant possible. Embodiment is often denied to women, not out of desire but out of psychological necessity. A body that is constantly treated like an object for others or that is destined for fulfilling the roles of mother, sex object, or quiet servant is not one that understands sovereignty or owning oneself and certainly isn't encouraged in that self-possession. Overcoming the internal version of the external programming of cultural powers that suppress the female body is the goal of Embodied Transcendence. The crown lies on the other side.

CHAPTER 12

ABJECTION

You've probably heard the word *abject* before—like "living in abject poverty." Or perhaps you've heard it used in the phrase *abject horror.* Unless you're a trained psychoanalyst or you're into nerdy feminist film theory, you probably haven't used the word in too many other ways.[1] In this chapter, I borrow from Julia Kristeva, a Bulgarian-French psychoanalyst and philosopher. Her work focuses on what it means to be confronted by the most disturbing aspects of human existence and how those confrontations affect someone's individual experience of themselves. To be faced with Abjection means to confront our most complex and foundational understanding of being alive and embodied and all the natural pollution that comes with that (blood, urine, vomit, etc.) and the alternative, confrontation of the mortal remains, the corpse of someone (or something) who was once alive.

On the Queen's Path, this step is akin to looking down and finally taking note that all the parts that have been ripped from you in the Rendering didn't actually go anywhere. They've been rotting in a scratchy burlap sack that you've been pulling behind you throughout the whole journey. Each time culture, an important person, or even you yourself cleaved something off in the second quadrant, it got dropped in the bag. Body parts, dreams, ambitions, love, anger—whatever was stripped from you is in this fetid sack that you have every right to want to avoid. Looking is too painful and goes against all that we've come to know about ourselves. Looking in the bag makes us feel sick. Feeling sick makes us feel vulnerable. And feeling vulnerable is not something most of us have learned to embrace.

Kristeva's theories have been picked up and developed further by feminist scholars, especially those studying the representation of women in films, novels, and other media. In film theory, most scholars point to abjection as a primary symbol of horror movies. The body, especially the female body, is treated as an object of abjection. Kristeva's theory proposes that the body and its particular connection to what is materially real creates a rift in how people experience themselves and the world. Beliefs about what the female body expels, from menstrual blood to babies, simultaneously defiles and elevates the body. This duality is the nature of abjection. Something that is simultaneously sacred and profane upsets the balance and throws social understanding into confusion. Cultures create rituals and practices to help make sense of the boundaries between life and death, holy and mundane, innocent and corrupt. But it is the mixing of these meanings, and the ease of their conflation, that makes abjection possible according to Kristeva.

Which brings us to this step in the Queen's Path. We have crossed into the third quadrant from the second quadrant. Where the previous quadrant focused on the woman's experience in Cleaved and thus rendered her into either a MISOR or a MIPE, this new quadrant focuses on her experience in the Depths. This area, whether we are discussing the deepest aspect of the unconscious or the darkest places in the shadows of the self, is filled with dangerous ideas, banished traumas, and unrealized dreams and desires. In life, this is the unimaginable place. In stories, this place represents the dark, unexplored realms. A writer or director might represent this as a forest, a haunted castle, or some other traditionally scary environment. The important thing to remember about this part of the journey is that there is real danger that a woman who gets stuck here won't survive this place. A woman who isn't transformed in the third quadrant will be stuck in either a metaphorical or actual death. This is as true for real women as it is for characters in stories.

After the harrowing ordeal of the Hunt, anyone would want to rest. The woman is worn the eff out. Her body, spirit, and psyche have used all their resources. But Abjection doesn't allow for a moment of repose. A woman who has been hunted through the second quadrant into the third will be dragging the hopes and dreams of her divided self with her. She'll struggle to bear the weight of the Divide into the next phase. She is lugging the aforementioned bag of her discarded parts. Even worse, in it, she may be dragging the body of her sister-self with her. It is invisible but still bears the dead weight of a corpse. Where she goes, the bag follows, eventually becoming an impossible psychic burden.

If this language seems heavy-handed, it is meant to be. The term *abjection* refers to things that we feel sickened in the presence of. It points to the aspects of life that we avoid. Corpses, vomit, blood, feces, urine, rot, maggots—all these represent the fundamental idea of abjection. In this experience is the avoidance of, indeed, terror of, an encounter with the most base aspect of being a living, material creature. This flesh will one day be without a soul and will need to be disposed of. The excrements of the body are vile and act as vectors for disease. We cannot imagine the true horror of murder or the infinite toll of war. The collective psyche creates systems and institutions to manage these. We defer these ideas to those systems rather than face them head-on. When horror flashes before us, or hints at the edges, we avoid it. In films, we close our eyes; in the real world we create abstractions. We avoid the reality of these things because they are so real as to be reviled and feared.

This is not precisely because we fear death—we have created cultural symbols and systems to help us manage the experience of those fears. It is because when there is a fundamental encounter with the physical, material reality of death, decay, and destruction, it is too much to bear. The material reality is outside our cultural systems of meaning. The symbolic systems, religious explanations, and cultural artifacts that we have created to manage cannot hold up in the face of the aftermath of war, the disgust of defilement, or even the experience of being in the room with the corpse of a loved one. To be in the place of Abjection means that nothing is true and everything is true simultaneously.

If you've ever confronted the unimaginable pain of losing a child, surviving a natural disaster or war, or the betrayal of incest (to name a few), you have stood in the place of Abjection. To stand in this place is to lose all the meanings that have been given to us. For some of us, this might mean we go a little (or a lot) mad. Some people reject this place, refusing to recognize the terrible defilements. They put their faith in the systems that manage our fears: religion, law, family. They look away from the terrible, trying desperately to make the world fit something that makes sense. The systems of belief make sense. But the systems exist for us; we don't exist for the systems. If we are to gain our freedom, we must question those structures and systems. That doesn't mean that the previous life or even the systems themselves are meaningless, just that their meanings were contrived. Most systems don't run deeply enough to help us in this place.

Abjection demands that we look at the things as they are, not as we would wish them to be. The veil is torn down; the lens is broken. The realest of real stands before us, with us. In acknowledging this revulsion, we must risk breaking the things we believe in or even breaking ourselves and the things we believe define us. Abjection requires that at the very least, we accept that the burlap sack is ours. All that nastiness belongs to us. We may not have created it, but we cannot escape it.

This is how we enter the Depths. Bedraggled. Exhausted. Stripped of Meaning. Confused. Laid bare. But as therapists like to say, "The only way out is through." But it's not so simple. To go through Abjection, we must examine ourselves within the context of our unique lives and ask the very difficult questions. What parts of this are mine? What beliefs were given to me? What do I actually want? What are the worst parts of my history? What are the most base aspects of my personality? How did I participate in creating the worst parts of this experience? How do I fit in the world? Did I create any monsters? Did I facilitate any of this horror? Am I responsible? How does the person I was expected to be match the person I am becoming?

After the Hunt, however, most of us are not in a generous, Zen-like state to ideally answer those questions. Instead, we are depleted, losing our connections to ourselves and the people around us who once meant the most to us. At this point, most of us forget what it was like before the Divide came to get us. We forget what it felt like in the undifferentiated innocence of childhood. Worse, we long for an innocence we struggle to remember. We believe that innocence is a stand-alone state, as opposed to the beginning of a system of self-awareness. There is a sense that if only we could get our innocence back, if only the pain of the separation of the Divide wasn't the thing we feel most, then all would be right with the world. The systems of domination and hegemony tell us that this place, Abjection, is the problem. We are in contact with both the holy and the impure—and that defiles us. As women, we are told that it is our fault—the sin of Eve returned to keep us in our place. But that is a system telling us the limits, not our own lived experience. And the primary function of any system is first and foremost to guarantee its own survival.

In contrast, to be in Abjection can be freeing. Once you see the horror of the world, you have confronted the most profound and simple place of existence. You have confronted the ground of being. If you can learn to tolerate this place, and maybe even treat it with kindness, you can walk through to the next step on the Queen's Path. To avoid or otherwise run away from Abjection is a sure way to be trapped in it. The unconscious will not tolerate being ignored, so if you won't look at it consciously, it will haunt your dreams and motivate your unconscious desires. If you've experienced the Hunt, you have no choice but to traverse the dreaded, swampy, disgusting, and vile step of Abjection. The only way out is through.

How the MISOR Experiences Abjection

The MISOR goes through her life expecting or enjoying the protection of family, culture, or other systems. She has spent her whole life trying to be the "good girl." She has followed the rules and expects to have earned the benefits of having done so. There are several possibilities for the MISOR in Abjection. If she has been hunted by a suitor, or has hunted for a husband, she will be looking for her Happily Ever After (HEA). The HEA is a fantasy, an ideal that is presented to her as the reward for living up to a cultural standard. Achieving the HEA means she will have a permanent protector and partner. She will have children and grandchildren. Her family and the broader culture will treat her like a "lady." Indeed, she will expect to be treated this way.

But as most older or former MISORs will tell you, the HEA is an illusion. Did you ever notice that the HEA is at the end of the fairy tale? You don't hear any more about the protagonist afterward. Have you ever wondered why? It's because once she's married, the story is over. She doesn't have to strive anymore. She is no longer a unique individual but the paramour at best and the possession at worst of her very own pseudo–Prince Charming. She dies to her old self. She is her role and her role alone. This is often quite confusing for her. She did everything right! Wasn't this what was expected of her? To marry and have children? To be a "good girl" and marry a "good man" who will take care of her and their children? Wasn't she supposed to want to be protected and cared for?

Abjection can live in marriage quite easily. I've seen it when a partner can't live up to the ideals they have for themselves. I've seen Abjection arrive when confronted with addiction, financial losses, the death of an important person, or illness. I've treated women (and men) who face Abjection when their idealism must give way to reality. Maybe marriage is more difficult than expected. Or perhaps their sex life isn't fulfilling. Sometimes the members of a couple have never learned to regulate their own emotions, expecting that partnership will provide the calming influence that can center them. When that doesn't materialize, or when a woman is suddenly faced with the loss of an important ideal, where does she go? A MISOR will go to her family or to an established authority like a rabbi, minister, imam, or priest. If marriage fails her, if she finds herself getting divorced or losing an important relationship, she may find herself confronting the reality that shows up with Abjection. She will revile the options before her. This is not what she wanted. Divorce was not in her plan. The risk is that Abjection may break her.

She is also found in the historical but mythologized Roman story of Lucretia, who committed suicide after having been raped by the son of a wicked king. Her story was considered one of womanly virtue: rather than live with the shame of having been raped, she killed herself by violently stabbing herself to death but not before exacting a vow of vengeance from her male relatives. This story is touted as the birth of the Republic of Rome. Vengeance for Lucretia inspired the public to overthrow the tyrannical Estruscan kings.[2]

In movies, she's Elle Woods, who is ready to walk away from it all when she realizes her professor was trying to seduce her, that she wasn't succeeding in a meritocracy after all. She's Miranda Priestly in *The Devil Wears Prada*, who plays the ultimate game of chess and betrays her allies to maintain her position of power as the editor of the famed fictional *Runway Magazine*. When faced with Abjection, the MISOR will reinvest in the authority she relies upon. Often, though, a MISOR who has no power or for whom authority is weak will simply die. In fairy tales, we often are told of a queen who died in childbirth—the ultimate sacrifice of a woman to her role.

The MIPE in Abjection

Animus possession may sound like a horror movie title, but it actually comes from Jungian psychology.[3] This idea is one of the closest I can think of when describing what happens to the MIPE in Abjection. Prior to the sexual revolution of the 1960s, it was a relatively new idea that women and men each had a contrasexual unconscious aspect to their personality. Jung described this as a woman having an interior masculine aspect that he called the *animus*, and a man having an interior feminine aspect that Jung named the *anima*. Both words come from Latin and basically translate to "spirit" and "soul." In brief, the anima for a man and animus for a woman are deep aspects of the unconscious. For a person to become a healthy, whole individual, they must integrate this unconscious aspect into their identity. If they do not, then the banished aspect will run the unconscious like a poltergeist in the psyche. According to Jungian psychology, a woman who is animus-possessed will become hard, ruthless, argumentative, and difficult. A man who is anima-possessed will become wishy-washy, overly emotional, and indecisive.[4]

To me, these ideas are outdated. In psychology, we no longer have sex-essentialist ideas of what it means to be a man or a woman. We don't align the personalities of women as somehow less logical because of the presence of XX chromosomes or because she presents feminine to the world. We expect that people of all genders are equally capable of and in need of love, nurturing, logic, depth of thought, awe, joy, vulnerability, and all the other experiences that make us human. Anima and animus possession don't fit in quite the same way they did in Jung's time of writing. However, for this one particular instance on the Queen's Path, I find some interesting correlations.

The MIPE has also been through the Hunt and landed at the gate to the third quadrant exhausted and spent. Often, the MIPE has not had the benefit of generosity or grace offered to her from the world at large. She has always been an outsider. Meeting Abjection after being chased makes her angry, depressed, hurt, even vengeful. If she was the one doing the hunting, then her Hunt very likely was to survive or at the very least was an effort to prove once and for all that she is valuable. She did everything she could to be successful. She likely used her gifts to show her family, her community, or the important people around her that she was worthy. And yet, like all women, regardless of whether they are MIPE or MISOR, she was still chased to the point of exhaustion. She has been broken by something. She has not been allowed to win on her terms and being a MIPE, she's pissed about it.

Her likely response is to work more, be more, do more. Whatever her magical gifts are—whether it's her intelligence, beauty, sex appeal, magical powers, athleticism—the MIPE upon entering Abjection will confront the horror and the reality by doing more, perhaps even perverting the order of things in her world. In classical mythology, she is Medea killing her children or Arachne, who was transformed into a spider after winning a weaving contest against the goddess Athena. Athena was infuriated that she could find no fault with the mortal's weaving and cursed her as a result. Or she is Medusa, cursed by Athena (again) to become a monster after being raped in Athena's temple, the original victim-blaming story. In the movie *Promising Young Woman*, she's Cassandra visiting the bachelor party of the men who drove her friend to suicide, planning to torture the worst offender, making him wear the initials of his victim carved into his body. In *The Woman King,* Nanisca is confronted by the return of the man who violently raped and impregnated her and has to confront her own internal monster as well as the child she gave away so that she could remain in service to the king.

The MIPE in Abjection can double or triple down on her role. If she's a warrior, she'll get tougher. If she's an intellectual, she'll get more logical. If she's a miner, she'll dig deeper. If she's a pilot, she'll fly higher. If she's a murdering sociopath, she'll be more murderous and sociopathic. You get the idea. One of the core problems for the MIPE in Abjection is that what she does can be so risky that it becomes deadly. The harder you push, the less you notice the risks. Associating abjection with Jungian animus possession is apt here. She is possessed as though by an outside force. But it's really the sack of discarded parts in the unconscious underworld that is motivating her behavior.

Different Paths: Same Fate

I'm not saying every MISOR or MIPE will do something horrible, but Abjection will be the worst experience of a woman's travel along the Queen's Path. The MISOR dies metaphorically in the HEA. The MIPE is hunted for her power. Either way, the MISOR or MIPE is haunted by the aspects of herself that she has been forced to deny. And if she can't see herself differently, she'll become a story on the evening news, like Andrea Yates, the Texas mom who killed her five children in a bathtub,[5] or Idaho mom Lori Vallow, who killed her two children to remove them as obstacles in the way of a desired romance.[6]

Addiction, obsession, depression . . . these are all risks to both the MISOR and the MIPE in Abjection. We can never know what is happening in someone else's heart and mind. But we can look at the archetypal patterns before us and know that there is a way through. Also, as I mentioned before, this step along the path is not a one-and-done kind of step—it can be the miserable gift that keeps on giving. If you feel stuck in Abjection, hating everything, wanting things to change and generally banging your head against the wall, then take a moment to assess. Sit in your room for an hour, or if you can, go away for a weekend and spend some time figuring out whether or not you're doubling down on your role, avoiding the burlap sack of discarded parts. If you can stomach it, look inside the bag. What is the first part that you see?

For me it was the sweet, mothering part of me. I spent decades of my life trying to climb ladders, banishing this aspect of myself. First, I was scaling the rungs of entertainment. I was good at running productions and enjoyed the attention to detail and the machinery of a movie set. But when Abjection came for me, I struggled to traverse the interior gulf. I abdicated and ran to something else, grad school. I had a fellowship, and the director of the research arm that funded my tuition and gave me a stipend that placed me doing research on of, all things, the *entertainment business* because I had experience in that world! Every time I had to confront Abjection, I ran to a different goal. Pretty soon there was no more running. Nightmares started to invade my nights, forcing me to look in the sack of rotted parts. When I got to grad school to become a therapist, the "mothering" part of me that I had rejected in my MIPE identity had to show up in a big way. To be a therapist is to help other people have a corrective nurturing relationship that is all about them. When I made peace with the mothering part of me, I was finally able to emerge from Abjection.

Remember Sarah from Chapter 10? She was the actress with the controlling mom and got a big break on a television series. As we worked through her treatment, the starring role became a challenge. Sarah's inner world was in conflict, and the turmoil made the outer world unrelenting. We were routing out the false self. Sarah had forced her psyche to submit to wholly unobtainable external beauty standards in response to the curses and marks given to her by her mother. Sarah started to pay attention to what she wanted rather than to what she had been trained to like. The more she paid attention to her inner life, the more angry and confused she became. She found that she disliked the rigid ballet work she had committed most of her life to. She liked country music, anathema to her mother's East Coast standards. The more she embraced the parts of herself that she had been taught to reject, the more agitated she became. While for me this was a normal but very uncomfortable part of healing, Sarah was struggling. She was looking into the burlap sack.

Soon she started to dislike her character on the show. She couldn't identify with her. Sarah began to associate the character she played for her job with the character she had played for her family. The aspirational character she played on the show felt a thousand miles away from her real life. She felt that she was miscast. She wasn't this fake model type at all. She liked being a little boring and wearing flat shoes, T-shirts, and jeans. She toyed with chopping her hair off, but that would have caused problems for her with her agent, the show's producers, and the network. Every part of her job was invested in the Divided Sarah. Her real self was just starting to catch up. Sarah had no desires to prove anything to her mother anymore; indeed she wanted to rub the new Sarah in her face. When the show wasn't renewed, Sarah was relieved. The morning after the last episode was shot, Sarah changed her appearance drastically—going from long dark wavy hair to a platinum pixie cut. The following week, she bought a pickup truck. A few months later, she got a tattoo.

This state is the scariest of all of them. There is real danger here of losing yourself. This is the place where addiction, mental illness, violence, and harm all live and thrive; read the tragedy of Amanda Yates's life to see how bad it can get. It is in this place where irrevocable choices can be made. Also, if we have unresolved trauma, we may make a loop that pulls the Hunt and Abjection into a constant cycle. This is what is happening in addiction. Beyond this stage, though, are the immediate steps to sovereignty. One cannot be a Queen without having been in the despair and horror of Abjection. This is where "realness" gets a new definition. It also can look like the place of rejection, or at least the place where we are tempted to reject everything we've learned on the journey and double down on the cultural expectations given to us. If we do, then we get stuck in Abjection. We will become rigid, frightened, and anxious, always

the Queen's path

trying to make the world around us meet our expectations. The real freedom is not in controlling the outer world and all our relationships, roles, and goals but in understanding the inner world with all its desires, tastes, and longing.

The difficult trick of mastering Abjection is to stop fighting the "shoulds." Therapists have a joke that we sometimes share with our clients, when the person sitting before us keeps repeating the word *should* over and over again. We often say, "You're shoulding yourself." This is a light joke, basically pointing out to our client that the word *should* is the emotional equivalent of pooping yourself. When in Abjection, the woman has no choice but to face the repugnant and vile horrors of materiality. But to traverse Abjection, she has to stop resisting them. She can't fight them. She must look at them, maybe even embrace them. At the very least, she must relax in their presence. When she can do that, she can cross beyond the most dangerous threshold into the one that holds the possibility of transformation, Choice.

Why This Is the Danger Quadrant

We don't like to look at the worst of ourselves. It is a known psychosocial reality that we often scapegoat people who are symbols of our failings. This is true whether we are talking about individuals, families, or society at large. This is why victim blaming is such a problem in our society. It is why we haven't ended hunger or war. We want these things, but it hurts too much to look at both what it would cost us and the cost it has already wrought. We are not prepared to face the abject horror of our actions or inaction. As a result, the systems of separation, scapegoating, and subjugation are set in motion against classes and individual people who make us uncomfortable. Why? Because it is much easier to place our anger on the people who are calling out the problems than to face the challenges that would force us to change. It would be easier if they'd just shut up. As the next two examples show, there are real consequences for those who refuse to submit. The world is not kind, and whether in real life or in the stories we tell the risk for women is very real.

222

Ending in Abjection: Princess Diana

I vividly remember waking up to the news on August 31, 1997. The first image when the TV hummed to life was of a crumpled and nearly indistinguishable black car crushed under a tunnel. The images were taken at night, and the sky beyond the tunnel was blueish black. The hulking mass of metal was shiny but no longer resembled a car. I was filled with horror looking at the image before I even read the chyron at the bottom of the page: "Princess Diana Killed in Paris Car Crash." I remember feeling dizzy and sick to my stomach. Diana was not even 10 years older than I was. How could she be dead?

The world awoke that morning in tears to news of the sudden loss of 36-year-old Princess Diana, chased to her death by the paparazzi through the streets of Paris. There is scarcely a sadder real-life story of Abjection than the life of Princess Diana. She had done everything in her power to live as a MISOR under the protection of her husband's powerful family. But while Diana had not intended to live her life as an outspoken critic of the monarchy, she was also unwilling to be a victim to its inconsistencies, vicissitudes, and shame. By acting outside of the protection of the Crown, Diana was soon cast onto the track of the MIPE. And once you're on that track, it is very difficult to return to the MISOR's world of naïveté and protection.

Once she had fallen to the MIPE path, her presence was even more a lightning rod for the press. Ever since her engagement to Charles the Prince of Wales, the tabloids and worldwide press had grown hungry for images of her. The fairy-tale romance was a welcome distraction from AIDS, Margaret Thatcher's austerity policies, and the frustration of the working class. But once Diana had started to call attention to her plight, once she had voiced her frustration, she no longer fit the portrait of the silent, obedient, protected princess. After her two sons were born, she seemed to take more ownership of herself, much to the frustration of the other royals. Diana did as she pleased, albeit anxiously. She was the People's Princess, going where other royals would not, like AIDS-stricken townships in Africa. The people of the world loved her, and many paparazzi made a full-time career of following her every move.

Diana had tried many times to dissuade the rabid photographic hordes who chased her everywhere. She confronted them when they followed her on a ski vacation with her children. She avoided them when possible. But still they hunted her. The purpose of the Hunt is to objectify the woman being hunted. She's a trophy, prey. Whether she's a MISOR being pursued as a wife or a MIPE being pursued as a rebel, she's an object. The purpose of the Hunt is to remind her, and the world, of that status.

At the time of her death, Diana had recently gotten divorced, placing a foot onto the Commit step, assuring her role as a MIPE. She also started a romantic liaison with Dodi al-Fayed, the son of Egyptian billionaire Mohammed al-Fayed. Dating the foreigner provided another hard tap dance on the MIPE step. Had Diana survived the accident, she would have had the opportunity to go through the steps of Choice and Embodied Transcendence. Indeed, her life was set in motion for both. She would have eventually stood as a model against other royals, like the queen, and indeed after her death, there was a severe backlash against the royal family. As her children matured, she would have had the opportunity to stand in the place of a royal mum herself, as a counterpoint to Queen Elizabeth. But Diana never got the chance. She was hunted for the sport of royal watching, of trophy collecting. She was a trophy because of her royal name and her MIPE status. The more magical she became away from the royal family, attending to people maimed by land mines, visiting New York with Mother Teresa, and being photographed by Mario Testino for *Vanity Fair* magazine, the more isolated, powerful, and endangered she became.

Ending in Abjection: *Promising Young Woman*

In Emerald Fennel's 2020 film *Promising Young Woman*, Cassie Thomas's life is motivated by the loss of her best friend, Nina. We never learn how Nina's life ended, only that she was violently raped at a party where Nina and several other medical students were in attendance. Many of the students watched. Everyone knew about the rape, but no one would commit to holding the rapist and the observers accountable. Since this awful event, Cassie has been exacting revenge on the "nice" guys who feign wanting to help women when they're drunk in public, but who are actually just predators out for an easy target.

Cassie spends almost the entire movie in the second quadrant. We learn about her OUT, her curse and her mark, and her brief blindness. She is a MIPE through and through, always smarter than her peers, confounding her parents with her behavior and desires. The Hunt has encapsulated virtually the entire film, with Abjection basically finishing out Cassie's story. The movie is all Quadrant II until the last act, when crossing into the third quadrant Cassie goes to the cabin where Al Monroe, the man who raped Nina years earlier before a crowd of onlookers, is having his bachelor party.

Cassie goes dressed in a sexy nurse costume, replete with cotton-candy wig and red heels. As she walks up the driveway to the cabin, the Britney Spears hit "Toxic" plays in a minor chord in the background, giving deep resonance to the animus possession at work for Cassie. She comes into the party, and all the men in attendance protest that no one hired her. Indeed, no one did, but no one fears the sexy stranger. They presume one of the partygoers is lying. Cassie lines them up to give them shots from a tainted bottle of vodka, the liquid spiked with something to render them unlikely to interrupt her. She gets Al into the bedroom, where he tells her that he doesn't want to "do anything" because he loves his fiancée. He isn't very sincere, letting her handcuff him to the bed, watching her as she moves around the room in her costume. He asks her name, and she gives him the name of the woman he raped at the party, Nina Fischer. Naturally, this causes Al some alarm.

Cassie then goes on to explain what's going to happen to Al. She is going to carve Nina's initials into his flesh. She doesn't claim that she's going to kill him or his friends—which she could have done, given their state and Al's being handcuffed to the bed. No, she's going to mark him too. If Nina had to wear the mark, then Al's going to have one too. But this is where the tragedy unravels. Al manages to free one hand just as Cassie is about to begin carving into his flesh with her scalpel. Even one-handed, he is much stronger than she is. He uses his greater physical power to get on top of her and suffocates Cassie with a pillow by putting his knee on her face, all with one hand still cuffed to the bed. As the Margaret Atwood quote goes, "Men are afraid women will laugh at them, and women are afraid men will kill them."[7] There's no more apropos ending to sum up that truth.

The next morning, Al is in the bed with Cassie's body when his buddy Joe comes in to check on him. At first Joe thinks that the nurse/stripper/Cassie is passed out on the bed after a raucous night of sex. Soon he learns that she's dead and that Al killed her. Rather than face the music, they devise a plan to dispose of Cassie's body and go on like nothing happened. Joe comforts Al for his guilt and his fear of losing everything, rather than either of them thinking about the dead girl lying right next to them.

In some workshops and classes where we've discussed this film and the Queen's Path, I've had a handful of students offer that the movie doesn't end in Abjection but in Choice. In the film, a series of messages, cards, and evidence finds its way to important people, including a lawyer and the police. As a result, Al and Joe are arrested at Al's wedding. In this way, Cassie's decision to leave a trail of breadcrumbs lest she not return foreshadowed her choice to be with Nina in death rather than continue living in a world that is so cruel and unrelenting for women. I think those participants had a good point. Cassie's story ends in Abjection, but the movie ends in Choice. Either way, the film ends in the third quadrant, with Cassie not getting to enjoy sovereignty, at least not in this world.

Exercise

Draw an image that expresses the feelings of Abjection you've experienced on this step of the Queen's Path. If it feels easier to write about it in words, then express Abjection in prose or poetry. You can express it in a story, a journal entry, or any way you choose. I personally like pastels for this exercise. The pastels allow me to not be focused on making some recognizable image but allow me to explore color and shapes. In my own journal, this step often looks like the shape of claws or the black of oblivion scrawled in black and gray oil pastels. The important aspect of this exercise is to let yourself feel the experience of Abjection rather than just describe it intellectually. The forces that move in the unconscious are often best suited to creative forms of expression. Feel free to let your creativity take over with this exercise.

CHAPTER 13

CHOICE

After the experience of carting around the rotting bag of discarded parts and then pulling them out to look at them, the next step on the path may seem rather benign. If you survive Abjection, the step afterward at first glance may look easy. In novels, films, and other narratives, this is almost always the point of the crescendo in the story. The protagonist "chooses" to save her sister-self, or she sacrifices something to save the day. But in real life, the Choice step on the Queen's Path is the consequential decision to move out of Abjection and into radical acceptance.

In psychotherapy, radical acceptance is best known as a tenet of acceptance commitment therapy or ACT. This form of therapy is one of the many forms of cognitive behavioral therapy or CBT. What I like about ACT is that though it is a form of CBT, it is not as rigid. The outcomes in ACT are far more lasting, and the tools also endure much longer with clients. The core idea of ACT is to create emotional and psychological flexibility. Achieving that begins with radical acceptance.

But before you roll your eyes at the page, let me explain a little bit. Here's what radical acceptance is not. It is not an invitation to suffering. I see patients come into my office engaging in what I like to call the "Misery Olympics." Women especially have been enculturated to never sing their own praises or draw attention to their successes. Though it isn't pleasant, women are allowed to critique, complain, and cajole. But it's frowned upon if we do too much of this directed at others, so instead we direct it back to ourselves. The result is a competition of who can suffer the most, as though you'd earn a medal worth parading around the grocery store or dog park that other women could see.

Most people misconstrue what the word *acceptance* in *radical acceptance* means. They believe that acceptance is the same thing as allowing, embracing, or endorsing. But acceptance in therapy is not embracing pain and struggle. The experience of radical acceptance is simply learning to go toward a painful feeling when necessary. Most people never bother to assess whether a difficult experience is useful or appropriate. They simply avoid the pain. This is normal! We are wired to avoid pain. Our nervous systems help us regulate and care for ourselves by indicating when something is painful. Avoiding pain is adaptive. That notwithstanding, trauma is not something our psyches and nervous systems are expected to endure on a regular or constant basis. The sheer level of stress and trauma that we live with in our current world is extraordinary. In the wild, animals aren't exposed to constant stress. They endure occasional stress, and then their nervous systems regulate by shaking, moving, and being with their community. Human culture has devolved to the point that we don't do any of those things anymore. Instead, we have grown to believe that stress is a normal, everyday fact of life.

When I explain radical acceptance to my clients, I do it with an analogy because stories are much easier to remember, and ACT uses metaphors for almost everything, so that makes it easy. So here's my favorite analogy to explain radical acceptance. You've saved your money for a year to take a wonderful vacation to Paris. You have your passport all ready. You've bought fashionable but comfortable shoes for walking down the Champs-Élysées. You're going to meet your girlfriends there and drink champagne at Le Café Marly next to the Louvre. It's going to be spectacular. You get on your plane, super excited. When you land eight hours later, you're not in Paris at all. You're in Rio de Janeiro. Now, Rio is nice, but it's not where you expected to be. Your clothes are all wrong, and your girlfriends are already in Paris. What do you do? Do you cry and scream and find the nearest airline pilot to yell at? Do you get together with the other passengers and demand a new flight? Do you take hostages until you get your way? Or sit in the Rio airport bathroom and have a two-hour crying jag? Radical acceptance says that the first thing you must do is take a deep breath and notice where you are. Don't worry at first how you got here. Right now, the important thing is taking stock, so that you can use your best problem-solving skills to move forward.

If you move without informed choice, you are likely to return to the Hunt, which will put you right back into Abjection. Yes, you'll wind up at the door of Choice again, but is that really how you want to move? Perhaps taking a deep breath would make it a little easier. Look around. You're in Rio. It's filled with life; there is wonderful music. The food is great. The people are beautiful and helpful. The beach is a wonder. Okay, still don't want to stay? Totally fine. Now that you've had time to breathe and take stock, do you want to try to get to Paris? Go home? Someplace else? Once you've taken stock and examined how you feel, you can really move forward. If you want to get to Paris, you'll need to find an airline representative to help you or charter a plane or get some other transport. You'll no doubt feel a little self-conscious arriving after your friends, so you'll need to plan for that emotionally. Radical acceptance is not being afraid of difficult emotions. It's basically learning to be comfortable being uncomfortable. Most of us try to outplan or overcontrol to avoid this feeling. But the avoidance of negativity makes us rigid and unyielding. Sovereignty demands flexibility.

Phoebe's Story

I have a client named Phoebe whom I've been seeing for a long time. Phoebe came to L.A. at the ripe old age of 16 to become an actor. Her parents sent her with her 22-year-old cousin and some frequent flyer miles to come back home to Virginia every few months. Within a year, Phoebe's cousin had decided she didn't like being the caregiver for a teenage actor. Her cousin moved to Northern California, six hours away, to live with her boyfriend. Rather than Phoebe's parents collecting her and moving her home for the last year of high school, her parents decided she was old enough to be on her own working. She was, after all, very responsible. She completed all her homework for her online school. When she worked, she was always off-book, which meant she had memorized all her lines, even if she had just received the script the night before. She never missed an audition, and she was always the first on set when she had work. What they couldn't see from 3,000 miles away was that Phoebe was down to 80 pounds. Showing up on set first was motivated by more than being responsible. She was terrified of making a mistake. She needed the positive, affirming response she received from the cast and crew just to make it through the day. A nod in the wrong direction or a raised eyebrow could set off earthquakes of deep panic.

When Phoebe first started therapy, she was just beginning recovery from her deadly eating disorder. She had gotten herself as far as she could alone. By the time I met her, she was 23 and had been living on her own in L.A. for 7 years. She was pretty, charming, and funny. She had maintained a romantic relationship all this time with her boyfriend from high school in Virginia. He had gone to college and medical school while she was working and living on her own in Los Angeles.

Phoebe felt like she was far behind her peers. She had never had appropriate mirroring. Her parents had misinterpreted her drive to be a successful actor as healthy ambition rather than a profound need for positive mirrors. Growing up the youngest of three siblings in a very competitive household made Phoebe *hungry* for meaningful attention. Her parents, both successful lawyers, ran their own firm representing high-profile politicians and government agencies. Her two older siblings had attended prep schools and succeeded in competitive sports. Her brother was a track star, and her sister an accomplished equestrian. Both had gone on to receive Ivy League college educations. Phoebe saw herself as a failure compared to her parents and siblings. She hadn't gone to college, didn't compete in sports, and lived far away from her family's life of achievements, parties, and capital-city gossip. Phoebe was a MIPE, always outside of her family's life and expectations and never enjoying their protection.

As she worked through the sense of abandonment she felt and the subsequent absence of mirroring in her life, Phoebe started to do better. She gained a healthy amount of weight. She adopted two dogs. She broke up with the high school boyfriend, whose attention had become stagnant and controlling. She was feeling good about herself and decided to take a martial arts class. That's where she met Jeremy.

A tall, strong, athletic man, Jeremy was the picture of what Phoebe had been raised to want in a partner. He had just graduated from law school, was studying for the bar, and was funny, smart, and charming. He was very romantic and matched her in subtle ways that she found very appealing. She resisted a relationship at first, as she was just beginning to learn about herself and what she wanted in life. She was rethinking her career as an actor and attending community college to eventually transfer to a four-year program. She had become fascinated by writing. Her nightly dreams were filled with images of paper, houses, and books.

Jeremy was persistent. He courted her . . . pursued her. Phoebe was the object of the Hunt. You're reading this book, so you know what happens next. Phoebe had to navigate the Hunt and Abjection before getting to Choice. At first, she allowed herself to be pursued. She even liked it. No one had ever demonstrated the kind of desire for her that Jeremy had. And he was someone who fit her family's expectations. Jeremy was an attorney from a good family. Phoebe wouldn't be the black sheep bringing another black sheep home to Thanksgiving dinner.

Phoebe let herself be caught in the Hunt. The two officially became a couple. At first, it was amazing. Jeremy was attentive. He got her. Phoebe felt seen. Jeremy appreciated her creativity. He thought she was beautiful. But one night out with friends, the veneer started to crack. Jeremy had tickets to a hockey game. His firm had a suite at the stadium, and they were meeting some of Jeremy's colleagues there after a romantic dinner. Phoebe had put on something edgy and attractive but not sophisticated: a mini skirt and dramatic top that had been hand-painted by an artist friend. The outfit was completed with a pair of flat Doc Martens boots. When they pulled into the parking lot, Jeremy gave her a passionate kiss . . . and then slapped her *hard* across the face. He told her she was going to embarrass him in front of his colleagues in those ridiculous clothes and ordered her to stay in the car until he returned. Phoebe was in shock. She didn't know what else to do, so she stayed in the car.

Pretty soon, the physical abuse was a normal way for Jeremy to express his anger or manipulate Phoebe. He started to want ridiculous demonstrations of her loyalty and affection. He became jealous of how much she loved her dogs. He would tell her she was worthless, that no one would ever love her but him, and she should be glad to have him. Without him, she was nothing (this is a big clue to being in Abjection). He'd critique her clothes or her hair. Rather than fight, she'd ask him how he wanted her to dress or wear her hair. He wouldn't give her an answer. He told her to figure it out. And if she got it wrong? You guessed it, more abuse. All this was a mixture of Hunt and Abjection. Jeremy would pursue, she'd get caught, and he'd denigrate her. She didn't know how to fight. She just kept trying to be the perfect girlfriend, her MIPE self, trying to impress Jeremy with her intelligence, her sex appeal, and her creativity, then she'd submit. She reembraced the role every single time, only to find it putting her right back in the same place. Phoebe was in Abjection and couldn't see her way out. She'd get sucked into the Hunt again, thinking "maybe this time will be different." Except it never was. When she finally told me what was happening, the abuse had been going on for over a year.

No one can pull someone out of or forward on the Queen's Path. The only thing anyone can do, even a therapist, is to accompany the woman on the path, hold her hand, and point out the usual hiding places of monsters and trolls. As Phoebe got pulled in a constant loop dragging her through Commit, Hunt, and Abjection, over and over again, my job was to be the person offering loving support and gently pointing out the pattern. It would be months before Phoebe could find herself in Choice. When she finally did, she described it as perfectly as anyone ever had to me. She said she was completely depleted and could not see what was next. She could see some options, though they weren't very clear, and there were far too many. She was looking at objects that didn't seem to have a purpose, as though she was supposed to understand how it would help her. Everything felt like a challenge, as though it was physically, emotionally, and psychologically expensive. She was frustrated that her choices weren't more obvious. There were no neon signs that said, "Happiness this way!" They were subtle yearnings and tastes that told her which way to point her cracked glass slippers.

Since we're on the Queen's Path, the Choice step we are facing comes on the heels of Abjection. Which means that what we're using our radical acceptance skills for is looking at some of the worst things in our lives. We might have to look at periods of abuse. Or perhaps we are looking at our worst behavior. Maybe we're confronting addiction. It might be that we're looking at something that isn't a bad thing we've done but a reality that will exact a price in the world, like a woman loving another woman, leaving a difficult relationship, or accepting that you're transgender. We have to pull out the bag of discarded parts and decide what to keep and what to discard. We can't take it all with us; it's too much. But we must take the things that from this point forward will define who we choose to be in the world. It's the step of Choice because it's for us to choose not only which direction to go in but also what to take with us and who we choose to be moving forward. The end of Abjection is always either being killed by the process or doing away with the dead parts of us that cannot serve us. Then we pick up the ones that can define us in our sovereignty. We must be careful to treat the discarded parts as respectfully as we can. They're still us, so treat their going-away with the reverence of a funeral.

The Mirror at the Edge of the Forest (Reprise)

Remember the gilded mirror at the edge of the forest from Chapter 9? You had to break the mirror to move forward out of the Enchanted Forest. Now, battle worn and staring in the mirror, you are being asked to take stock of the woman who looks back at you. You may remember from that chapter that the mirror is encircled by a gilded frame. And in the frame are symbols of the scenes of your life. Traumas and triumphs tell the story of your life as you reflect. To move forward, you must choose what you will take with you. You can't take the whole mirror, nor can you take all the pieces. You have to choose a handful of memories to take with you as you move forward.

The step of Choice is critical to our own stories as well as the narratives we encounter that enlighten the Queen's Path. To choose is to affirm your sovereignty, agency . . . and worth. To make a choice is to reject the idea of subjectivity. Even if you find yourself in an impossible situation: prison, living under a totalitarian state, or living with an abusive parent or spouse, taking Choice back into your hands is the window that will ultimately lead to freedom. Even if you have to behave like a subject to save your life (speaking to women held captive by tyrannical regimes or subcultures, or to women who have been subjugated by abusive families), you can make internal choices that will save your soul. Choosing will free you. It is not what you choose that breaks the curse but the fact that you choose at all.

Choice as the Door out of Abjection

After returning to Los Angeles from my own Abjection experience, I was stuck. I was seeing a new psychoanalyst. I was in graduate school again. I was working in a visual effects studio. One of the people in my department was engaged in flagrant sexual discrimination. The head of the human resources department heard my complaint and then asked me if I was sure I wanted to make an official report. I might be branded a difficult woman and never work in the movie business again. I was horrified. This was one of the worst moments in my life. I couldn't understand what had happened to me or why. I had done everything I was expected to do. I had subjected myself to the high-wire act of always performing. Everything I had ever done was to prove to some real or invisible external force of authority, i.e. God, that I deserved a good life. I sat in my therapist's office, words bursting out in a staccato fury: "I did everything right. Why isn't life loving me back?" I said it over and over again, "Why can't life love me back?" To me, loving life meant that I was obedient, dutiful. That's how you're supposed to behave, right? Loving someone means submitting. It didn't mean I *actually loved* my life. It meant I tried hard to always be a "good girl." Even as a MIPE, I always endeavored to be "good."

My therapist looked at me, perplexed. "I don't think it works like that." I stared at him. I begged him to explain it to me. He struggled to find the words. Finally, he said, "You just *love* your life. That means that you make the life *you* want, regardless of whether or not someone approves. You don't need anyone's permission to love your life. Life will not love you back for your obedience. Life will love you if you love how you live, what you do, and enjoy every moment."

Mind. Blown.

There is *zero reward* for being a pretty, obedient object. I had to choose. In choosing myself, I would have a life I loved. Loving life meant loving *my* life, choosing experiences I would love. Loving life meant doing things that I loved. I would never learn to love myself by hoping someone else would do it first. There is no real reward for becoming smaller. You can't submit yourself free.

The MISOR in Choice

Some of the clearest metaphors of Choice come through movies and other cultural products. One of the easiest to relate to in the last decade can be seen in Disney's *Frozen*. If you haven't seen the movie lately, have a look. It will surprise you how clearly this film fits the Queen's Path. The flagstone on the path representing Choice is played out first by Anna. Elsa is told by the evil Prince Hans that the eternal winter Elsa released killed her sister. This news devastates Elsa, and she drops to her knees (she's still in Abjection). Meanwhile, Anna, who is not in fact dead, has the opportunity to get "true love's kiss" from Kristoff, the ice vendor who helped her find her sister earlier. But when she sees that Elsa is about to be murdered by Prince Hans, Anna steps in to protect her sister with her last breath before being transformed into a block of ice. Anna chooses an act of true love for her sister over "true love's kiss." You might recall this would have been the MISOR's Abjection ending. The MISOR in Choice is almost always stepping into the role of her exiled MIPE sister. Anna in *Frozen* takes the power from Prince Hans. You'll see shortly that each has to step into the other's domain to fully exercise Choice.

The MIPE in Choice

The MIPE's choice is often misunderstood. She is doing less, and as such most people see this as less difficult, but it is actually much more challenging. Where the MISOR has to step from passivity into power, the MIPE has to soften. She must relax, step back, take a breath, and reverse her forward drive. If she pushes (a MIPE staple) in Choice, she will find herself continuing the pattern of Hunt, Abjection, Hunt, Abjection, Hunt, Abjection. For a MIPE, the Choice to relax, slow down, and allow herself to go slowly will make it possible for her to move through the third quadrant. For a MIPE, this means being a little more like the MISOR. She has to be receptive; she needs to allow. She cannot make something happen. She can't use her typical powers. Sticking with talking about Disney's *Frozen*, when Elsa, the MIPE in the story reaches Choice, she realizes that love will thaw the ice and end the eternal winter. It is not something she has to do; rather it is something she must feel. The MIPE must let go of control, the drive for power, or her need to win.

What Choice Is and Is Not

Choice is not the place where we solve the problems of the world. But it can look and feel like that sometimes. Choice is the act of reviewing and deciding what to do next. But it isn't the grasping, action-oriented place of achievement. It is a deep place of looking for profound knowledge of who we are and what we desire. In this way, Choice becomes a radical act. Yes, I am that. No, that one is not mine. I am a trained equine therapist, and one of my favorite exercises is to take clients out to the big enclosure where my three horses live together in a herd and ask the client if they can tell which pile of shit belongs to each horse. Inevitably, they start down the road of examination and logic. They're comparing size of horse to size of poop pile, they're asking which ones are male versus female; they're really trying to answer the question. And the truth is that unless they stood there and watched all day, there's no way to know. Next I invert the question: "Do you know whose poop it's not?" Again, they run down possibilities, almost to a person they look at me incredulously and say, "Mine?" Exactly. The origin of shit doesn't matter. What matters is figuring out if it's yours or not. For me, the responsibility for the horse shit is mine; they're my horses. But it's still not my shit. My clients have no need to worry about the horse shit. They have no claim on it. That doesn't mean that they won't be affected by it. They could walk in it and track it home or in their car. They could find themselves face down in it if they slip and fall. Just because it isn't your shit doesn't mean it won't affect you. But once you figure this little nugget out, you're free to make decisions. Choice is about feeling into what works for you and what the right decisions are for yourself.

In my experience, the choices women have to make in this step are almost always about reconciling with the parts of themselves they have had to throw out to survive. The mother who had to give up being a stay-at-home mom after her husband died. The doctor who had to give up practicing medicine after a cancer diagnosis. The woman who, after a marriage and children, realizes that she is in love with another woman. Women have to pick up those discarded pieces, examine them, and reimagine what it means to reintegrate them into their being after the pain of Cleaved, the Hunt, and Abjection.

In narratives with female protagonists, this often looks like two characters exchanging roles or one character returning to an old skill set or habit. In Disney's *Frozen*, it's Anna standing up for her more powerful magical sister, Elsa. Elsa in turn has to be more receptive and relational to make the eternal winter cease. In 1985's *The Color Purple*, it's Celie standing up to Albert while Shug is quiet and placating to get them out of the house safely. In Patty Jenkin's 2017 *Wonder Woman*, it's Diana facing Dr. Maru while holding a tank over her head and realizing that love is what she sees in humans, and it is love, not power, that will drive her efforts to defeat Aries. It is Nanisca in Gina Prince Bythewood's *The Woman King* choosing to save her sister soldiers and face her rapist, knowing she is abandoning her chances at leadership in the king's guard. In Greta Gerwig's 2023 *Barbie*, it's Barbie asking permission of her creator Ruth Handler to become human, only to be told that there is no one to ask. Barbie doesn't need permission to become human. She only needs to choose.

As mentioned earlier, it is the act of choosing that is freeing, not the results of the choice. Though the results themselves can lead to wonderful outcomes, it is the power to choose and the knowledge of that power that makes the difference. Following immediately on the heels of Abjection makes Choice more challenging in one sense. We are spent of our resources and don't have the usual cadre of protections to help us along the way. However, that emptiness can also make things plain. It is much easier to see before us when all the rules, routines, and roles are stripped bare.

Taking options and choices away from people is one way to colonize or oppress them. A choice that is removed or obstructed from view is unavailable. By the same token, too many possibilities creates a challenge that can render someone incapacitated, overwhelming them to the point that they cannot discern between them. Standing in the place of Choice and deciding to reunite with parts or aspects of the self that were discarded to make others more comfortable is a radical act. This step toward sovereignty asks that you accept the authority of your own inner desires, preferences, or identity rather than the one(s) that are given to you. Reuniting authority and responsibility are critical to wearing the crown of sovereignty. You direct your life's imperative and claim authority over your life and decisions.

Exercise

What dilemma is facing you right now? What would happen if you didn't need permission from anyone? What would it feel like to just move? Would you feel safe? Can you identify any important decisions that you are waiting on permission to make? Can you imagine the possible outcomes if you didn't bother with permission but just moved on your own imperative? What part could you adopt from the MIPE or MISOR (the opposite of your track) that could help? Do you need to be more active? More relaxed?

CHAPTER 14

EMBODIED TRANSCENDENCE

When a woman is undergoing the internal transformation of the Queen's Path, the last step of the underworld is that of embodiment. That is not to say that she is disembodied prior, but rather that up until this part of the journey, she has been a passenger within a body whose meaning has been mediated by others. Culture, family, religious institutions—they have all told her who she is allowed to be. The path through the Hunt and Abjection have shown her the perils of subjectivity. Choice has shown her that she has an imperative to see her body as the first terrain of her own domain. Any Queendom she might expand into begins with the sovereignty of her own body and her right to its inviolability.

For the last several hundred years, most religious practices in the West have promoted transcendence as a goal. The body, with its needs, desires, and functions, is often portrayed as less important than the mind or soul. The focus has been on denying the material world of the body in favor of the world of the spirit. As such, any sensations, celebrations, or joy in the body has at best been played down and at worst been fully rejected and treated as mortal sin. Rarely do we ask why transcendence has been given to us via this route.

There are historical and political reasons. The imprint of Greek thought is still with us to this day, and among the classical philosophers, logic and reason were believed to be the highest virtues.

There is the history of the Christian tradition eschewing any physical pleasure in exchange for eternal life. In addition, there is a long history in hegemonic cultures to entreat people to hope for a better world in the next life to make them more compliant in this one. This world is grim; the next one will be better. Just keep hoping and working, and you'll earn a better life next time. Combine that with the warmongering that has been the hallmark of the last several thousand years, and you will find cultures had to make the afterlife a form of doctrine; otherwise, life was utterly unbearable, and no one would have bothered to do any work, go into battle, or belong to any kind of social system that would risk a lifetime of incessant misery.

If you've ever studied social sciences like anthropology or psychology, you probably know that shame is a powerful social tool. It is used to keep people behaving according to the rules set by the culture. Our brains and nervous systems are most at ease when we belong to a group. Whether that's a tribe, a family, or a pickleball team, people need to belong to feel safe. The minute you start taking that sense of safety away, cultural norms also start to ebb. Shame is used as a threat to keep people thinking about their place in whatever group they belong to. If the girls on your high school prom committee all wore a certain style of clothes, for example, chances are good that belonging to the group meant upholding that sense of taste, and if you didn't, you might have been made fun of. Similarly, if you really like your pickleball club, chances are good you would defend your right to stay a member. You'd defend the integrity of the club if suddenly there was someone misbehaving or preying on members of your league. Other group members know that if they share publicly that Gladys has been cheating on her husband, or that Diane has been abusing her dog, then shame dictates that those behaviors must improve so that Gladys and Diane can be welcomed back into the league just in time for the big tournament next month. Shame has kept them in line and reminded everyone that there is a standard to uphold.

Reflecting on Female Corporeal Subjectivity

Body shaming is one of the oldest tools in the book used to keep women in line. Even in Classical Greece, the name "amazon" given to the legendary female warriors was a form of body shaming. The word itself means "without a breast." The Amazons were mythologized as terrifying barbarians with one breast. The story was that Amazon women were forced to chop off the right breast to be able to tightly pull the string of a bow in battle. But the Amazons weren't a story made up to frighten little Greek children. The real Amazons were Scythian warriors.[1] The Greeks did not like independently minded women. Their culture promoted the belief that women were to be seen and not heard. Women should be kept in private homes, not parade about the polis. And if women did have to go out, how they should dress and act in public was legally prescribed. You can imagine that under these strict guidelines, the idea of marauding women who were capable of riding horses, shooting bows and arrows, and governing themselves was anathema to the "cultured" Greeks of the ancient Mediterranean. The nomadic Scythian culture expanded from what is now Iran to the Caucuses. Some of the tribes separated into bands based on sex. Women lived and fought together and once or twice a year would gather with other Scythian bands of men. This type of independence was terrifying to the Greeks. They shared stories of the Amazons to dissuade Greek women from getting too uppity. Do you want to be a one-breasted, muscular freak or a proper Athenian lady?

Body shame is a cultural bedrock. Girls are taught to be ashamed of their female bodies almost as soon as we realize we're bound for womanhood. In 1970, the age most girls started dieting was 14. By 1990, that number had plummeted to eight years of age.[2] By age 10, 80 percent of American girls have been on a diet. In research on women's opinions about their bodies, more than half report feeling ashamed of what they look like and believe the size or shape of their body is responsible for everything from poor romantic prospects to lack of career advancement.[3] Further, slurs and insults about the body are used far more often against women than against men.

More than a third of women reported having experienced or knowing someone who has been the target of body-shaming slurs either in person or on the Internet. Over 94 percent of teenage girls report being bullied via body shaming, and 57 percent of girls from age 12 to 20 believe that their experience of being bullied is because of their physical appearance.[4]

Being disconnected from our bodies is unfortunately "normal" for most women. The binary of the cultured world as masculine and the natural world as feminine has reinforced the idea that the body is dangerous and that women's bodies are downright evil. Women across cultures are held responsible for men's responses to women's presence. Most men feel free, even compelled, to comment on a woman's appearance, despite what she wants or desires. In our culture, a man is somehow less of a rapist if the victim was scantily dressed. The implication is clear that a man's physical drives are somehow more powerful than his will. A man can be charged with a "crime of passion" if he hurts or even kills his woman partner after learning of, or suspecting, her infidelity. The sentences for crimes of passion are also shockingly lower than those for premeditated crimes, at least when committed by men. Men who kill their intimate partners receive prison sentences from 2 to 6 years, whereas women who commit the same crime often spend 15 years in prison.[5]

The worldwide COVID pandemic and subsequent lockdowns drove this point home in earnest. Domestic violence increased in large numbers in every statistical study. In Italy, researchers found that 89 percent of femicides in 2020 happened in the domestic sphere.[6] Their research points to the fact that the home is actually the most dangerous place for women. The World Health Organization reports that 1 in 3 women have been the victim of intimate partner or sexual violence.[7] This makes violence against women one of the largest health concerns in the world. Add to these sobering statistics that a remarkably low 9 percent of women are killed by strangers.[8, 9] Do the simple math, and you realize that means that in fact 91 percent of murdered women are killed by people they know. These numbers also point to the fact that women's safety at home is a major human rights issue that is scarcely addressed. We don't discuss it nearly enough in the media or see action in public policy.

In conservative, religiously driven cultures, women are often forced to cover their bodies, hair, or even their faces. The reasoning? To protect men from their own impure thoughts. This is true whether we are talking about conservative Mormons in Idaho, Hasidic Jews in Williamsburg, or Shi'a Muslims in Iran. The rules of modesty endure for the same reasons, to protect men, and, by default, women. Women are expected to behave in a way that doesn't tempt men. If women "behave," then men won't have a reason to hurt them. The unspoken implication is that the powers of women, sex, and attraction are so compelling that men don't have the capacity to maintain any realistic purchase on self-control if women aren't following the rules set out for them by . . . men. That's the rationale anyway. Of course, it's just another way for women to be kept in the Divide, but most of us don't figure out it's a trap until we ourselves or someone we love is hurt even when she was following the rules. The "What Were You Wearing" exhibits that tour college campuses and community centers share examples of clothing worn by victims of sexual assault. The exhibit pairs the testimony of victims with the clothes they wore at the time of the assault.[10] The goal is to demonstrate that most victims were wearing everyday clothes that would normally be considered unremarkable. It combats the myth that the way someone dresses has anything to do with their victimization by a rapist.

Shame in being a girl or woman is baked into almost all global cultures. Have we ever really spent time examining the mechanics in our individual lives? I have been body shamed too many times to count. From my mother worrying that I wore a size 6x as a first grader, to my dad telling me I needed to be skinny to be loved at age 12, all the way to strangers on the street cat-calling me as an anorexic 20-year-old, or a guy on the Santa Monica pier calling me a dike when I was 22 because I had a shaved head, or a stranger calling out that he "liked fat girls" while walking to my car to have dinner with a friend when I was 29. Maybe my experience is unusual, but in talking to friends and patients, the evidence supports my claim that my experience is normal for most women.

The Obedient Object

The body is by default the canvas onto which any establishment of power is projected. Why do police have authority? Because they can arrest you and bring your body (habeas corpus) to jail or to court to answer for any alleged crime or wrongdoing. Up until recently, men had legal authority over their wives. A woman's consent to sex was presumed in marriage until the 1970s, meaning that a husband could not be accused of raping his wife. All 50 states had repealed these laws by 1993. But the penalties have been slow to change. For example, it wasn't until 2021 that the law in California changed so that rape within marriage now carries the same penalties for rape outside of marriage.[11]

Authority over the spouse and children holds as a tenet of many conservative religious traditions, regardless of faith, sect, or denomination. In many religious texts, women are instructed to obey their husbands. The authority of the household is given to the patriarch of the family. But it is the body that the head of the household ultimately has control over. A dominating partner cannot know whether or not they have invaded the mind of their spouse or children, but they can see the effects they have on their behavior. If a wife and children are obedient with their bodies, their behavior will provide the confirmation the dominating partner needs to know that their authority is being heeded.

What do all these depressing statistics have to do with this last step in the third quadrant? Plenty! Most women will have gone through their adolescence and young adulthood learning what their culture expects of women. Most of us can describe what is expected of us or recognize obedience even if we struggle to comply. The expectation that our bodies will be compliant—thin, regulated, emotionally contained, attractive, available, hardworking, and quiet—is everywhere. We learn this from the time we are little girls. We learn to "be nice." We learn deference. We learn to keep the peace. We learn to be small. The effect is ultimately that we feel disembodied. Our bodies are instruments of submission, not the holy vessel of our incarnate being.

Embodiment

Have you ever used your body in an unexpected way? Did it make you feel physically strong? Did you learn to dance? Learn to ride horses? Maybe you've achieved a physical goal you didn't think you were capable of? Like running a marathon, taking a 100-mile bike trip, or hiking for 10 hours straight? Or maybe you've done something even more powerful, like had a baby or survived cancer?

The body is more than a vehicle for our mind and spirit. It is not a meat suit that takes commands from the brain. The body is the ground of being, the seat of our existence. Your body is the miraculous evidence of your presence in the world. It carries the DNA evidence of thousands of years of history and destiny. You are simultaneously the evidence that all those people existed before you, AND you are a unique version of self that has never existed before. If the Hunt was the most challenging part of the Queen's Path to write and think about, this step on the path for me is the most rewarding, the most exciting.

The result of traversing the third quadrant and successfully navigating Abjection and Choice is to arrive fully at the experience of the power you have in your own material being. Your body. To stand in the truth of embodiment is to realize the miracle of being a fully realized person, a woman, in a body that is wholly important and not subject. Your body is yours. Your being is indispensable. Your physicality is essential to your presence. You matter. Your being matters. You are not disposable. You are essential. You are not interchangeable. You are exceptional and singular. Standing in this revelation renews your identity as an empowered and fully embodied woman. Your body is perfect, regardless of what you think it looks like or how you'd like it to look or feel. It's perfect right now. It is the conduit of all your unique experience. It is the evidence of the unfolding of your life. In every molecule, inch of flesh, scar, tattoo, eyelash, or wrinkle, there is the *sacred you*. That you has lived your whole life unfolding, taking in and transforming experience into knowledge, knowledge into embodied wisdom, and inviolable body into sacred being.

Carl Jung developed many of the ideas, and wrote extensively about the different functions and developmental stages of the individual psyche. Of these, one of the most important is the transcendent function. The way it is conceived of in Jungian terms, the psyche must evolve and change for the person to individuate, or truly become themselves. One of the core theoretical precepts of depth psychology is that there is an unconscious self in relationship with the everyday, logical conscious mind. The unconscious can contain Freud's repressed and exiled parts, but from a Jungian perspective, the unconscious is more than the repository of our most hidden aspects. The unconscious guides the individual toward their most authentic self. When unconscious material comes forward in partnership with consciousness, this can open a new realm for the individual. They transcend their earlier life and embody a new place.[12, 13]

For a woman on the Queen's Path, embodiment is the transcendent place of womanhood. It is the acceptance, celebration, and power of her material being. It is her woman-ness that sets the stage for her becoming a Queen. When a woman's body truly belongs to her and is not reviled, shamed, subjugated, or objectified by her, then she emerges from the underworld of the unconscious. When she doesn't submit her physical being and thus everything that goes with it—her mind, her soul, her desires, her ambitions, her love, her intelligence—she is ready for the crown. She has embraced, elevated, and fought for all the things that make her . . . her.

Embodied *Barbie*

At the end of the 2023 *Barbie* movie, our newly human protagonist has made the round of the Queen's Path. She has hunted for Gloria and Sasha. She has been hunted by the Mattel bosses. She has been hunted by stereotypical Ken to be his long-term, long-distance, low-commitment, casual girlfriend.[14] She has faced Abjection, lying on the ground depressed in Barbieland and later in the Weird House of Weird Barbie. Barbie's version of Abjection was recognizing that she wasn't perfect anymore. She couldn't be perfect anymore. Gloria reflects this back to her transitioning her from Abjection to Choice. I mentioned it earlier, but it deserves a brief reprise here. Barbie faces her creator, Ruth Handler, and asks permission to become human. Ruth responds by telling her the ultimate truth about becoming a Queen. There is no one to ask, because permission cannot be given. Becoming yourself is a choice. By choosing, Barbie asserts her own impera. She owns her own reason to be. In the final scene of the film, we see Barbie's ultimate embodiment, foreshadowed by her sporting Birkenstocks as she gets out of Gloria's car. Barbie, renaming herself Barbara Handler, shows up for her first-ever gynecologist appointment. Barbie finally has a real woman's body.

QUADRANT IV

Resplendent

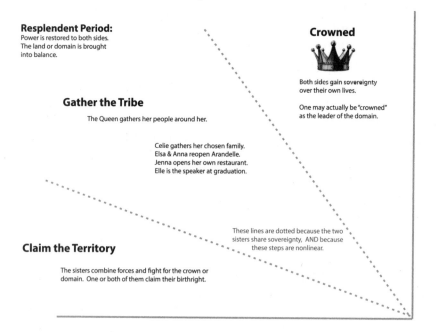

Resplendent Period:
Power is restored to both sides.
The land or domain is brought
into balance.

Crowned

Both sides gain sovereignty
over their own lives.

One may actually be "crowned"
as the leader of the domain.

Gather the Tribe

The Queen gathers her people around her.

Celie gathers her chosen family.
Elsa & Anna reopen Arandelle.
Jenna opens her own restaurant.
Elle is the speaker at graduation.

These lines are dotted because the two
sisters share sovereignty, AND because
these steps are nonlinear.

Claim the Territory

The sisters combine forces and fight for the crown or
domain. One or both of them claim their birthright.

The fourth quadrant is named Resplendent because of the way that a woman appears (and hopefully feels) when she is standing in her full authenticity and majesty. The glory of sovereignty shines through her. She occupies a new place once she has succeeded in owning the terrain of her body and being. In moving out of the embodiment step and crossing into the fourth quadrant, we leave the World of Invisible Forces and Mystery and return to the World of Visible Power and Form. The work she has done in the underworld of the second and third quadrants will now be visible to not only herself but also everyone in the conscious world of day-to-day experience.

Once a woman arrives in the fourth quadrant, the steps no longer follow a particular order. They can happen in rapid succession or in reverse order. She claims her territory, gathers her people around her, and gets a symbol of her queendom—for our purposes, she is crowned. In stories, this is usually a short part of the last act. The symbols can be anything from owning a home, ascending a throne, being crowned, or standing in a royal garden. In the film *The Woman King*, it is Nanisca returning victorious to Dahomey, and being named the Woman King, ascending the throne next to King Ghezo. In 1985's *The Color Purple*, it is Celie standing on her own land, surrounded by all her friends and family as her sister and children return. In 2023's *Barbie*, it's Barbie going to the real world and being supported by Gloria and Sasha as she goes for her first gynecologist appointment.

In real women's lives, these steps can be challenging. Asserting your domain can take years. Sometimes it takes a long time to even figure out what your domain is. Do you need to return to school for it? Leave an unhealthy relationship? What is the limit of the domain? What do you love about having or defining your own place? How do you decide what to keep and what to let fall away to feel safe? Is a domain as simple as a home? Or is it all of it: career, home, money? Only you can decide.

In gathering the tribe, it can take time to find our people, learn to trust them, and invest in our mutual well-being. Rising to the steps of the throne may seem inevitable, but most of us don't notice it until we've already done it. You're standing there, crown on your head, wondering what everyone else is looking at—and it's you! They're looking at a woman who has claimed her sovereignty and runs her own queendom. These last steps are important for many reasons. To wield power over yourself, you must not be afraid of power and authority. In our culture, we are trained from birth that power and authority are not for women, so standing in this place and claiming that authority can feel wrong, or pushy. But we are talking about your authority, your power. Not power you wield over others but power you hold for yourself to drive your will and authority in the world. No matter your circumstances, you can hold that internal power and know that you and you alone hold the queenly power of your being. What you do with it is up to you.

CHAPTER 15

CLAIM THE TERRITORY

The first terrain that a woman must claim is herself. That can only happen if she has first made the journey through the underworld terrain of the second and third quadrants. As she reemerges into the light of the conscious world in the fourth quadrant, the unknown terrain of the unconscious starts to make sense. What had been a mystery is now a known aspect of the woman on the Queen's Path. She has connected the unconscious material to the conscious world. She is transformed. Her body is her own; she has reclaimed the lost parts of herself that were cleaved from her in the Divide. She has made peace with her Curses and her Marks. This is the last part of the journey. She is ascending the steps to claim her crown.

The step before this one, Embodied Transcendence, is the final critical piece, the culmination of all the others. Reclaiming and asserting the terrain of her own body, the woman on the Queen's Path is now unencumbered. She doesn't have to submit to the authority of culture, job, or her family. If she does acquiesce, it will be because she chooses, for her own purposes. The spell is broken. No one else holds the imperative that moves her anymore. She chooses for herself.

Walking into this place is disorienting. Think about it from the perspective of leaving the Enchanted Forest. When you've been in the forest for a long time, you've become accustomed to the darkness of the canopy covering the woods, even in the daytime. You pick your feet up and high-step through the brush. You wear layers to keep you warm and protect you from the grabby branches of the magical trees. When you stand at the edge with the sunlight hitting your face, you might enjoy the light and the warmth, but it's disorienting. Your eyes will need a little time to adjust to the brightness. You feel a little dizzy taking in the wide expanse beyond the edge of the woods.

Stepping out from the underworld journey of the second and third quadrants is like that. You're moving from the deep world of your inner life to the bright light of the world you share with everyone else. The outer world is now different because your inner world is completely changed. You are no longer a captive. Your self is no longer a debt paid to others. You belong to you. Now you get to make sure the world knows it. You will now live your life from the place of sovereignty. And to do that, you must now make a queendom for yourself. The domain you create doesn't have to be anything fancy or expansive. It can be as simple as your own room, apartment, or job or as vast as your own multinational corporate empire. Either way, the first step toward the crown is to Claim the Territory.

As I mentioned earlier, first you Claim the Territory of the self, which you've already begun in the embodiment step. The next step is for you to expand this domain outward from your body to the immediate expanse of the domain that is yours to control. But what is that immediate space? That is for you to define. Take a few minutes and think about what that space is for you. Have you even considered what your domain is? If you haven't defined it, what would you like it to be? You don't have to worry about it being static. As you grow, your domain will grow too. We don't go through this process only once; we may go through it several times in our lives. Each time you emerge from Embodied Transcendence, you have the opportunity to expand, redefine, or remake your domain.

First Define the Territory

Imagine that the domain you are set to rule is an actual country. Would you like to name it? Is it an island? Does it border another country? What does the terrain look like? How big is it? Below you'll find an example from a workshop I gave for some clients. It's one of my all-time favorites.

The Queendom of Dorothlandia

The sovereign domain of Dorothlandia is a monarchy with holdings that span from the central Alps to a system of small islands in the northern Mediterranean. There is a peninsula that stretches from its alpine borders with France, Switzerland, and Italy, all the way to the sea, where the country extends into fingerlike islands that expand from the peninsula. The mountain regions enjoy cold temperatures where skiing is a regular pastime. The more southern areas enjoy warmer climates similar to France's Cote d'Azur. The beaches are pristine, and the water is a deep cobalt blue. Dorothlandia was first colonized by the expansion of the warring armies of Margereterra and Howardistan. Before becoming its own sovereign domain, all the resources of Dorothlandia were previously dedicated to paying the taxes and dues of Margereterra. This was due to the reparations due to the inhabitants of Dorothlandia following the revolt that secured the nation's independence in the summer of 2005. Today, Dorothlandia is primarily a monarchy that produces artistic exports, including novels, paintings, and documentary films. Its wealth is held in its beautiful natural resources; its financial stability is provided by its creative exports and consulting fees.

As you might imagine, Dorothlandia's monarch is named Dorothy. For the majority of her life, she lived in the shadow of her mother, who was angry and bitter because her marriage ended when Dorothy was only six years old. For the majority of Dorothy's life, she tried to "make it up" to her mom. She tried to be her mom's best friend. She provided for her financially. As an only child, Dorothy had no one else to rely on when it came to her mom. In her 30s, and desperate to have a life separate from her mom, Dorothy started therapy. She had some modest success in her creative life as a television writer but felt that she couldn't risk living out her full creativity while her mother needed financial support. As she traversed the Queen's Path, Dorothy realized that the terrain she needed to claim was more than her job. It was also her right to assert that while she could help her mom, her obligation to herself and her own future required that she not sacrifice her own life to take care of her.

Within a year of confronting her curses, marks, and her own Divide, Dorothy figured out that she had felt the shame of her parents' divorce for most of her life. She couldn't recall if her mom had made her feel guilty when she was a child, but she vividly remembered her constant feelings of shame in high school. Dorothy's mom told her regularly how she had given up her dreams to get married and be a mom, only to be dumped and left to scramble to take care of herself and her daughter. Dorothy felt she owed her mom. The way Dorothy received it, she owed her entire existence to her mom's sacrifice. But that pressure was soon hollowed out in therapy as she worked through the pain and sadness that Dorothy had never let herself feel. She had never been allowed to miss her dad, because he had abandoned her and her mother. She had never felt comfortable asking her mom for anything because her mom had always had to work so hard to pay the bills. Dorothy had never expected her mom to go out of her way, because her mom had given up her dreams of being a journalist to support her daughter. Her mom worked as a secretary at a local university and never let Dorothy forget that the people in her department had been given more opportunities than her mom had ever had, even though she was just as smart and talented.

Dorothy's mom retired, and Dorothy contributed to her income to make sure that her mom always felt safe and appreciated. But Dorothy never told her mom the percentage of her income she was giving to support her. When her mom retired, Dorothy started giving her mom about 30 percent of her income. By the time she came to therapy, it was about 55 percent. Dorothy felt that she couldn't reduce the number because her mother would never survive. She approached her mom's care from the perspective of a little girl desperately trying to prove her worth to an angry parent.

Dorothy's mom wasn't the bad guy here. Dorothy had gotten stuck in the Divide. She wanted to be the MISOR to her mother's reluctant and bitter MIPE. She wanted to make it up to her. But they never discussed it. As she worked through the Queen's Path in therapy, Dorothy disclosed that she'd been living on dollar-store groceries and could not contribute to a retirement account because so much of her income went to her mother's care. Dorothy didn't make a bad living, but she was sending out more than half of her monthly take-home pay to support her mom. It took more than a year for her to build the confidence to talk to her mother about finances. Dorothy was not prepared for what happened next.

Dorothy approached her mom with a great deal of apprehension. She didn't expect that she'd make any huge changes in her mom's life, but maybe she'd be able to get a small percentage of money back to put toward her own retirement. When she told her mom that she needed to make some changes, her mom let out a sigh of relief. Her mom expressed her deep gratitude but admitted that Dorothy had been overcontributing for a long time. They had an honest and transparent conversation about finances, for the first time, and it turned out that Dorothy could reduce her contribution to her mom by about 60 percent and her mom would still be more than fine. What's more, her mom had taken the extra money and had been saving it for years. She wrote Dorothy a check for a substantial sum of money, a good portion of which went to fund a retirement account for Dorothy.

The newfound financial windfall of the big check and the ability to hold on to more of her income left Dorothy feeling a bit overwhelmed. She decided to take a much-needed vacation to Europe, where she had longed to go since she was a little girl. This new freedom also liberated Dorothy's own creativity. She had always wanted to be a novelist. Believing she had to provide an ever-growing sum of money to support her mom, she spent all her spare time on extra hours and projects to help supplement her income. With an extra sum at the end of each month, Dorothy had spare time that could be dedicated to her own creative endeavors.

Dorothlandia became the domain Dorothy invested her time and energy into. She took a series of novel writing classes through a well-respected writing program. She took up painting. Within a year, she completed a first novel and sold it. It didn't win any awards or make her famous, but Dorothy was living *her* life, not the life of the daughter who owed her mom. She hadn't abandoned her mother but had finally been honest with her about what was possible and reasonable. Dorothy's mom agreed. She had never expected her daughter to sacrifice her livelihood or her dreams to take care of her. Once Dorothy had emerged into the fourth quadrant and claimed her territory, she and her mom were both free. Dorothy was the Queen of Dorothlandia, and her mom was no longer the ghost haunting the underworld of Dorothy's life.

How to Define Your Territory

One of the hardest realities in becoming an adult is learning (and accepting) that the only forces that can tell you your destiny are the ones who want to control it . . . and thus, you. Whatever name you give to the divine—God, Goddess, Jesus, Allah, or Hashem— God isn't keeping a hidden book with your secret destiny locked away until you're ready to receive it. Only the deepest part of you can guide you. If there is no place that God is not, then that means that God is in you too. That deep self holds the power to make decisions and choices that challenge you to step into your character. Your destiny is defined by your character, not your job, your bank account, or your family.

Think about it from the perspective of how most people live their lives. They are afraid of falling out of favor with the divine, their family, or their community. Accepting the authority of culture, religion, or an institution is safety. Indeed, for some people in repressive regimes or violent families, it isn't a choice; it's life and death. Those women have to create sovereignty that is more interior than exterior. This can be a delicate balance but one that will make room for the woman's eventual survival and success. If you are in a dangerous situation, know that your acceptance of that external authority is a choice you can make to save yourself now so that full sovereignty can be yours when it is safe to emerge out of that external control. For women who aren't living in peril, we get the choice to accept or reject any external authority. Notice that *choosing* to submit is still exercising sovereignty. It is the choice that makes the difference.

In defining your territory, you will also need to determine what you keep and what you discard of old belief systems, anarchic structures that you may have once dedicated yourself to, and relationships that you may have grown past or that aren't a fit anymore. This doesn't mean you drop them whole cloth. Quite the contrary—you are making conscious decisions about what you want in your life. You are deciding what the boundaries of your domain are and what values rule that domain. If you grew up religious, and that is an important value to you, I am not suggesting that sovereignty demands that you give up your faith. What I am asking is that you approach it with conscious awareness. Your faith is a choice, and it is has even deeper meaning if you dedicate your life to it out of awareness rather than obligation or heritage. This same principle applies whether we're talking about faith, relationships, or work. Consciousness and choice will now be guiding principles. They'll show up in places you never realized could be governed by your own decision making.

Let's start with values. Have you ever sat down and truly defined what is important to you? I don't mean have you ever thought about it . . . I am asking if you've ever written it out and considered it carefully and thoughtfully? Most of us haven't. The first time I did this, I made a bullet list. The more I wrote, the more I wanted to write because defining the motivating principles of my life suddenly became centrally important. In making your own values document, I encourage you to first be completely honest. You don't have to share this with anyone. Also don't be afraid to make mistakes. Expect change! This document will go through multiple iterations and revisions over the course of a lifetime. I would argue it's basically the Constitution of Dorothlandia (insert your country's name here). The first statement, like the U.S. Constitution should set out the governing principles of your domain. Let's look at the preamble to the U.S. Constitution to give us a little guidance.

> *We the People of the United States, to form a more perfect Union, establish Justice, insure domestic Tranquility, provide for the common defense, promote the general Welfare, and secure the Blessings of Liberty to ourselves and our Posterity, do ordain and establish this Constitution for the United States of America.*[1]

The preamble states who is making the statement, for what purposes, and proclaims their intent to establish a governing document for the country that would become the United States. When the document was written, the United States wasn't a reality; it was an idea. If you are American or have studied U.S. history, you know that the Constitution went through several drafts and later also required multiple amendments over the course of the history of the country to ensure equity and parity in the law. Almost all those governing principles can be found in the very simple preamble. Yours doesn't have to be so concise. Let's look at another one.

The preamble to the French Constitution was rewritten after World War II. It is much more verbose than its American counterpart. This document spells out its values very clearly. Following the cataclysmic destruction that France suffered during the war and throughout its occupation by Nazi Germany, that's no surprise. As a result, the rights proclaimed on behalf of the people of France restated and refined the principles that had motivated the French Revolution over 150 years prior:

> *On the morrow of the victory achieved by the free peoples over the regimes that had sought to enslave and degrade humanity, the people of France proclaim anew that each human being, without distinction of race, religion or creed, possesses sacred and inalienable rights. They solemnly reaffirm the rights and freedoms of man and the citizen enshrined in the Declaration of Rights of 1789 and the fundamental principles acknowledged in the laws of the Republic.*
>
> *They further proclaim, as being especially necessary to our times, the political, economic and social principles enumerated below.*

The law guarantees women equal rights to those of men in all spheres.

Any man persecuted in virtue of his actions in favour of liberty may claim the right of asylum upon the territories of the Republic.

Each person has the duty to work and the right to employment. No person may suffer prejudice in his work or employment by virtue of his origins, opinions or beliefs.

All men may defend their rights and interests through union action and may belong to the union of their choice.

The right to strike shall be exercised within the framework of the laws governing it.

All workers shall, through the intermediary of their representatives, participate in the collective determination of their conditions of work and in the management of the work place.

All property and all enterprises that have or that may acquire the character of a public service or de facto monopoly shall become the property of society.

The Nation shall provide the individual and the family with the conditions necessary to their development.

It shall guarantee to all, notably to children, mothers and elderly workers, protection of their health, material security, rest and leisure. All people who, by virtue of their age, physical or mental condition, or economic situation, are incapable of working, shall have the right to receive suitable means of existence from society.

The Nation proclaims the solidarity and equality of all French people in bearing the burden resulting from national calamities.

The Nation guarantees equal access for children and adults to instruction, vocational training and culture. The provision of free, public and secular education at all levels is a duty of the State.

The French Republic, faithful to its traditions, shall conform to the rules of international public law. It shall undertake no war aimed at conquest, nor shall it ever employ force against the freedom of any people.

Subject to reciprocity, France shall consent to the limitations upon its sovereignty necessary to the organization and preservation of peace.

France shall form with its overseas peoples a Union founded upon equal rights and duties, without distinction of race or religion.

The French Union shall be composed of nations and peoples who agree to pool or coordinate their resources and their efforts to develop their respective civilizations, increase their well-being, and ensure their security.

Faithful to its traditional mission, France desires to guide the peoples under its responsibility toward the freedom to administer themselves and to manage their own affairs democratically; eschewing all systems of colonization founded upon arbitrary rule, it guarantees to all equal access to public office and the individual or collective exercise of the rights and freedoms proclaimed or confirmed herein.[2]

Your preamble can be somewhere in between the American and the French versions in length and specificity, but hopefully these give you an idea of how simple or complex you can be in developing a governing document for your territory.

Yes, I actually want you to write this out for yourself. I am not going to ask you to write out an entire constitution, but I do think that defining the values of your domain in writing is very useful. I know you're probably thinking that this is a lot. Writing it all out seems silly. You know what you value! I ask you to give this process the benefit of the doubt. Writing out what you value and why has a way of catalyzing your expectations. When you put it in writing, things become more real, less amorphous. Any lack of structure only serves the forces of external power. Here are a few questions to answer as you develop your preamble.

1. What area of your territory is the most vulnerable? Is it the borders? Or maybe it's the interior?

2. What is the most critical guarantor of security for your territory? Is it a home? Money? A partner? Your children? Creativity? Your career?

3. What breaches to your territory do the most damage? Bad relationships? Insecure finances? Loneliness? Needy friends? Unequal partnerships? Addiction?

4. What does someone who wants to have a relationship with your country need to respect the most? What kinds of values would you require for an alliance? (There will be more about this in the next chapter.)

5. How independent is your territory? Does it require support at this time? Which is more critical? Independence? Positioning toward alliance? Or is your territory dependent right now?

Now, spend a little time to write the preamble to your constitution. What do you want to tell the world about your territory, your Queendom?

Name of Territory: _____

_____

Values:

Authority & Responsibility

_____

_____

Financial

_____

_____

_____

_____

_____

Creative

_____

_____

_____

_____

_____

Governing

_____
_____
_____
_____
_____

Decision Making

_____
_____
_____
_____
_____

Other

_____
_____
_____
_____
_____

Why the Values Matter Now

You've been through the darkest part of the Queen's Path. You've had the proverbial snot knocked out of you, and now you're creating a new world for yourself. You've survived being Cursed and Marked, Blind, Divided, the Hunt, and Abjection. You've sorted through the rendered pieces and chosen (Choice) what to reintegrate into your life. Finally, you've reclaimed the body, wondering in the marvel of you (Embodied Transcendence). You now get to create the life you want. This requires a container. Having a container for your territory is like having a glass to pour water into. If you're thirsty, you *can* drink from the faucet or pour the water onto the table or floor to lap up. But it's more enjoyable, controllable, and sanitary to pour it into a glass to drink from. The container of your territory tells you exactly what the boundaries of your domain are. It also gives you the possibility of concentrating the energy in a particular place rather than spilling it into other people's domains where your goals, effort, and love will be in service to someone else, watered down, or negated.

The values you define mark the boundaries of the territory you are creating and claiming for yourself. Being a therapist, I talk about boundaries a lot. It's one of my favorite things to discuss with my clients because it's a place that most people never get to discuss. It's wonderful to work with clients to expand their tool kits. Boundaries aren't what most people think. They aren't all hard, rigid walls that keep people out. The most effective boundaries are flexible and well-discussed and don't feel risky. They have available ways in and clear consequences when they're breached.

Thinking about the borders of your territory as the boundaries you would like for the container of your queendom makes me think of the way we talk about boundaries. The French word for *border*, like the one you cross at the edge of a country is *frontière*, similar to the English word, *frontier*. The etymology of this word is relevant: "the front of the land that faces the outside or in war, the enemy." Your borders create the container of your territory. Your territory concentrates your power. From this territory you create the seat of sovereignty.

CHAPTER 16

GATHER
THE TRIBE

Now that you've claimed the territory of your Queendom, the next step secures the allies and collaborators that will help support you. No territory exists without support and alliances. A woman can best realize her queendom with other sovereigns who recognize her authority over her own life. Without allies and support, we are all at risk of being subjects to those who would keep us in a subordinate position. Gathering the tribe is about finding the like-minded women and allies who will shore us up when we feel sad or exhausted. It is about building a structure that supports us and that permits us to support other women. By doing so, we create and sustain networks of Queens and their domains. The frontiers of those united Queens will be the power that stands up to the efforts to disempower women individually and collectively. The number of allies and supporters doesn't have to be enormous. The agenda doesn't have to be political. A handful of good friends and formal connections with other women is enough.

The brilliant 2022 Oscar-winning film *Women Talking* shows the power of Gathering the Tribe. In this film, director Sarah Polley uses a gathering of women in an isolated religious community of Mennonites to raise the issue of how women respond to systemic abuse. The film is based on real events from a book of the same name by Canadian author Miriam Toews. The wives, daughters, and even the smallest children are being drugged and raped by the men in the community. The women and girls wake with no memory but are covered in bruises. Their isolation, inability to read, and ignorance of the world around them make them particularly vulnerable to being overwhelmed by the men and the rigid rules of the commune. In the film, the women gather to discuss and vote on whether they should stay and do nothing, allowing the abuse to continue; stay and fight, and thus possibly break the rules they consider sacred; or leave and risk being on their own but maintaining both their individual integrity and their collective faith. If you haven't seen the film, I highly recommend it. It makes profound and realistic depictions of all the ways that women struggle with our place in society. Spoiler alert, if you don't want to know what happens in *Women Talking*, stop reading now—go watch the film and come right back.

The women meet in the hayloft of a barn while the men go to town to handle a legal matter. The women vote by making marks on a chalkboard, and the initial vote is a tie between staying to fight and leaving. The women elect three families to discuss the situation and reach a consensus, and the other women agree they will adhere to the decision made by this smaller group of representatives. There are several women who are angry and who want to stay and fight. Motivated by a need for justice to be served, their mothers and grandmothers eventually talk the angry women out of this stance. They do this by acknowledging the individual pain of the angry women, the righteousness in their anger, and their sorrow at having been complicit in other matters that made this level of abuse possible. In the end, the women decide to leave the colony. They will take their children with them, including the boys up to age 15, but no boy 12 or older will be forced to go with his mother. The women of the colony decide on sovereignty together.

Another one of my favorite stories of women forging connections to uphold their own sovereignty is in the Greek play *Lysistrata*. In this story by the Greek playwright Aristophanes, the women of warring Greek states band together to deny sex to the men until they agree to finally end the misery of the Peloponnesian War.[1] The play is a bawdy comedy, making fun of everyone in the effort to make a point about the cost of war and the reasoning some people will engage in to keep it going. To be fair, Aristophanes was no feminist, but the depiction of women aligning their interests and efforts to bring about change is as relevant today as it was 2,500 years ago.

We see this in movies like the 1985 version of *The Color Purple*, where, in the final scenes of the film, having claimed the territory of her home and business, Celie Johnson gathers her family of choice around her. It comes together in one long and almost silent scene, where Celie and all the people she's loved stand around on the porch, in the field, staring at the strange sight of a car coming down her long driveway. This finally brings the story full circle as her sister and children stand in the driveway, their colorful clothes flagging their arrival from Africa. Celie is finally reunited with her children and sister after decades of separation. The same theme can be seen in every film with a female protagonist. If she achieves sovereignty (as we've discussed some stories end in Abjection), then she will Gather the Tribe around her. We can look at Patty Jenkins's 2017 *Wonder Woman*. Diana Prince is surrounded by her closest friends and allies, eventually joining the Justice League. It is true of Greta Gerwig's 2023 *Barbie* movie. Barbie leaves Barbieland to live in the real world. There, she is supported by her human friends Gloria and Sasha in starting her life as a "real woman" in Los Angeles.

Whether you look in the works of ancient Greece or the blockbuster movies of the last several years, you see the same model: women supporting other women. We must stand together and shore up other women so that all of us enjoy the crown of sovereignty. Who are your supporters? While having close friends is great, it doesn't have to start with friends. It can start with organizations you support. Perhaps it is through an organization like Women in Media, United Methodist Women, Hadassah, the National Organization for Women (NOW), the International Alliance of Women, a local Goddess Circle, a Red Tent meet-up, or any other group or organization that promotes women supporting other women. Maybe it's in a local chapter organization that does work for victims of domestic violence or girls in foster care. What matters is that the values align with what is important to you and that it connects you with like-minded women who want sovereignty for themselves and other women.

In your relationships with friends, sisters, daughters, or co-workers, where do you see people's sovereignty being compromised? At work? Is it at school? What about in public spaces? What about in private organizations? Do you want to have an influence there? Consider that your well-being is also connected to the well-being of other women around you. When you stand in your sovereignty, you give other women permission to do the same.

Recognizing the Allies

People who don't believe in women's sovereignty are not reliable allies. Sadly, there are many women who, whether they admit it or not, support the subjugation of women. In doing the research for this book, I attended a debate put on by an organization called the Free Press. This group of journalists tends to lean more to the right than I am comfortable with, but I cannot deny they have uncovered some egregious abuses of political power on both the left and the right. The debate was entitled "Has the Sexual Revolution Failed?" It brought together very loud and erudite voices on the right and the left. Representing the right were podcaster Anna Khachiyan and British writer Louise Perry; on the left, writer and founder of Ex-Muslims of North America Sarah Haider and musician Grimes.

Right out of the gate, all four women basically negated the premise of the debate. These four women enjoyed a life made possible by the sexual revolution, regardless of where they sat on the political spectrum. None of them were so blind as to say that they weren't the beneficiaries of policies and practices that made women's sovereignty possible. I was familiar with the arguments made by Sarah Haider and Grimes. To be fair, I wasn't there to have my own point of view reinforced. The most interesting arguments were made by the women representing the right. Anna Khachiyan basically argued that the question wasn't whether or not the sexual revolution had failed, but if it was over. She argued that the sexual revolution was over and that women had won! She argued that we should proceed with the assumption of our sovereignty, not spend our time bemoaning the lagging influence of patriarchy. Louise Perry also offered that while there was no doubt that women had benefited from the impact that political feminists had fought for, was there anything to look at in our collective past that might be instructive? Have we rejected the advice of our foremothers simply because they are our own mothers and grandmothers? Shouldn't we consider the possibility that they have wisdom to impart? I can't argue with either of their arguments—they are worth thoughtful consideration.

Throughout the debate, the women rarely made arguments against each other. They didn't discuss whether or not women were capable; they were the obvious examples of women's capacity for complex thought and powerful rhetoric. They discussed whether women's rights needed to be fought for, and in that, I would have to argue that the women on the left held sway—women's rights weren't secure. The overturning of *Roe v. Wade* in the United States and the stance of politicians around the country who were waging war on women's reproductive rights won the night for me. But the discussions led by Anna Khachiyan and Louise Perry greatly moved me. They weren't saying that women should go back to the kitchen, not work, or not contribute to society. They were arguing that we should not avoid the difficult discussion of what is happening to men in our culture and to include the possibility that the fight for the equality of women may be over at least in terms of the expectation that women are as capable as men in any endeavor where they are given the opportunity to learn, train, and prepare in the same manner.

While I bristled at some of the humor shared throughout the night, neither the right and left side participants, nor the evening's host, the Free Press founder, Bari Weiss, left me thinking that they were anti-women. While we might disagree on some of the ideals or maybe even the methods, I'd call all of them sisters in the cause for women's sovereignty. That being said, the theatre was alive with the laughter and frequent random professions of love from right-wing supporters, mostly toward Anna Khachiyan. After the debate was posted online, the comments were not as generous. Online I saw misogyny in full bloom, mostly from angry people, though to be fair, there were some excellent comments. The sheer and expected offensiveness of some of the online participants was some of the most rancid I've encountered. It speaks to the political moment. The divisive issues of the sexual division of labor and the expectations that natural is the same as right and good are alive and well.

Engaging the Frontiers

Looking back at the values that you established in the last chapter, can you use these to determine the places you want to find like-minded women as potential allies? What were your values? Were they based on something important to you? A role? Like your job? Or motherhood? What about the values you wrote down that related to any important political views? Or perhaps you listed values that had to do with health or lifestyle issues. Maybe they had to do with religion or cultural concerns that are important to you. Go find your sisters! Support them; support their organizations. Plan dinner parties or salons and invite people over. Host meetings of people at your home or in places like local coffee shops. Create groups to work through this book together! Support one another, recognizing that we are not all alike, and we aren't going to agree on everything. But one thing is certain: every single one of us deserves to enjoy our own sovereignty. No one should be a subject to another person. Not. A. Single. One. Of. Us.

Exercise

Who are your allies? What do they look like? How do they speak? Where can you find them? My guess is that there are some that you have only tenuous connections to. Can you spend some time identifying who some of these women are? You could create a group of Queens who are ready for their own queendoms. Gather them to your home and sign an accountability alliance. You could read this book together and map out your own path to the crown.

CHAPTER 17

CROWNED

You rule! Now you can relax . . . sort of. You're putting that crown on your head and beginning to live fully in your queendom. That's not to say that you're going to be sitting atop your throne while ordering the peasants to bring you bon-bons as you shout, "Off with their heads!" That's not ruling; that's dominating. Ruling is more fun, more collaborative, and more difficult. From this point forward, your sovereignty is yours. No one gets to take it from you . . . and they will try.

Wearing your crown means that you have accepted your worth. Think about the Queens you already know and respect. Some of the most well-known include Michelle Obama, Taylor Swift, Malala Yousafzai, Oprah Winfrey, and Beyoncé Knowles. No one tells these women what to do, how to be, or who can come into their lives. They live in their sovereignty every day. Living in that place requires some new skills. Some of these will have come through the work you've done to get you here, and some of them will be new.

Sitting in your sovereignty will undoubtedly make you a target for other people's negativity. That's their projection and insecurity, not yours. And while it may be frustrating, make you sad, or create hurt feelings, it's not your problem. How other people see you is none of your concern. You can never be good enough to escape other people's projections. Hold on for one second and let that sink in further:

You can never be so good that you escape other people's projections.

That's a lesson we must learn to overcome the Divide. There are people who benefit from the Divide—they typically want only their way to persist. They don't care if it means that other people are hurt. They can only see their struggles, and they only care about their outcomes. Those people aren't worth fighting or working with. Sometimes we have no choice, in the workplace or in politics, for example. But that marker in someone means you will always have to watch your back with them.

In the next few pages, I'm going to include some of the most critical skills necessary for reigning your queendom. This isn't about power over other people; this is about power over yourself. Your domain is all about you. You needn't worry about what other Queens are up to. As you go through this list, you may think of other skills you want to develop—that is wonderful. Feel free to augment this list for your own purposes. Your queendom. Your rules. Your skills.

The Queenly Talents

Kindness

You may remember from earlier in the book that we discussed "being nice" and how dangerous it is for women. The experience of being nice is about being small, diminutive, and not rocking the boat. Being kind is very different. It is giving difficult news with as much sensitivity as possible. It is timing your actions for the least harm. It is remaining aware that there is another person at the other end of a decision. Kindness also means listening to others attentively, which also happens to be the next talent. It differs from niceness in all these ways. Niceness is almost always about keeping the status quo. Kindness is about being authentic while still being concerned with the well-being of those you care about. That is not the same as providing for their feelings over your own.

Listening

This lost art is a challenge for many people. To truly listen means giving your attention to the other person. It means to tune in to their feelings, observe their body language, and stoke your own curiosity about what is happening for or to them. Listening is not waiting for important concepts and jumping in with your opinion. That is buffoonish, coarse, and dismissive. A Queen listens so that she can not only understand her allies, friends, and strangers but also have a full understanding of the situation before her. She is curious because it serves her to have as much investment and information as possible. Knowing those around her, whether in her family or her work, deepens her connections to others and promotes loyalty from them. This type of loyalty is forged in deep understanding and compassion, not necessity and insecurity.

Skills Assessment

Knowing what you're good at and what you're not is critical in maintaining your domain. If you hate to do any financial tasks, then try and hire someone or take a class. If you hate to cook, or are terrible at it, get a meal plan. We live in a world where it is possible and relatively simple to find capable, affordable people to help with tasks that we aren't good at or don't want to do. Need help with keeping your body healthy? Classes, meal plans, workout clubs. Need help with cleaning? Housekeepers. Need help with writing? Graduate students are great for this. Need help with managing money or a budget? Even your bank or credit union will have resources. Look for people who can augment your skills. Don't let fear of not having absolute control over everything keep you slaving away at the things that you dislike or aren't talented in.

It's important, though, to notice that as Queen, you get to assess the skills of those with whom you work or engage in projects. If your co-worker Shelly is an excellent designer and a terrible public speaker, it doesn't help either of you if you don't assess those skills. Either you take on the public speaking role, find someone better, or help Shelly develop those skills. If you're great at public speaking and only a modest designer, then own that reality and commit to it publicly. Give Shelly the credit for her talent—that's being an ally to another Queen. There is no harm at all in elevating people who have more skill in an area than you do. This builds trust in the people around you and shows that you are an honest broker. It also frees your mental, emotional, and psychological overhead. If you don't have to do or be everything, you can create a robust interdependence with other Queens rather than a fragile, brittle independence or an enmeshed, mushy, co-dependence.

Character Assessment

There is probably no question more critical than this one as you take the crown: Who is with you? Do you know them? Are they trustworthy? Have you discerned what they're getting out of being in your company? Do they benefit in some way that you haven't considered? There are a lot of people who want to be adjacent to power. When you have control over yourself and your destiny, people often project onto you that you have some secret power that they don't have. They act as though you have access to some special information that they don't. The truth is, of course, that the power you have mastered can be available to anyone who works hard to master themselves. This simple mystery often eludes people.

Many years ago, I ran an organization that served people in the goddess movement. I had a collaborator who had at times been a great friend to me, and at other times she would lose her cool and either blow up at me or make very poor decisions. The members of this organization would frequently come to me and tell me about mistakes my colleague had made or the ways that she had made them uncomfortable. Sometimes she had mistreated people. I often found myself defending her to others. I frequently confronted her, though this was not always met with generosity from her.

I realized too late that I had more loyalty than sense. It wasn't until she turned on *me* that I saw what they were talking about. She was vicious when she felt insecure and intimidated people to get her way. I should have done a better job listening to what people were telling me. When one person tells you something, it's okay to question it. Two is not a pattern . . . but three is. If you see a pattern in someone, believe your observations. The stories we tell ourselves about behavior are rarely the full story. But behavior matters. Why someone does what they do is ultimately less important than the fact that they do it. If someone's behavior is a problem, it is kind to try and understand why they behave that way. But kindness and forgiveness are not how you manage someone else's (or your own) unacceptable behavior. You must hold people accountable for their behavior, even as you have compassion for their reasons.

Patience

Rarely when someone is in a rush, a bad situation, or under pressure do they benefit from quick decision making. In almost every situation, there is a benefit to taking a pause, even if momentary, to get as centered as possible. Desperation serves only the person with the upper hand. Patience is necessary when you're a Queen because you have an obligation to think about things that are bigger than the "right now." Your reputation, financial security, and sense of self are more important than the resolution of a quick decision.

The best way to learn to cultivate patience is to do so when the stakes are low. Think of it as practice. If you are in a restaurant with friends and everyone has ordered, can you take your time? Ask questions? Maybe try it out as an experiment. When you do this, notice how uncomfortable it makes people around you. People long for certainty; they would rather be certain about a negative situation than live with the uncertainty of either good or bad. Most people suffer more because they wind up in unpleasant or unhealthy situations that could have been avoided if they'd felt safe to take their time. I often talk to my clients about whether they feel they have enough data to make a decision. If they don't have enough data, then the answer is, "Wait for data." When you have enough data, decide.

If you feel your own anxiety creeping up, ask yourself what is the worst thing that could happen in the absence of a decision? Is it that someone else will be upset or frustrated? Why is their frustration or upset your responsibility? This is an important place to find any lurking subjectivity. That isn't to say that in important relationships we don't have responsibility to those closest to us. But if you're always the one responsible for feelings or you find yourself always doing the work of regulating your emotions or expectations because someone else cannot, then that is a *big* problem.

When you feel pressured to make a decision too quickly, take a breath and offer to come back to the decision tomorrow. In the meantime, observe not only your process but that of the people around you. Are you (or they) frustrated? Angry? Is a pause inappropriate? Is what is being asked too much? Not enough? If you struggle to regulate your own anxiety, take up a mindfulness practice, like box breathing. Or choose something a little more focused like the Havening Technique, which pairs a physical movement with a distraction technique. If those don't feel right, find or invent another method to help you feel more grounded as you manage your feelings. Reflect on the decisions and slow down your thoughts and feelings. Waiting for data is never a bad idea.

Strategy

Have you ever had to play a game that required that you look ahead? What about something like chess, where you need to hold several possibilities in mind at once? Developing the capacity for strategy begins with taking in the possibilities before you as dispassionately as possible. That means that while you are examining them, you have to be careful not to show too many of your own cards. By withholding any evidence of your excitement, fear, concern, or dread, you can more easily move the machinery toward your benefit. Remember that the person who is the most patient has the greatest advantage. The benefits of almost any situation flow toward the person who has the greatest toleration for uncertainty.

This doesn't mean you aren't invested. It means that you have the most coverage. So, if you know that the house you want to buy has 10 other interested buyers, then you have to figure out how to slow the process down to your advantage. If you can't slow it down to your advantage, then you get to decide if it is worth the price being asked. If there is real value, whether real in terms of price or the house being the one you've always wanted, then weigh for yourself what your maximum price is in advance. The same goes whether you're buying a house, car, business, or anything of value. You get to look at the twists and turns that may surface and how each of those will impact you and your goals. Decide in advance your risk tolerance. Don't get pulled into someone else's power struggle. The person who has the most power in any situation is the one who can most easily walk away.

Action

When do you take action? When you are ready, of course. That means that you act decisively—neither impulsively nor too late. If you take no action, do so with intention. For example, you need a new car. Your old car is in working order, but you have a particular price point you need to reach. The best time to buy a new car is typically in December and January. This is especially true for a vehicle that has a model change. If you get a pushy salesperson, don't be afraid to walk away. You are the person with the power in this situation because you're the buyer. If you have a down payment and good credit, you're in an even better position.

Know where you stand so that you can take decisive action while maintaining your position as much as possible. If you know you are not in the most favorable position but have to take some action, get the best understanding of the circumstances possible before making the call. Don't let anger or frustration cost you positioning. Be honest with yourself about where you stand. If you're the new person in the workplace, you haven't yet built enough social capital to make demands or ask for favors. Act with awareness, intention, and understanding. And as much as possible, use diplomacy in your efforts with others. Diplomacy requires that we have as broad and global a view as possible. What does the situation look like up close? What about from 20 feet away? What about from the other party's point of view? What about from the 30,000-foot view downward? Try and give yourself the opportunity to look at any given situation from as many points of view as possible. This will take some practice at first.

Diplomacy

The work of a diplomat is to convey meaning with as much subtlety as possible to be effective but as much directness as is warranted to accomplish the necessary goals. Being a diplomat means to use all the other tools in this list as well. Being a diplomat also means to bring some value to the table in negotiating. To cut to the chase, let me add that I also like to steer people away from using the word *compromise*. When approaching any discussion or negotiation, if one party or both parties feel that there will be compromises, it usually means they go in with defenses up. Compromising almost always makes people feel like they are at a disadvantage. If you know ahead of time what is critical to you, then a negotiation doesn't have to be negative. Attending to any interaction from a diplomatic perspective will benefit you the most when you know what's important to you and hopefully what's most important to the other people involved. By approaching from the perspective of kindness, sovereignty, and respect, you can make decisions based on what's best for you without being inconsiderate of the others involved.

Distress Tolerance

When therapists talk about someone having flexibility, we are often discussing their capacity to tolerate frustration or distress. While it may seem like a simple thing, it is quite complex. I once was in a couple's counseling session with a couple I had been seeing for months. I had struggled to make sense of why they were in therapy. In session, they seemed like they had a good rapport with one another and were committed to improving their communication skills. Their patterns of arguing were particularly impressive, with each one making effort to see the other person's point of view. One day, I disagreed with a point one of the pair made. I described their respective positions as quite different. In this one instance, Josh was immediately hurt by the things his fiancée was saying. When Diana heard a criticism in this situation, she seemed to take it more in stride. She was being very thoughtful, where he was reactionary. What was soon clear was that Josh could not tolerate the possibility that I didn't agree with him. He exclaimed that she thought and felt exactly the same as he did, or she wouldn't behave in that way. When I offered that perhaps she didn't, he got angry and stormed out of my office. Josh couldn't tolerate the distress he felt in confronting the idea of the difference between them and the possibility that the authority figure in the room, me, had not agreed—or that I hadn't remained 100 percent neutral. What came out of this was the realization that when there was a power struggle between them, the weight of my opinion seemed to be used as a tiebreaker. This for me felt like a challenging and uncomfortable position as the therapist. My goal is usually to behave in a universal approach trying to look at every situation as dispassionately as possible. That's not always possible. I'm just as human as my patients, and try as I might, my own beliefs will creep in from time to time, for better or worse.

The important takeaway from this encounter with Josh and Diana was that they had different capacities for distress tolerance. Josh had to work much harder for it. Diana's was more easily accessed. The "why" of that distinction isn't as important as the reality that they had different comfort levels with unresolved emotions. Josh needed resolution more quickly than Diana. For them, we had to come up with a scale. If he was at an 8/10 in distress tolerance and she was at a 3/10, they needed to wait until Josh was more regulated. And the two of them had to be careful not to escalate and make his worse. Also, Josh had to work with his individual therapist to identify and work on noticing his frustration earlier.

What is your level of distress tolerance? To sit on the throne of sovereignty, you will be best served by expanding this skill, no matter how amazing (or not) you are at it already.

Discipline

Most people admire discipline. I cannot tell you how many times clients will come in, especially around the beginning of the year, and bemoan their lack of motivation. They want strategies at having more discipline. They want to wake up earlier and work out six days a week. They want to recycle everything. Most of my clients bemoan their lack of motivation as the culprit. The mistake that most people make is that they conflate discipline with motivation. I am not motivated to get up and write at five in the morning. I am disciplined because I've trained myself to do so. I dread getting up early; discipline means I get my ass out of bed and do the things I am not motivated to do. I don't always succeed. I may get out of bed at seven, but I still write, even if it's only for 15 minutes. Discipline means paying attention to your body as you feel anger rising within. Discipline means not eating the fourth cookie when they taste so good. But be attentive—motivation is different. Being motivated generally means we look forward to something. It feels good. We want to do it. The commonality between the two is that they have the same or similar results. People often feel good when they've accomplished some task that took either discipline or motivation. But the result shouldn't be conflated with the means of getting there. If you feel good either way at the end, you can use that as motivation. But they are not the same thing. Discipline is doing something no matter how motivated (or not) you are.

The Crown

If we look at popular culture, whether it's movies, video games, or novels, the end of a woman's sovereignty narrative almost always has some symbolic crown. It is either an actual crown, like in 2017's

Wonder Woman or 2014's *Maleficent*. Or it can be metaphorical; in *Barbie* the eponymous character is sporting a pair of Birkenstocks. In 1985's *The Color Purple*, both sisters Celie and Nettie have their hair braided in intricate crown braids. In *Legally Blonde*, we find Elle Woods as the class speaker at her law school graduation, the traditional mortar board atop her head. What is the symbol of your queendom? It can be a crown, a throne, or maybe a flag. I personally like crowns because of the completeness of the symbolism. I own myself. I am a Queen. You are a Queen. I have sovereignty over myself; I am beholden to no one. You have sovereignty over yourself. You are beholden to no one but yourself.

The Final Gift

A Queen never doubts her worth. Her confidence and self-love emerges not from a negative place of being above or over others, but from having done her work. She has earned her seat on the throne. Having sovereignty over oneself is about owning your own life and your own imperative. You don't give away what gives you meaning in your life to satisfy someone else's whim or taste. Your love, dedication, service, talent, and gifts are not for someone else to plunder. You decide what is important and belongs in your domain; you don't depend on others to do that for you.

If you'd like a symbol and are so inclined, perhaps the most appropriate gift you can give yourself is your very own tiara or crown. It needn't be something you actually wear on your head. Maybe it's a beautiful crown that sits on a pillow on your desk. It could be a piece of art that hangs on your wall. It could be a ring in the shape of a crown. I've seen beautiful bracelets and necklaces sporting the word *Queen* on them. It can be anything to remind you that you have made this journey and have come through the Queen's Path as a whole person. You have made your world better. In improving the world for one woman, it is improved for all of us. Your journey matters to me. It makes me better. And hopefully mine makes the world safer and richer for you. If every one of us stands arm in arm in our sovereignty, the world will be a beautiful place for women and for everyone in the world who may not realize that they matter. By promoting sovereignty for ourselves, we show everyone else, women and men alike, that it is not just possible, but also necessary that we as individuals own ourselves. We are what sovereignty can look like. Sovereignty for everyone starts with sovereignty for you. Work that crown. You've earned it.

CONCLUDING
THIS ROUND
ALONG THE PATH

Welcome, Your Majesty! You have successfully navigated the Queen's Path! The crown is yours. Sovereignty imbues every step you take. Now that you have entered this rarefied space, you will see things very differently. You will see other women and maybe even a few men tripping as they progress through the same steps you've trod. They can't be saved from the path. They can't skip any of the steps. And they can't make the journey from a theoretical perspective. Every one of us must experience it for ourselves. You can help someone else by steering them away from the place where the dragon hides its treasures or from where the troll haunts the base of the bridge. But they must place their own feet along the steps; it is what brings them to sovereignty.

The Queen's Path is an archetypal structure, which means that it has an architecture that impacts everyone, even though each person's experience will be their own unique journey. It's like a bridge. To cross a river, almost everyone uses the bridge. Whether you're walking or in a vehicle determines part of the journey. What kind of car you're in, how fast you're going, and where in the car you're seated will color your experience of the bridge, as will the behavior of other drivers. Everyone has a "bridge" experience, but no two crossings are the same. In addition, you may get to cross this bridge or multiple bridges in your life. The Queen's Path is something you'll navigate more than once. But now that you've made the circuit once, the steps will be much easier for you to recognize next time.

What you do with your sovereignty is your decision. That is what sovereignty is all about. The most amazing (and challenging) aspect of discovering my own sovereignty has been understanding that my life is my own; it is not *for other people.* There is no one who can give me permission to live my own wild, royal, or insane life. How I live it is a matter of my own choice. I presume my own power from the get-go. I no longer assume that there is someone from whom I need permission, blessing, or validation. That makes every decision a very different experience from where I was before going through the Queen's Path.

When I was trapped in my role as a MIPE trying to fit into the MISOR track, I negotiated submission everywhere. As a MIPE, submission was not my natural way of being in the world. I used it as a tool to get needs met, or to fit in, but it always felt completely foreign to me. With sovereignty, I no longer see my decisions as negotiations for permission to have power. Instead, I make decisions about how I use my power, not whether or not I get to have it. That has meant different career decisions, choosing friendships differently, and navigating a marriage as an equal, not a subject. It has made all the difference in the world.

What will you do with your sovereignty? How will it impact you to navigate your world differently? Does it feel foreign to have power? Maybe even unsafe? That is completely normal. It feels odd at first, like someone who has been bound all her life suddenly noticing that there is no chain holding her to the ground. True sovereignty can feel like being untethered at first. But once it starts to become part of how you make decisions, you won't tolerate anything less. Your authenticity will become dependent on your sovereignty. And that, my dear Queen, is a very good thing.

I will also offer a word of warning: Whether you have been a compliant MISOR or a willful MIPE, people will resist you asserting your sovereignty. Don't be put off by this. It is normal that people who have experienced you one way will be uncomfortable with change. Treat it tenderly but firmly. Your sovereignty is not up for discussion. That doesn't mean that you can't listen or learn about the other person's experience or desire. Remember that sovereignty is not tyranny. Sovereignty doesn't mean ruling your life with an iron fist and forcing everyone around you to bow to your will. Sovereignty is recognizing your own power and coming to every encounter with the presumption that your will matters. No one gets to decide for you unless you agree to let them.

There will be people who want to cast you in your sovereignty not as a Queen but as a MIPE. Let them. They don't know what they're talking about. Rule your domain magnanimously and let the haters and finger-pointers tire themselves out with their outrage. You know your worth and what you have had to learn and do to claim your sovereignty. The only reason they want to make you a villain is because of their own fear of being cast in that role. They are still stuck in the Divide, and they are the only ones who can get themselves out of it. They are on their own journey, and most of them will fight to protect the system that keeps people in submission. They feel safer in a role than with themselves.

If you have always been a MISOR, you will probably have an easier time negotiating with people but will find it more difficult to stand in your power. Don't back away from your sovereignty. Assert it firmly. The people around you may struggle with this at first, but they will eventually get it if they are capable. They may struggle because they fear you having power will mean you want power over them. Just treat them as your sovereign peer and move along your path. A Queen doesn't bow to anyone else, especially someone who wants to rule others as a tool to compensate for their own insecurity. If they matter to you, feel free to introduce them to the idea of sovereignty. If they aren't that important, then perhaps your time as friends, co-workers, lovers, or partners has come to an end. If you have been a MIPE, sovereignty will sometimes feel familiar, but it will force you to soften. You cannot rule as a sovereign with only a desire for power as your guiding light. As a MIPE, you have likely been denied power and feel safer when you make your own decisions. Be mindful that power is not the same as sovereignty.

Whether you began your journey as a MISOR or a MIPE, you have made the same journey as every other woman who has found her way along the Queen's Path. Sovereignty means you have authority, responsibility, and grace. You have found the power in your being, faced and reclaimed the parts that culture would have you deny, and done the challenging work of claiming your domain and gathering your tribe. You have survived the Hunt and faced Abjection and Choice. If you feel that there is any place on this journey that you need to go back and revisit, do so. The steps are here for you to work through. You may find that one or more steps show up for you more than others; that is okay. We all have aspects that are more challenging. I have found that the third quadrant is the place where most women revisit. Once you start excavating in the deepest places, you're sure to find more aspects of you that long for the light of your attention. It's like an archaeological site. Once you find one artifact, you're likely to find a whole lot more as you dig deeper.

If you have not gathered your tribe, perhaps start a Queen's Group. You can work through this book or just meet once a month or quarter to visit with each other. Perhaps offer a theme to help organize discussions of sovereignty and any royal challenges you may face. Compare with other Queens. You're sure to have similar issues. Working with other women and forming alliances is a great way to help bolster your own sovereignty. Women need other women who assert their sovereignty as peers and role models.

Just because you assert your sovereignty doesn't mean that men, patriarchal institutions, and even other women are going to just lie down and say, "Oh! That's right, you're a Queen now. By all means, Your Majesty, go forward." I wish it were that simple. No, you will have to defend your sovereignty, just like any monarch must defend their domain. But it will be worth it. You will be much clearer about what you allow in and out of your life. You will know that your power is your own, and that though people and institutions may want to take it from you, it is your divine right to wholly own yourself.

This journey has been the most challenging and rewarding of my life. I am delighted that you have found the way to claiming your own crown. I am humbled to be the one to have rediscovered this pattern. It is my discovery but not my invention. The Queen's

Path has been here all along, just waiting for us to find it. The path is not new, but it is newly uncovered, so it might be unfamiliar to those around you. That's okay. The more of us who reclaim our sovereignty, the more comfortable those we love will become. My work has been to uncover the stones along the path. Your work is to walk it and find your own unique queendom. The Queen's Path it is not mine; it is ours. As women, we have a new way of defining our path to freedom, security, and power. Sovereignty is both the path and the destination. Use it wisely and share it, especially with women you love.

Long may you reign!

APPENDIX

Queen's Path Narrative Example

Wonder Woman (2017) by Patty Jenkins

Quadrant I

Remember that the first quadrant is part of the World of Visible Power and Form. In both Quadrant I and IV, the main character can tell where the external power is. In Quadrant I, she doesn't have it; it resides with someone else—in this instance, her family and the queendom of Themiscyra, Paradise Island, home of the Amazons.

In the first quadrant, we learn who Diana is. We are introduced to her in the present, working as a fashionable curator in the Louvre in Paris. She sets us up for the Once Upon a Time (OUT) from her comfortable space in the present. The first quadrant will tell us what her own personal Once Upon a Time was. It will tell us the story of her beginnings and reveal what was lurking at the edges.

This quadrant is titled Undifferentiated or Chimaeric because nothing is set in stone yet; the journey won't have a shape until Diana is set on either the path of the MISOR or MIPE. Her mother, Queen Hippolyta, would like to keep her home, living out a life of protection and not fulfilling the role she was destined for. In the first quadrant, we will learn alongside Diana that she has a curse and mark that make her different from all the other Amazons. We will also see that Diana and her mother, Queen Hippolyta, who acts as her first mirror, are both blind. Diana is blind to her true nature as a goddess among Amazons. And Hippolyta is blind to the reality that Diana cannot hide from her true nature.

1. Once Upon a Time

We meet Diana of Themiscyra as a bounding seven- or eight-year-old girl. She is running through the streets of her mother's domain. She is admiring all the warriors in training and joyfully imitating them. The head of her mother's army, General Antiope, notices Diana imitating the moves of the warriors as they engage in their various forms of training. But soon we see Diana's tutor is looking for her, and when she spots her surveying the field of warriors in training, she calls out her name. Diana knows she's in trouble and takes off running, only to be (literally) caught by her mother.

2. Cursed and Marked

Antiope trains Diana in secret, and when her mother, Hippolyta, finds out, she is at first angry. But Antiope reminds Hippolyta that they cannot protect Diana from her destiny. She is not like the other Amazons. This reveals for the first time any knowledge that Diana is "different." Hippolyta redoubles and tells General Antiope that she'll have to train Diana harder; she'll have to make sure that Diana becomes a better soldier than even Antiope herself.

3. Blind

Diana is blind to her true nature and to her ultimate power. When she is training with the other Amazons and the general, she finds herself being challenged by Antiope, who is trying to get her to do more, be more vicious, and to take her skills and the possibility of battle much more seriously. At one point, Diana takes a defensive posture, kneeling down and crossing her arms to block a blow. When she does, an unknown power emerges from her, evidently catalyzed by this stance. It sends Antiope flying across the practice field. Diana is so shaken, she leaves training. She finds herself on the beach, where she sees Steve Trevor's plane crash into the sea.

Diana and all the Amazons are blind to what is happening in the world. Diana rushes out to the water to save Steve. But soon the island is under siege as the Germans follow Steve Trevor to the shores of Themiscyra. In addition, Diana is naive and believes that the god of war, Aries, is actively responsible for the world of war that Steve Trevor introduces to her world. She isn't wrong, but she is blind to how the world works and why the people around her dismiss her.

Quadrant II

We are now crossing the threshold from the World of Visible Power and Form (the Upper Hemisphere) into the World of Invisible Forces and Mystery (the Lower Hemisphere).

Moving from the first quadrant to the second is the first shift for the protagonist. It's an early transition and as such it is very difficult. Indeed, this may be one of the first profound challenges of her life and identity. Traversing into the World of Invisible Forces and Mystery turns the world upside down. The rules of the World of Visible Power and Form don't operate the same way in this mystery world. In this world, she has to confront the collective unconscious and how it affects her. She also has to confront her own inner unconscious and all the unspoken rules that have helped create the inner world of her psyche. Conflict, pain, and challenging relationships play out in the confrontation between the inner world and the outer.

4. Rendered

As the protagonist is moving from Blind into the World of Invisible Forces and Mystery, the world gets more complex. The Divide starts to open up. The forces of the Divide are archetypal, but the particular details are unique to her. It's coming for her specifically with all of her fears, loves, desires, and flaws. The Divide will also be fearsome because it will be more meaningful and personal as her closest people will be involved. At this moment, it will be clear what side of the Divide she is expected to occupy: Maiden in Search of Relationship (MISOR) or Magical, Isolated, Powerful, and Endangered (MIPE). For Diana, the first of these moments happens when she decides to leave Themiscyra.

5. The Mirror

Her mother surprises her as she is leaving the island with Steve Trevor. In this moment, Hippolyta tells Diana that if she leaves, she won't be allowed to return. This seals her firmly on the track of the MIPE. The Mirror Encounter will happen multiple times in a story and might happen multiple times in a real woman's life. It is in this experience that she is confronted with what it means to be a MISOR or a MIPE. This can come in an encounter with another woman or with a role she expects to conform to. For Diana, it comes for the first time when her mother comes to tell her good-bye. Diana has another of these moments when she arrives in England and is shopping for new clothes with the help of Steve's secretary, Etta Candy. In these scenes, we see Diana literally looking in the mirror and seeing the mismatch of her MIPE self with the confining clothes of the period and place. Etta is the MISOR trying to help Diana's MIPE understand the way women comport themselves in England.

6. Commit

On the Queen's Path, this is the first time we see the character fully commit to either the MISOR or MIPE track. She accepts what her role defines for her, whether that is to her advantage or is painful for her. In Patty Jenkin's 2017 *Wonder Woman*, this is one of the most famous scenes from the film. Diana is traveling to the front with Steve and their band of spies and saboteurs. Her goal is find Aries; their goal is to find (another mirror to Diana) the evil chemist Dr. Maru and stop her from creating a bomb that would change the course of the war toward the Germans' favor. As they approach the front, Steve admonishes Diana that she cannot do things her way; she doesn't have the power. They are in "no-man's-land," and she cannot cross the front to get to the town of Veld that is being held by the Germans. After several instances of Steve "correcting" her, Diana is finally pushed to her limit at the idea of "no-man's-land" and responds that she "is no man." She dons Antiope's tiara given to her by her mother; she then proceeds to demonstrate all her MIPE abilities to cross the front and break the logjam of the German occupation of the town.

7. The Hunt

Once she's crossed the front and successfully retaken the town of Veld, Diana gets more serious about her pursuit of Aries. She comes to the conclusion that Aries must be disguised as the evil German General Ludendorff. Steve is dedicated to finding his collaborator, Dr. Maru, who has devised a deadly new poison. Diana is committed to finding and destroying Ludendorff because she believes he is actually the god of war. Her pursuit of Ludendorff takes her from a ritzy party to an airfield where the poison is loaded on a plane, ready to reignite the German offensive. Diana kills Ludendorff but nothing changes. Diana expects that everything will stop immediately upon Ludendorff's death. But once she kills him, the soldiers are still working to get the chemical bomb loaded and ready to be deployed.

Quadrant III

The Hunt takes us into the third quadrant. We are still in the World of Invisible Forces and Mystery. This is the most dangerous quadrant because it is possible that the story ends here. A MISOR who is pursued through the Hunt into marriage can die because of the risk of the Happily Ever After (HEA); she ceases to exist as an individual and succumbs to living a role. A MIPE can be hunted in an effort to subordinate her—or she can be the one doing the hunting and lose herself in revenge or be consumed by her ambitions. She can fail to find the positive mirror in choice or not find her embodiment. If any of these happen, the story is effectively over, and she will not reach sovereignty.

8. Abjection

It is in this place that the protagonist is at the greatest risk. She loses herself, her identity, her love, her ideals, her life, her goals, or maybe all of it. She is facing the worst of life and will be brought to the brink of destruction. It is possible that she can't overcome the gravity of the forces bringing her to the lowest place she can go. There are several aspects of Diana's Abjection. First Diana realizes that Sir Patrick, who has been her ally, is actually Aries, the god of war. She tries to kill him, only to realize that the "god killer" weapon she believed would end Aries forever didn't work at all. That's because Diana herself is the weapon, something that her mother and aunt knew but never told her. Also Steve Trevor dies. He sacrifices himself flying the chemical bomb out of range where the fewest number of people will be hurt or die. Diana is devastated by the loss and immediately begins to rampage against Aries.

9. Choice

This is the place that is the transition out of Abjection. Without choice, there is no way for the MISOR or MIPE to overcome the Divide and become sovereign. Aries is goading Diana to choose destruction and come to his side. Diana is devastated by everything she's seen, by the loss of Steve, and by the anger at not having succeeded in her goal. As Aries encourages Diana to destroy Dr. Maru, we see the expected facing of the MIPE or MISOR with her counterpart. This is a great example of having a positive MIPE coming up against a negative MISOR in Dr. Maru. The character of Dr. Maru is protected by her membership in the Nazi hierarchy. Everything she does is in support of the Nazi cause. Just because she's a villain doesn't mean she's a MIPE. In Diana's choice, she stands over Dr. Maru holding a tank over her head. Diana makes the choice not to take her revenge on Dr. Maru, and this shows her "who" she is. Diana chooses love over hate. And this enables her to turn her power on Aries.

10. Embodied Transcendence

This moment is wholly dependent on the circumstances of the individual woman; whatever she needs to reunite the divided pieces in herself will need to be expressed in her physical body. She will have to use her living, corporeal identity to realize her own power. Diana does this very well. When she is fighting Aries, she is getting battered. This weakness is because she has just come out of Abjection and is depleted. As she reflects during the fight, she notices that the gauntlets she is wearing on her arms are absorbing the power being hurled toward her. This is the power of the "god killer." Diana realizes that her unique power is her ability to receive and magnify power. Whatever Aries does to overpower her, she absorbs, observes, and redirects back to him. The filmmakers symbolically illustrate her transcendence by having her serenely float above him while conducting the absorbed power between her hands. When she's concentrated it enough, she looks down at Aries, and with the crossed arms of her power/boundary, she sends it right back to him, this time obliterating him and his influence (for now). Boundaries, it turns out, are a girl's best friend. Her power in her body has transformed her world; she has vanquished the enemy by simply returning his destructive power back to him. In doing so, she overcomes the Divide and takes the final step toward her sovereignty.

Quadrant IV

The return to the World of Visible Power and Form from the underworld energies of the lower hemisphere are important. The woman reentering the world is doing so with a deeper understanding of her power and what she brings to the world. That doesn't mean she won't make this journey more than once; indeed she'll likely make it a few times in her life. For Diana, we see that she makes the transition from MIPE to United Queen with both heartbreak and strength. She has endured and overcome the pain of being divided, and all that has entailed: being cursed and marked, having blindness, cleaving, mirroring, being hunted, experiencing abjection, making a choice, and having an embodied transcendence. All that's left is for her to acknowledge her own sovereignty. One of the ways we know this is coming for Diana is that as soon as she has vanquished Aries, her predictions come true. All the soldiers on the airstrip seem to come out of the fog of a painful war. Diana was right all along. If Aries—the personification of war—isn't there to focus their rage, the soldiers lose their warring behavior. In movies, narratives, and stories, this next set of steps doesn't have to unfold in this strict order. They can happen all at once, or they can be short and symbolic. In real life, these are ongoing efforts. But once we know them, we can recognize them in both narrative and life.

11. Claim the Territory

In her fight with Aries, Diana realizes that the only force that can overcome the darkness of war isn't more power or greater armaments—it's love. She uses this power as she redirects Aries's destructive force back to him. We have seen Diana's loving nature throughout the film like a trail of breadcrumbs to this moment: being surprised at the cost of war on the bodies of soldiers, not comprehending why frightened people are whipping horses to get them through muddy terrain, and stopping to talk to terrified mothers along the way to the battlefield. It is her memory of loving Steve that reminds her of what she's fighting for. Diana believed that she could stop war and bring peace. But what she learned was that she needed to bring love, and that love would bring some battles but also could bring peace. This is the territory she claims in the end of the film.

12. Gather the Tribe

This is when we recommit or connect to our people. Who are the people that "get" us? Who do we want to be around? What values are important enough to share with the like-minded and like-hearted? In *Wonder Woman*, this is a short scene that reunites Etta

Candy and the crew that worked with Diana and Steve. They gather in a square in London amid thousands of other people celebrating the end of the war. Diana looks lovingly at Steve's photograph on the wall with all the other lost heroes. She has a tearful moment of connection and steps back into the crowd. Humanity is her tribe.

13. Crowned

For real women, this experience is basically the knowledge of one's own gifts, worth, and the assertion that you matter, regardless of what culture tells you. Your gifts and uniqueness are indispensable to humanity. In *Wonder Woman*, this is again another short scene. We are returned to the present day in Diana's office at the Louvre, where she is looking at the photograph of her, Steve, and her companions from the day they liberated Veld. The photo was sent to her by Bruce Wayne, reflecting that he knows that she is different. It is the first bid to inviting her to join the Justice League, a new tribe for her to participate in. The film ends with a short monologue about what Diana learned on her journey. The last image sees her launch herself into the Parisian sky with the diadem, gauntlets, and clothes of her Amazon origins. The crown is the fitting symbol for her new role, a fully embodied version of herself, with no one telling her how or who to fight.

ENDNOTES

Introduction

1. Campbell, *The Hero's Journey: On His Life and Work*.
2. Murdock, *The Heroine's Journey*.

Chapter 1

1. Solomon, *The Art of Frozen*.
2. Kahneman, *Thinking Fast and Slow*.
3. United Nations General Assembly, Universal Declaration of Human Rights.
4. United Nations Inter-Agency Network on Women and Gender Equality, "25 Years After Beijing: A Review of the UN System's Support for the Implementation of the Platform for Action 2014–2019."
5. Ibid.

Chapter 2

1. Machiavelli, *The Prince*.
2. Parker, Horowitz, and Stepler, "On Gender Differences, No Consensus on Nature vs Nurture."
3. Pettitt, *Ladies Like Us: A Modern Girl's Guide to Self-Discovery, Self-Confidence and Love*.
4. Ibid.
5. Andelin, *Fascinating Womanhood: A Guide to a Healthy Marriage*.
6. Ibid.
7. Clark and Baird, *Girl Defined: God's Radical Design for Beauty, Femininity, and Identity*.
8. Clark and Beal, "Topics."
9. Clark and Baird, *Girl Defined: God's Radical Design for Beauty, Femininity, and Identity*.
10. Doyle, *Untamed*.
11. Donegan, "For Too Many Girls, Teenage Years Are a Time of Unwanted Attention from Older Men."
12. Raj, "India Struggles to Eradicate an Old Scourge: Witch Hunting."

Chapter 3

1. Yalom, *Birth of the Chess Queen*.
2. Ibid.

3. Lopez, "Chapter 1."
4. Jung, *Aion: Researches into the Phenomenology of the Self.*

Chapter 4

1. Campbell, *The Hero's Journey: On His Life and Work.*
2. Mayor, *The Amazons: Lives and Legends of Women Across the Ancient World.*

Chapter 5

1. Stone, *When God Was a Woman.*

Chapter 6

1. Yousafzai and Lamb, *I Am Malala: The Girl Who Stood Up for Education and Was Shot by the Taliban*, Kindle Edition.
2. Ibid.
3. Ibid.
4. World Health Organization, "Female Genital Mutilation."
5. Fey, *Bossypants.*

Chapter 7

1. Levack, *The Witch-Hunt in Early Modern Europe.*
2. Hook and Ben-Yehuda, "European Witch-Hunts."
3. Goode and Ben-Yehuda, *Moral Panics: The Social Construction of Deviance.*

Chapter 8

1. Febos, *Girlhood.*
2. Phelian, "How Céline Sciamma Subverts the Male Gaze in Portrait of a Lady on Fire."
3. Berger and Dibb, *Ways of Seeing.*
4. Mulvey, "Visual Pleasure and Narrative Cinema."
5. Gauthier et al., "The Potential Scientist's Dilemma."
6. Forciniti and Zavarrone, "Data Quality and Violence Against Women."
7. Petersen, Maier, and Seligman, *Learned Helplessness: A Theory for the Age of Personal Control.*
8. Specter, "Why Are Women Now Required to Cover Their Arms in the Missouri State House?"
9. Zhou, "Why School Dress Codes Are Sexist."

Chapter 9

1. Woodward and Gerson, "Mirroring and the Development of Action Understanding."
2. Jung, *Aion: Researches into the Phenomenology of the Self.*
3. Ayunin, "Eve, the Existing Abject (Postmodern Feminist Study toward the Story of Adam and Eve in Bible)."

Chapter 10

1. Moyer et al., "Stress-Induced Cortisol Response and Fat Distribution in Women."
2. Cai et al., "A D2 to D1 Shift in Dopaminergic Inputs to Midbrain 5-HT Neurons Causes Anorexia in Mice."

Chapter 12

1. Creed, *The Monstrous-Feminine: Film, Feminism, Psychoanalysis.*
2. "Lucretia | Roman Heroine, Death & Roman Republic," Britannica.
3. Hannah, *The Animus: The Spirit of Inner Truth in Women.*
4. Jung, *Animus and Anima: Two Essays.*
5. McLellan, "Mental Health and Justice."
6. "Lori Vallow Is Sentenced to Life without Parole for Murders of Her Kids JJ and Tylee and Her Husband's Ex-Wife Tammy Daybell," Daily Mail Online.
7. Atwood, *Second Words.*

Chapter 14

1. Mayor, *The Amazons: Lives and Legends of Women Across the Ancient World.*
2. Greco, "Most Girls Diet by Age 10, and Other Depressing Facts about Body Image Development."
3. Lickteig, "Social Media."
4. Ibid.
5. Chalabi and editor, "Are Women Punished More Harshly for Killing an Intimate Partner?"
6. Forciniti and Zavarrone, "Data Quality and Violence Against Women."
7. Abramsky et al., "What Factors Are Associated with Recent Intimate Partner Violence?"
8. World Health Organization, "Levels of Domestic Violence Increase Globally, Including in the Region, as COVID-19 Pandemic Escalates."
9. Violence Policy Center, "When Men Murder Women: An Analysis of 2020 Homicide Data."
10. "Art Exhibit Powerfully Answers the Question 'What Were You Wearing?'" HuffPost Women.
11. Manshoory, "Marital Rape."
12. Miller, *The Transcendent Function: Jung's Model of Psychological Growth through Dialogue with the Unconscious.*
13. Jung, "The Transcendent Function."
14. *Barbie*, Fantasy Comedy.

Chapter 15

1. "The U.S. Constitution," Constitution Center.
2. Refworld, "Preamble to the Constitution of 27 October 1946."

Chapter 16

1. Aristophanes, *Lysistrata and Other Plays.*

BIBLIOGRAPHY

Ablin, Jacob N. et al. "Distinctive Personality Profiles of Fibromyalgia and Chronic Fatigue Syndrome Patients." *PeerJ* 4 (September 13, 2016): e2421. https://doi.org/10.7717/peerj.2421.

Abramovitz, Beth A., and Leann L. Birch. "Five-Year-Old Girls' Ideas about Dieting Are Predicted by Their Mothers' Dieting." *Journal of the Academy of Nutrition and Dietetics* 100, no. 10 (October 2000): 1157–63. https://doi.org/10.1016/S0002-8223(00)00339-4.

Abramsky, Tanya et al. "What Factors Are Associated with Recent Intimate Partner Violence? Findings from the WHO Multi-Country Study on Women's Health and Domestic Violence." *BMC Public Health* 11, no. 1 (February 16, 2011): 109. https://doi.org/10.1186/1471-2458-11-109.

Ahituv, Yosef. "Modesty and Sexuality in Halakhic Literature." Jewish Women's Archive. Accessed May 6, 2023. https://jwa.org/encyclopedia/article/modesty-and-sexuality-in-halakhic-literature.

Al-shammari, Huda Aziz Muhi, and Nidaa Hussain Fahmi Al-Khazraji. "Ideological Representation of Women's Oppression in Margaret Atwood's *The Handmaid's Tale*: A Critical Discourse Analysis." Al-Adab Journal, no. 138 (September 15, 2021): 15–22. https://doi.org/10.31973/aj.v3i138.1771.

Alhakk, Nour. "Not Shocking: Devout Religious Followers Have Better Sex Lives." *ILLUMINATION* (blog), September 4, 2022. https://medium.com/illumination/not-shocking-devout-religious-followers-have-better-sex-lives-11c969349524.

Amazon.com. "Thank You." Accessed May 6, 2024.

Andelin, Helen B. *Fascinating Womanhood: A Guide to a Healthy Marriage*. Santa Barbara, CA: Pacific Press, 1963.

Appel-Slingbaum, Caren. "The [Jewish] Tradition of Slapping Our Daughters." The Museum of Menstruation and Women's Health." Accessed February 11, 2023. http://www.mum.org/slap.htm.

Apperson, Virginia, and John Beebe. *The Presence of the Feminine in Film*. Newcastle on Tyne, UK: Cambridge Scholars Publishing, 2008.

Aristophanes. *Lysistrata and Other Plays*. Boston: Addison Wesley, 2008.

Atwood, Margaret. *Second Words: Selected Critical Prose 1960–1982*. Toronto, ON: House of Anansi Press, 1995.

Avens, Roberts. "Imagination in Jung and Hillman." In *Imagination Is Reality*. Putnam, CT: Spring Publications, 1980.

Axelrod, David B., Carol F. Thomas, and Lenny Schneir. *Merlin Stone Remembered*. Woodbury, MN: Llewellyn Publications, 2014.

Ayunin, Qurrota. "Eve, the Existing Abject (Postmodern Feminist Study toward the Story of Adam and Eve in Bible)." *PARADIGM* 2, no. 1 (June 29, 2019): 41. https://doi.org/10.18860/prdg.v2i1.6708.

Bakalar, Nicholas. "Safety: Car Crashes Pose Greater Risk for Women." *The New York Times*, October 31, 2011, sec. Health. https://www.nytimes.com/2011/11/01/health/research/women-at-greater-risk-of-injury-in-car-crashes-study-finds.html.

Bakalar, Nicholas. "Women at Greater Risk of Injury in Car Crashes, Study Finds." *The New York Times*. Accessed May 9, 2023. https://www.nytimes.com/2011/11/01/health/research/women-at-greater-risk-of-injury-in-car-crashes-study-finds.html.

Bakar, Faima. "Half of Women Experience Body Dysmorphia. Here Are the Signs." HuffPost UK, November 23, 2021. https://www.huffingtonpost.co.uk/entry/half-of-women-experience-body-dysmorphia-here-are-the-signs_uk_619cb77ee4b07fe20110697b.

Balkwill, Stephanie. "The Sūtra on Transforming the Female Form: Unpacking an Early Medieval Chinese Buddhist Text." *Journal of Chinese Religions* 44, no. 2 (2016): 127–48. https://muse.jhu.edu/pub/1/article/708669.

———. "The Sūtra on Transforming the Female Form: Unpacking an Early Medieval Chinese Buddhist Text." *Journal of Chinese Religions* 44, no. 2 (n.d.): 127–48.

Barbie. Fantasy Comedy. Warner Bros. Pictures, 2023.

Barstow, Anne L. *Witchcraze: A New History of the European Witch Hunts*. Reprint. New York: HarperOne, 1995.

Batuman, Elif. "Céline Sciamma's Quest for a New, Feminist Grammar of Cinema," *The New Yorker*. Accessed May 5, 2024. https://www.newyorker.com/magazine/2022/02/07/celine-sciammas-quest-for-a-new-feminist-grammar-of-cinema.

Bayless, Kacen. "Missouri House Faces Backlash for Women's Dress Code Rule." *Kansas City Star*. Accessed May 5, 2024. https://www.kansascity.com/news/politics-government/article271158062.html.

BBC News. "What Did St Paul Say about Women?" November 18, 2014, sec. Magazine. https://www.bbc.com/news/magazine-29513427.

Beardsworth, Sara. "Kristeva's Idea of Sublimation." *The Southern Journal of Philosophy* 42, no. S1 (March 2004): 122–36. https://doi.org/10.1111/j.2041-6962.2004.tb01020.x.

Beauty and the Beast. Buena Vista Film Distribution, 1991.

Becvar, Dorothy. "Tracking the Archetype of the Wise Woman/Crone." *ReVision* 28, no. 1 (2005): 21–23. https://api.semanticscholar.org/CorpusID:144444048

Ben-Yehuda, Nachman. "The European Witch Craze of the 14th to 17th Centuries: A Sociologist's Perspective." *American Journal of Sociology* 86, no. 1 (1980): 1–31. https://www.jstor.org/stable/2778849.

———. "The European Witch Craze of the 14th to 17th Centuries: A Sociologist's Perspective." *American Journal of Sociology* 86, no. 1 (July 1980): 1–31. https://doi .org/10.1086/227200.

Berger, John, and Michael Dibb. *Ways of Seeing.* London: Penguin Books, 1972.

biblestudytools.com. "The Top Bible Verses about Women's Roles in Scripture." Accessed April 19, 2023. https://www.biblestudytools.com/topical-verses/bible-verses-about-womens-roles/.

Birkner, Gabrielle. "Parsing the 'Menstrual Slap.'" *The Forward*, February 24, 2010. https://forward.com/life/126293/parsing-the-menstrual-slap/.

Bologna, Caroline. "Fierce T-Ball Players Redefine Squad Goals with 'Frozen' Themed Team Photo." *The Huffington Post*, June 17, 2015, sec. Huff Post Parents. http://www.huffingtonpost.com/2015/06/17/frozen-girls-softball-team_n_7606528. html.

Brave. Walt Disney Studios Motion Pictures, 2012.

Brazelton, T. Berry, Stanley J. Greenspan, and Benjamin Spock. *Winnicott on the Child.* Cambridge, MA: Perseus Publishing, 2002.

Briere, John. "When People Do Bad Things: Evil Suffering, and Dependent Origination." In *Humanity's Dark Side: Explorations in Psychotherapy and Beyond.* Washington, DC: American Psychological Association, 2012.

Brittanica.com. "Lucretia | Roman Heroine, Death & Roman Republic." Britannica. com. Accessed November 26, 2023. https://www.britannica.com/topic/Lucretia-ancient-Roman-heroine.

Brittanica.com. "Margaret Thatcher, Prime Minister of United Kingdom." Biography & Facts. Britannica.com. Accessed February 9, 2023. https://www. britannica.com/biography/Margaret-Thatcher.

Brittanica.com. "Miley Cyrus, American actress and singer." Biography, TV Shows, Songs, & Facts. Britannica.com. Accessed February 23, 2023. https://www .britannica.com/biography/Miley-Cyrus.

Burack, Emily. "The True Story of Princess Diana's Death." *Town & Country*, November 16, 2023. https://www.townandcountrymag.com/society/tradition/ a45737126/princess-diana-death-true-story-explained/.

Burke, Tarana. *Unbound: My Story of Liberation and the Birth of the Me Too Movement.* New York: Flatiron Books, 2021.

Butler, J. *Archetypal Psychotherapy: The Clinical Legacy of James Hillman.* New York: Routledge, 2014.

Cai, Xing et al. "A D2 to D1 Shift in Dopaminergic Inputs to Midbrain 5-HT Neurons Causes Anorexia in Mice." *Nature Neuroscience* 25, no. 5 (May 2022): 646–58. https://doi.org/10.1038/s41593-022-01062-0.

Cain Miller, Claire, Sarah Kliff, and Larry Buchanan. "Childbirth Is Deadlier for Black Families Even When They're Rich, Expansive Study Finds." *The New York Times.* Accessed May 10, 2023. https://www.nytimes.com/interactive/2023/02/12/upshot/child-maternal-mortality-rich-poor.html.

Campbell, Joseph. *The Hero's Journey: Joseph Campbell on His Life and Work.* Vol 7. New World Library, 2003

Campbell, Joseph. *The Hero with a Thousand Faces.* New York: Pantheon Books, 1949.

Carruthers, Mary. "The Wife of Bath and the Painting of Lions." *PMLA* 94, no. 2 (March 1979): 209–22. https://doi.org/10.2307/461886.

Chalabi, Mona, and Mona Chalabi Guardian US data editor. "Are Women Punished More Harshly for Killing an Intimate Partner?" *The Guardian,* January 12, 2019, sec. News. https://www.theguardian.com/news/datablog/2019/jan/12/intimate-partner-violence-gender-gap-cyntoia-brown.

Chan, Melissa. "Revisiting Andrea Yates 15 Years After She Drowned Her Children." *TIME.* Accessed October 6, 2023. https://time.com/4375398/andrea-yates-15-years-drown-children/.

Charlesworth, Tessa E. S., and R. Banaji Mahzarin. "Gender in Science, Technology, Engineering, and Mathematics: Issues, Causes, Solutions." PubMed Central. Accessed May 5, 2024. https://www.ncbi.nlm.nih.gov/pmc/articles/PMC6759027/.

Chaucer, Geoffrey. "The Wife of Bath's Prologue." In *The Riverside Chaucer,* 3rd ed., 105–16. Boston: Houghton Mifflin, 1987. https://archive.org/details/riversidechaucer0000chau.

Claremont de Castillejo, Irene. *Knowing Woman: A Feminine Psychology.* Boston: Shambhala Publications, 1973.

Clark, Kristen, and Bethany Baird. *Girl Defined: God's Radical Design for Beauty, Femininity, and Identity.* Grand Rapids, MI: Baker Books, 2016.

Clark, Kristen, and Bethany Beal. "Girl Defined." *Girl Defined.* Accessed April 21, 2023. https://girldefined.com/.

———. "Meet Us." *GirlDefined* (blog). Accessed April 28, 2023. https://girldefined.com/meet-us.

———. "Topics." *GirlDefined* (blog). Accessed May 2, 2023. https://girldefined.com/ topics.

Clark, Kristen. "7 Reasons I'm Not a Feminist." *GirlDefined* (blog), March 18, 2016. https://girldefined.com/7-reasons-im-not-a-feminist.

Collins, Suzanne. *The Hunger Games*. New York: Scholastic Press, 1990.

Conroy, Pat. *The Lords of Discipline*. New York: Open Road, 2010.

Cooper, Helen. "The Wife of Bath's Prologue." In *Oxford Guides to Chaucer: The Canterbury Tales*. New York: Oxford University Press, 1996.

Cosmopolitan. "Chelsea Handler Reveals Why She and Jo Koy Broke Up," December 28, 2022. https://www.cosmopolitan.com/entertainment/celebs/a42354061/why-chelsea-handler-and-jo-koy-broke-up/.

Costonie, Toni. *Priestess Miriam & the Voodoo Spiritual Temple: A Brief History*. New Orleans: Voodoo Spiritual Temple & Cultural Center, 2004.

Covington, Richard. "Mary Magdalene Was None of the Things a Pope Claimed." US News. Accessed May 20, 2023. https://www.usnews.com/news/religion/ articles/2008/01/25/mary-magdalene-was-none-of-the-things-a-pope-claimed.

Crane, Susan. "Alison's Incapacity and Poetic Instability in the Wife of Bath's Tale." *PMLA* 102, no. 1 (January 1, 1987): 22. https://doi.org/10.2307/462489.

———. "Alison's Incapacity and Poetic Instability in the Wife of Bath's Tale." *PMLA* 102, no. 1 (January 1, 1987): 20–28. https://doi.org/10.2307/462489.

Creed, Barbara. T*he Monstrous-Feminine: Film, Feminism, Psychoanalysis*. Popular Fiction Series. London: Routledge, 1993.

———. *The Monstruous-Feminine in Film: Film, Feminism, Psychoanalysis*. New York: Routledge, 1993.

Davis, Amy. *Good Girls & Wicked Witches: Women in Disney's Feature Animation*. New Barnet, Herts England: John Libbey Publishing, 2006.

Desert Flower Foundation. "What Is FGM." Accessed February 11, 2023. https:// www.desertflowerfoundation.org/en/what-is-fgm.html.

Didion, Joan. *The Year of Magical Thinking*. Vintage International. New York: Random House, 2006.

Dinshaw, Carolyn. "Good Vibrations: John/Eleanor, Dame Alys, the Pardoner, and Foucault." In *Getting Medieval: Sexualities and Communities, Pre- and Postmodern*. Durham, NC: Duke University Press, 1999.

Donegan, Moira. "For Too Many Girls, Teenage Years Are a Time of Unwanted Attention from Older Men." *The Guardian*, May 9, 2021, sec. Opinion. https://www .theguardian.com/commentisfree/2021/may/09/teenage-girls-unwanted-adult-male-attention.

Dougherty, N. J., and J. J. West. *The Matrix and Meaning of Character: An Archetypal and Developmental Approach*. Taylor & Francis, 2013. http://books.google.com/books?id=HoZEAgAAQBAJ.

Downie, Alison. "Christian Shame and Religious Trauma." *Religions* 13, no. 10 (October 2022): 925. https://doi.org/10.3390/rel13100925.

Doyle, Glennon. *Untamed*. New York: The Dial Press, 2020.

Driver, F. "Power, Space, and the Body: A Critical Assessment of Foucault's Discipline and Punish." *Environment and Planning D: Society and Space* 3, no. 4 (December 1985): 425–46. https://doi.org/10.1068/d030425.

Dubofsky, Chanel. "Daughter Got Her Period? Slap Her." Jewish Telegraphic Agency, February 10, 2023. https://www.jta.org/jewniverse/2015/daughter-got-her-period-slap-her.

Dumas, C. "On Film Studies and the Unconscious." *Camera Obscura* 27, no. 81 (2012): 38–67. https://doi.org/10.1215/02705346-1727455.

Dundes, Lauren. "Disney's Modern Heroine Pocahontas: Revealing Age-Old Gender Stereotypes and Role Discontinuity under a Facade of Liberation." *The Social Science Journal* 38 (2001): 353–65. https://doi.org/10.1016/S0362-3319(01)00137-9.

Dunne, Claire. *Carl Jung: Wounded Healer of the Soul: An Illustrated Biography*. New York: Parabola Books, 2000.

Dutton, Donald. *The Batterer: A Psychological Profile*. New York: Basic Books, 1995.

Edinger, Edward. *Anatomy of the Psyche: Alchemical Symbolism in Psychotherapy*. Chicago, IL: Open Court Publishing, 1994.

Ellroy, James. *My Dark Places: A True Crime Autobiography*. New York: Vintage, 2009.

England, Dawn, Lara Descartes, and Melissa Collier-Meek. "Gender Role Portrayal and the Disney Princess." *Sex Roles* 64 (2011): 555–67. https://doi.org/10.1007/s11199-011-9930-7.

Febos, Melissa. *Girlhood*. New York: Bloomsbury Publishing, 2021.

Federici, Silvia. *Witches, Witch-Hunting, and Women*. Oakland, CA: PM Press, 2018.

Feld, Brad. "Book: Against Our Will: Men, Women and Rape." Brad Feld, September 24, 2017. https://feld.com/archives/2017/09/book-will-men-women-rape/.

Feminism in India.com. "Manusmriti: The Ultimate Guide to Becoming a 'Good Woman.'" *Feminism in India*, January 10, 2018. https://feminisminindia.com/2018/01/11/manusmriti-ultimate-guide-good-woman/.

Fey, Tina. *Bossypants*. New York: Little, Brown, and Company, 2011.

Fitzgerald, F. Scott. *This Side of Paradise*. Dover Thrift Reprint. New York: Dover Publications, 1920.

Franz, Marie Louise von. *The Interpretation of Fairy Tales*. Revised. C. G. Jung Foundation. Boston: Shambhala Publications, 1996.

Freud, Sigmund. *The Interpretation of Dreams*. New York: Avon Books, 1965.

Fritz, D. W. "The Animus-Possessed Wife of Bath." *Journal of Analytical Psychology* 25, no. 2 (April 1980): 163–80. https://doi.org/10.1111/j.1465-5922.1980.00163.x.

Frozen. Family. Walt Disney Studios, 2013.

Gaille, Brandon. "29 Intriguing Crimes of Passion Statistics." *BrandonGaille.com* (blog), May 23, 2017. https://brandongaille.com/27-intriguing-crimes-of-passion-statistics/.

Gardam, Tansy. "Looking from the Outside In—Gender Representation in Animation." *Four Three Film* (blog), September 3, 2015. http://fourthreefilm .com/2015/09/looking-from-the-outside-in-gender-representation-in-animation/.

Gauthier, G. Robin et al. "The Potential Scientist's Dilemma: How the Masculine Framing of Science Shapes Friendships and Science Job Aspirations." *Social Sciences* 6, no. 1 (March 2017): 14. https://doi.org/10.3390/socsci6010014.

Gayman, Deann. "Study Examines How, Why Adolescence Halts Girls' Interest in Science," March 21, 2017. https://news.unl.edu/newsrooms/today/article/study-examines-how-why-adolescence-halts-girls-interest-in-science/.

Giving Compass. "Women Murdered by Men: 2020 Data," October 28, 2023. https://givingcompass.org/article/women-murdered-by-men-2020-data.

Glöckner, Andreas. "The Irrational Hungry Judge Effect Revisited: Simulations Reveal That the Magnitude of the Effect Is Overestimated." *Judgment and Decision Making* 11, no. 6 (November 2016): 601–10. https://doi.org/10.1017/S1930297500004812.

Goldman, Dodi (editor). *In One's Bones: The Clinical Genius of Winnicott*. Northvale, NJ: Jason Aronson, Inc., 1993.

Goldman, William. *The Princess Bride*. 30th Anniversary Edition. New York: Harcourt, 2013.

Goode, Erich, and Nachman Ben-Yehuda. *Moral Panics: The Social Construction of Deviance*. 2nd ed. Hoboken, NJ: Wiley-Blackwell, 1994.

Google search. "Sex Pistols, 'God Save the Queen.'" Accessed February 9, 2023. https://www.google.com/search?q=sex+pistols+god+save+the+queen&oq=se x+pistols+god&aqs=chrome.0.0i355i512j46i512j69i57j0i512l7.3567j0j7&sour ceid=chrome&ie=UTF-8#wptab=si:AEcPFx5TRTnca31vONqoNYlzoLKYWW9I o4JA99ZVqyY-gPmyoKoGglv3oCRyAbjkNyXtU8RFUXDnJnP7iGnb4YrAMKqb k1KMhLpKLNdWmShocdXpLGPHgDGTi86PIY7DdoMBPB1mswEDhkRRh3q HdML3SDNwMpyPLwIz8cxmzRjbfvcZgi-MP2o%3D.

Gordon, Aubrey. "The Economics of Thinness." *The Economist*. Accessed January 27, 2023. https://www.economist.com/christmas-specials/2022/12/20/the-economics-of-thinness.

Graves, Robert. *Food for Centaurs: A Collection of the Best of the Author's Short Stories, Essays, Poems*. Garden City, NY: Doubleday, 1960.

Greaney, Michael. "Violence and the Sacred in the Fiction of Julia Kristeva." *Theology & Sexuality* 14, no. 3 (January 2008): 293–304. https://doi.org/10.1177/1355835808091420.

Greco, Alanna. "This News about Body Image Is Damaging." *Bustle*, January 27, 2015. https://www.bustle.com/articles/60925-most-girls-diet-by-age-10-and-other-depressing-facts-about-body-image-development.

Green, Richard Firth. "'Allas, Allas! That Evere Love Was Synne!': John Bromyard v. Alice of Bath." *The Chaucer Review* 42, no. 3 (2007): 298–311. https://doi.org/10.1353/cr.2008.0005.

Greenberg, Eric J. "Dominance and Submission." *Jewish Telegraphic Agency* (blog), June 19, 1998. https://www.jta.org/1998/06/19/ny/dominance-and-submission.

Griffith, Nicola. "Men Are Afraid That Women Will Laugh at Them." *Nicola Griffith* (blog), November 8, 2014. https://nicolagriffith.com/2014/11/08/men-are-afraid-that-women-will-laugh-at-them/.

Groesbeck, C. J. "C. G. Jung and the Shaman's Vision." *Journal of Analytical Psychology*, Jul: 34, no. 3 (1989): 255–76. https://doi.org/10.1111/j.1465-5922.1989.00255.

Gross, Carol Cott. "My Mom Slapped Me When I Got My Period." *Kveller* (blog), June 13, 2017. https://www.kveller.com/my-mom-slapped-me-when-i-got-my-period/.

Hall, Calvin, and Vernon Nordby. *A Primer of Jungian Psychology*. New York: New American Library, 1973.

Hammond, Eleanor Prescott. *Chaucer: A Bibliographic Manual*. New York: Macmillan, 1908. https://archive.org/details/chaucerbibliogra00hammuoft.

Hannah, Barbara. *The Animus: The Spirit of Inner Truth in Women*. Vol. I. 2 vols. Polarities of the Psyche. Wilmette, IL: Chiron Publications, 2011.

Harris, Carissa. "Rape and Justice in the Wife of Bath's Tale." *The Open Access Companion to the Canterbury Tales*, 2017. https://opencanterburytales.dsl.lsu.edu/wobt1/.

Hayes, Steven C., and Kirk D. Strosahl. *A Practical Guide to Acceptance and Commitment Therapy*. New York: Springer Science & Business Media, 2004.

Hayes, Steven C., Kirk D. Strosahl, and Kelly G. Wilson. *Acceptance and Commitment Therapy: An Experiential Approach to Behavior Change*. New York: Guilford Press, 1999.

———. *Acceptance and Commitment Therapy: The Process and Practice of Mindful Change*. 2nd ed. New York: Guilford Press, 2011.

Hellenic Museum. "The Myth of Atalanta," December 20, 2021. https://www.hellenic.org.au/post/the-myth-of-atalanta.

Herrera, Alan. "Fox News Guest Has Unhinged Meltdown Over the Fact That Chelsea Handler Doesn't Want Kids." Second Nexus. Accessed February 16, 2023. https://secondnexus.com/jesse-kelly-chelsea-handler-childless.

Hill, Scott J. *Confrontation with the Unconscious: Jungian Depth Psychology and Psychedelic Experience*. London: Aeon Books, Ltd., 2013.

Hillman, James. *A Blue Fire*. New York: Harper & Row, 1989.

———. *Pan and the Nightmare*. Putnam, CT: Spring Publications, Inc., 1972.

———. *The Myth of Analysis*. Evanston, IL: Northwestern University Press, 1972.

Hockley, Luke. *Frames of Mind: A Post-Jungian Look at Cinema, Television, and Technology*. Chicago, IL: Intellect, University of Chicago Press, 2007.

Hollis, James. *Hauntings: Dispelling the Ghosts Who Run Our Lives*. Asheville, NC: Chiron Publications, 2013.

———. *The Archetypal Imagination*. Kindle Edition. College Station, TX: Texas A&M University Press, 2000.

Hook, D., and N. Ben-Yehuda. "The Great European Witch-Hunts: A Historical Perspective." *AJS; American Journal of Sociology* 88, no. 6 (May 1983): 1270–79. https://doi.org/10.1086/227806.

Horowitz, Juliana Menasce. "Wide Partisan Gaps in U.S. Over How Far the Country Has Come on Gender Equality." *Pew Research Center's Social & Demographic Trends Project* (blog), October 18, 2017. https://www.pewresearch.org/social-trends/2017/10/18/wide-partisan-gaps-in-u-s-over-how-far-the-country-has-come-on-gender-equality/.

How to Train Your Dragon 2. Family. Dreamworks Animation, 2014.

Hubback, Judith. "The Archetypal Senex: An Exploration of Old Age." *Journal of Analytical Psychology* 41, no. 1 (1996): 3–19. https://doi.org/10.1111/j.1465-5922.1996.00003.x.

Hundhausen, Evan. "Without Joseph Campbell There'd Be No 'Star Wars.'" GoshDarnBlog. Medium. Accessed May 12, 2023. https://medium.com/goshdarnblog/want-to-be-the-next-george-lucas-then-read-joseph-campbell-ed7f119b6d0b.

Hurwitz, Seigmund. *Lilith the First Eve: Historical and Psychological Aspects of the Dark Feminine*. Edited by Robert Hinshaw. Einsiedeln, Switzerland: Daimon Verlag, 2009.

Huxley, Elizabeth, and Boris Bizumic. "Parental Invalidation and the Development of Narcissism." *The Journal of Psychology* 151, no. 2 (February 17, 2017): 130–47. https://doi.org/10.1080/00223980.2016.1248807.

IsHak, Waguih William et al. "Quality of Life: The Ultimate Outcome Measure of Interventions in Major Depressive Disorder." *Harvard Review of Psychiatry*, Vol 19, No 5. Accessed September 25, 2023. https://www.tandfonline.com/doi/abs/10.3109/10673229.2011.614099.

Jacobi, Jolande. "The Process of Individuation: A Study in Developmental Psychology." *Journal of Analytical Psychology* 3, no. 2 (1958): 95–115. https://doi.org/10.1111/j.1465-5922.1958.00095.x.

Jean-Murat, Carolle. *Voodoo in My Blood: A Healer's Journey from Surgeon to Shaman*. Kindle. San Diego, CA: Bettie Youngs Book Publishers, 2012.

Jewish Virtual Library. "Eshet Hayil 'A Woman of Valor.'" Accessed April 19, 2023. https://www.jewishvirtuallibrary.org/eshet-hayil.

Jin, Xurui et al. "Women's Participation in Cardiovascular Clinical Trials from 2010 to 2017." *Circulation* 141, no. 7 (February 18, 2020): 540–48. https://doi.org/10.1161/CIRCULATIONAHA.119.043594.

Johnson, Paula. "Girls and Science: A Qualitative Study on Factors Related to Success and Failure in Science." *Dissertations*, June 1, 2004. https://scholarworks.wmich.edu/dissertations/1114.

Johnson, Robert A. *Inner Work: Using Dreams and Active Imagination for Personal Growth*. New York: HarperCollins E-Books, 1986.

Johnston, Ollie, and Frank Thomas. *The Illusion of Life*. Disney Editions. Burbank, CA: Walt Disney Productions, 1981.

Jones, Jennifer J. "Talk 'Like a Man': The Linguistic Styles of Hillary Clinton, 1992–2013." *Perspectives on Politics* 14, no. 3 (September 2016): 625–42. https://doi.org/10.1017/S1537592716001092.

Jung, C. G. "The Transcendent Function." In *Collected Works: The Structure and Dynamics of the Psyche*, 2nd ed., 8:67–91. Bollingen Series. Princeton, NJ: Princeton University Press, 1970.

Jung, Carl G. *Aion: Researches into the Phenomenology of the Self*. Translated by Gerhard Adler and R. F. C. Hull. Vol. 9, part 2. 27 vols. (Collected Works of C. G. Jung Vol. 9 Part 2). Princeton, NJ: Princeton University Press, 1979.

Jung, Emma. *Animus and Anima: Two Essays*. Putnam, CT: Spring Publications, Inc., 1985.

Jung, Hawon. "Women in South Korea Are on Strike Against Being 'Baby-Making Machines.'" *The New York Times*, January 27, 2023, sec. Opinion. https://www.nytimes.com/2023/01/27/opinion/south-korea-fertility-rate-feminism.html.

Jupta, Rudrani. "Dheere Bolo: Why Are Women Expected to be Demure Not Outspoken?" Accessed May 2, 2023. https://www.shethepeople.tv/top-stories/opinion/dheere-bolo/.

Kahneman, Daniel. *Thinking, Fast and Slow*. New York: Farrar, Strauss, & Giroux, 2013.

Kalsched, Donald. *The Inner World of Trauma: Archetypal Defenses of the Personal Spirit*. Kindle Edition. New York: Routledge, 1996.

———. *Trauma and the Soul: A Psycho-Spiritual Approach to Human Development and Its Interruption*. New York: Routledge, 2013.

Kellie, Dax J., Khandis R. Blake, and Robert C. Brooks. "What Drives Female Objectification? An Investigation of Appearance-Based Interpersonal Perceptions and the Objectification of Women." *PLOS ONE* 14, no. 8 (August 23, 2019): e0221388. https://doi.org/10.1371/journal.pone.0221388.

Khazan, Olga. "America's Deep Rift on Gender Issues." *The Atlantic* (blog), December 5, 2017. https://www.theatlantic.com/science/archive/2017/12/pew-gender/547508/.

Kieckhefer, Richard. *European Witch Trials: Their Foundations in Popular and Learned Culture, 1300–1500* eBook. Accessed May 6, 2024. https://www.routledge.com/European-Witch-Trials-RLE-Witchcraft-Their-Foundations-in-Popular-and-Learned-Culture-1300-1500/Kieckhefer/p/book/9781138969131.

Kittredge, George Lyman. "Chaucer's Discussion of Marriage." *Modern Philology* 9, no. 4 (April 1912): 435–67. https://doi.org/10.1086/386872.

Kleiner, Kurt. "Lunchtime Leniency: Judges' Rulings Are Harsher When They Are Hungrier." *Scientific American*, September 1, 2011. https://www.scientificamerican.com/article/lunchtime-leniency/.

Kolk, Bessel A. van der. *The Body Keeps the Score: Brain, Mind, and Body in the Healing of Trauma*. New York: Viking, 2014.

Kontis, Dimitrios, and Eirini Theochari. "Dopamine in Anorexia Nervosa: A Systematic Review." *Behavioural Pharmacology* 23, no. 5 and 6 (September 2012): 496–515. https://doi.org/10.1097/FBP.0b013e328357e115.

Lakshmanan, Manu N. et al. "An Archetype of the Collaborative Efforts of Psychotherapy and Psychopharmacology in Successfully Treating Dissociative Identity Disorder with Comorbid Bipolar Disorder." *Psychiatry* 7, no. 7 (July 2010): 33–37. http://pgi.idm.oclc.org/login?url=http://search.ebscohost.com/login.aspx?direct=true&db=psyh&AN=2010-16655-005&site=ehost-live&scope=site.

LaRocca-Pitts, Beth. "Anath: Bible." Jewish Women's Archive. Accessed May 6, 2023. https://jwa.org/encyclopedia/article/anath-bible.

Lechte, John. "Justice, Injustice and the Work of Julia Kristeva." *Theory, Culture & Society* 40, no. 6 (November 2023): 51–68. https://doi.org/10.1177/02632764221140762.

Lennon, Kathleen. "Feminist Perspectives on the Body." In *The Stanford Encyclopedia of Philosophy*, edited by Edward N. Zalta, Fall 2019. Metaphysics Research Lab, Stanford University, 2019. https://plato.stanford.edu/archives/fall2019/entries/feminist-body/.

Lesser, Elizabeth. *Cassandra Speaks: When Women Are the Storytellers, the Human Story Changes*. New York: HarperCollins, 2022.

Levack, Brian P. *The Witch-Hunt in Early Modern Europe*. 4th ed. Philadelphia, PA: University of Pennsylvania Press, 2000.

———. *The Witch-Hunt in Early Modern Europe*. 4th ed. London; New York: Routledge, 2015.

Lickteig, Beverly. "Social Media: Cyberbullying, Body Shaming, and Trauma." *The Child Advocacy Center of Lapeer County* (blog), November 2, 2020. https://caclapeer.org/social-media-cyberbullying-body-shaming-and-trauma/.

Lindner, Jannik. "Crime of Passion Statistics: Market Report & Data." Gitnux. Accessed December 6, 2023. https://blog.gitnux.com/crime-of-passion-statistics/.

Lipscombe-Southwell, Alice. "Why Are Girls Put Off Science?" BBC Science Focus. Accessed May 5, 2024. https://www.sciencefocus.com/science/why-are-girls-put-off-science.

Lipton, Emma. "Contracts, Activist Feminism, and the Wife of Bath's Tale." *The Chaucer Review* 54, no. 3 (2019): 335–51. https://doi.org/10.5325/chaucerrev.54.3.0335.

Loketch-Fischer, Minna. "The Relationships Among Modesty, Self-Objectification, Body Shame and Eating Disorder Symptoms in Jewish Women." ProQuest. Accessed December 5, 2023. https://www.proquest.com/openview/7b91b57fb69a011d8de40 6762ac42b96/1?pq-origsite=gscholar&cbl=18750.

Lopez, Kim Parker et al. "Chapter 1: Race and Multiracial Americans in the U.S. Census." *Pew Research Center* (blog), June 11, 2015. https://www.pewresearch.org/social-trends/2015/06/11/chapter-1-race-and-multiracial-americans-in-the-u-s-census/.

Lucherini Angeletti et al. "Anorexia Nervosa as a Disorder of the Subcortical-Cortical Interoceptive-Self." *Eating and Weight Disorders* 27, no. 8 (December 2022): 3063–81. https://doi.org/10.1007/s40519-022-01510-7.

Luminarium.org. "Jonathan Blake. Struggle for Female Equality in 'The Wife of Bath's Prologue and Tale.'" www.Luminarium.org, n.d. http://www.luminarium.org/medlit/jblake.htm.

Macdonald, Nathan. "The Imago Dei and Election: Reading Genesis 1:26–28 and Old Testament Scholarship with Karl Barth." *International Journal of Systematic Theology* 10, no. 3 (July 2008): 303–27. https://doi.org/10.1111/j.1468-2400.2008.00283.x.

Machiavelli, Niccolò. *The Prince*. New York: Reader's Library Classics, 2021.

Maglaque, Erin. "What Can the Wife of Bath Teach Us about Misogyny Today?" *The New York Times*, February 9, 2023, sec. Books. https://www.nytimes.com/2023/02/09/books/review/the-wife-of-bath-marion-turner.html.

Maguire, Gregory. *Confessions of an Ugly Stepsister*. New York: HarperCollins, 2000.

———. *Wicked: The Life and Times of the Wicked Witch of the West*. New York: HarperCollins, 2004.

Maleficient. Family. Walt Disney Studios, 2014.

Manager, Marketing. "Worldwide Survey Shows That Women's Health Has Declined." *Cary OBGYN* (blog), September 29, 2022. https://www.caryobgyn.com/worldwide-survey-shows-that-womens-health-has-declined/.

Manshoory, Shaheen. "What Is Marital Rape: California Laws and Penalties." Manshoory Law Group, APC, February 6, 2023. https://manshoorylaw.com/blog/marital-rape-california/.

Marcus, Emily. "Miley Cyrus Through the Years: From 'Hannah Montana' to Pop Sensation." *Us Weekly*, November 23, 2022. https://www.usmagazine.com/celebrity-news/pictures/miley-cyrus-through-the-years-music-love-acting-and-more/.

Mary. "12 Characteristics of a Godly Woman (How to Become a True Woman of God!)." *Healthy Christian Home*, December 23, 2017. https://healthychristianhome.com/characteristics-of-a-godly-woman/.

Masonheimer, Phylicia. "Dear Women's Ministry, Stop Telling Me I'm Beautiful." *Phylicia Masonheimer* (blog), January 2, 2017. https://phyliciamasonheimer.com/christian-womens-ministry/.

Mathewson, Clayton. *A Theoretical Study of Masculine Archetypes: Embraced and Rejected in Children's Cinema* (Dissertation). Carpinteria, CA: Pacifica Graduate Institute, 1999.

Mayor, Adrienne. *The Amazons: Lives and Legends of Women Across the Ancient World*. Princeton, NJ: Princeton University Press, 2014.

McCarthy-Brown, Karen. *Mama Lola: A Voodoo Priestess in Brooklyn*. Berkeley, CA: University of California Press, 2001.

McLellan, Faith. "Mental Health and Justice: The Case of Andrea Yates." *The Lancet* 368, no. 9551 (December 2, 2006): 1951–54. https://doi.org/10.1016/S0140-6736(06)69789-4.

McPhillips, Deidre. "Women's Health Got Worse in 2021, Global Survey Finds." *CNN*, September 21, 2022. https://www.cnn.com/2022/09/21/health/global-womens-health-index-2021/index.html.

Meehan, Dessa. "Containing the Kalon Kakon: The Portrayal of Women in Ancient Greek Mythology." *Armstrong Undergraduate Journal of History* 7, no. 2 (November 1, 2017): 8–26. https://doi.org/10.20429/aujh.2017.070202.

Merkatz, Ruth B. "Inclusion of Women in Clinical Trials: A Historical Overview of Scientific Ethical and Legal Issues." *Journal of Obstetric, Gynecologic & Neonatal Nursing* 27, no. 1 (January 1, 1998): 78–84. https://doi.org/10.1111/j.1552-6909.1998.tb02594.x.

Michel, Claudine. "Le pouvoir moral et spirituel des femmes dans le vodou haitien: la voix de Mama Lola et de Karen McCarthy Brown." *Numen* 50 (2003): 71–106. https://www.jstor.org/stable/3270556

Miller, Alice. *The Drama of the Gifted Child: The Search for the True Self.* Revised Edition. New York: Basic Books, 1997.

Miller, Jeffrey. *The Transcendent Function: Jung's Model of Psychological Growth through Dialogue with the Unconscious.* Albany, NY: State University of New York Press, 2004.

Miller, Kelsey. "Study: Most Children Start Dieting At Age 8." Refinery29. Accessed December 3, 2023. https://www.refinery29.com/en-us/2015/01/81288/children-dieting-body-image.

Minnis, Alistair. *Fallible Authors: Chaucer's Pardoner and Wife of Bath.* Philadelphia, PA: University of Pennsylvania Press, 2008.

Mitchell, Stephen A., and Margaret J. Black. *Freud and Beyond: A History of Modern Psychoanalytic Thought.* New York: Basic Books, 1995.

Moody, Robert. "On the Function of Counter-Transference." *Journal of Analytical Psychology* 1, no. 1 (October 1955): 49–58. https://doi.org/10.1111/j.1465-5922.1955.00049.x.

Moore, Thomas. "Honoring Symptoms as a Voice of the Soul." In *Care of the Soul: A Guide for Cultivating Depth and Sacredness in Everyday Life,* 3–21. New York: HarperCollins, 1992.

Morgan, Kenneth O. "Britain in the Seventies—Our Unfinest Hour?" *Revue Française de Civilisation Britannique. French Journal of British Studie*s 22, no. hors-série (December 13, 2017). https://doi.org/10.4000/rfcb.1662.

Morizot, Baptiste. *Ways of Being Alive.* Translated by Andrew Brown. Cambridge, UK: Polity Press, 2020.

Moskowitz, Lindsay, and Eric Weiselberg. "Anorexia Nervosa/Atypical Anorexia Nervosa." *Current Problems in Pediatric and Adolescent Health Care* 47, no. 4 (April 2017): 70–84. https://doi.org/10.1016/j.cppeds.2017.02.003.

Moyer, A. E. et al. "Stress-Induced Cortisol Response and Fat Distribution in Women." *Obesity Research* 2, no. 3 (May 1994): 255–62. https://doi.org/10.1002/j.1550-8528.1994.tb00055.x.

Mulan. Family. Buena Vista Film Distribution, 1998.

Mulvey, Laura. "Visual Pleasure and Narrative Cinema." *Screen* 16, no. 3 (October 1, 1975): 6–18. https://doi.org/10.1093/screen/16.3.6.

Murdock, Maureen. *The Heroine's Journey: Woman's Quest for Wholeness*. Boston: Shambhala, 1990.

Myers, Robert. "What Scars Say About Sex and Stereotypes." *SAPIENS*, August 13, 2020. https://www.sapiens.org/culture/scarification/.

Mythopedia. "Atalanta." Accessed May 15, 2023. https://mythopedia.com/topics/atalanta.

Naroditsky, Daniel. "How the Queen Chess Piece Became So Powerful." *The New York Times*. Accessed February 14, 2023. https://www.nytimes.com/2022/06/19/crosswords/chess/a-queen-in-any-other-language.html.

National Constitution Center, constitutioncenter.org. "The 0th Article of the U.S. Constitution." Accessed May 6, 2024. https://constitutioncenter.org/the-constitution/preamble.

National Constitution Center, constitutioncenter.org. "The U.S. Constitution." Accessed May 6, 2024. https://constitutioncenter.org/the-constitution.

National Institute of Mental Health (NIMH). "Major Depression." Accessed July 22, 2023. https://www.nimh.nih.gov/health/statistics/major-depression.

National Network of Depression Centers. "Facts (on Depression)." Accessed July 22, 2023. https://nndc.org/facts/.

Nature.com. "A Dopamine-to-Serotonin Circuit for the Treatment of Anorexia Nervosa." *Nature Neuroscience* 25, no. 5 (May 2022): 541–42. https://doi.org/10.1038/s41593-022-01064-y.

Neurodivergent Insights. "Insights of a Neurodivergent Clinician." Accessed December 13, 2023. https://neurodivergentinsights.com.

Nickel, Helmut. "'The Judgment of Paris' by Lucas Cranach the Elder: Nature, Allegory, and Alchemy." *Metropolitan Museum Journal* 16 (1981): 117–29. https://www.journals.uchicago.edu/doi/abs/10.2307/1512772?journalCode=met

Nicolaou, Elena. "How Princess Diana's Life Set Her Up For a Life as a Royal." *Oprah Daily*. November 15, 2020. https://www.oprahdaily.com/entertainment/a34329508/princess-diana-childhood/.

Oaklander, Violet. *Windows to Our Children: A Gestalt Therapy Approach to Children and Adolescents*. Highland, NY: The Gestalt Journal Press, 1978.

Oliver, Kelly. "The Male Gaze Is More Relevant, and More Dangerous, than Ever." *New Review of Film and Television Studies* 15, no. 4 (October 2, 2017): 451–55. https://doi.org/10.1080/17400309.2017.1377937.

Olza, Ibone et al. "Birth as a Neuro-Psycho-Social Event: An Integrative Model of Maternal Experiences and Their Relation to Neurohormonal Events during Childbirth." Edited by Anayda Portela. *PLOS ONE* 15, no. 7 (July 28, 2020): e0230992. https://doi.org/10.1371/journal.pone.0230992.

Oster, Emily. "Witchcraft, Weather and Economic Growth in Renaissance Europe." *The Journal of Economic Perspectives* 18, no. 1 (2004): 215–28. https://www.jstor.org/stable/3216882.

Paisley, Laura. "Ancient Buddhist Texts Reveal Shifting Perspectives on Women." *USC News*, April 14, 2017. https://news.usc.edu/120048/ancient-buddhist-texts-reveal-shifting-perspectives-on-women/.

Parker, Kim, Juliana Horowitz, and Renée Stepler. "On Gender Differences, No Consensus on Nature vs Nurture," December 2017. http://pewrsr.ch/2koqSO2.

Pathak, Ritambhara. "Implicit Bias in Healthcare: Maternal and Infant Morbidity and Mortality in Minority Patients." Master Essay, University of Pittsburgh, 2020. http://d-scholarship.pitt.edu/38499/.

People.com. "Miley Cyrus." Accessed February 23, 2023. https://people.com/tag/miley-cyrus/.

Peters, Edward, and Alan Charles Kors, eds. *Witchcraft in Europe 400–1700: A Documentary History*. Philadelphia, PA: University of Pennsylvania Press, 2000.

Petersen, Christopher, Stephen F. Maier, and Martin E. P. Seligman. *Learned Helplessness: A Theory for the Age of Personal Control*. Reprint Edition. Oxford, England: Oxford University Press, 1995.

Petite Maman. Drama. Pyramide Films, 2021.

Pettitt, Alena Kate. *Ladies Like Us: A Modern Girl's Guide to Self-Discovery, Self-Confidence and Love*. London: The Darling Academy, 2016.

Pew Research Center. "The Gender Gap in Religion Around the World." *Pew Research Center's Religion & Public Life Project* (blog), March 22, 2016. https://www.pewresearch.org/religion/2016/03/22/the-gender-gap-in-religion-around-the-world/.

Phelian. "How Céline Sciamma Subverts the Male Gaze in 'Portrait of a Lady on Fire.'" *The Quint*, June 21, 2022. https://www.thequint.com/entertainment/cinema/male-gaze-celine-sciamma-subversion-portrait-lady-on-fire-queer-film.

Pocahontas. Buena Vista Film Distribution, 1995.

Portrait of a Lady on Fire. Drama. Pyramide Films, 2019.

Portuges, Catherine. "Central European Twins: Psychoanalysis and Cinema in Ildiko Enyedi's My Twentieth Century." *Psychoanalytic Inquiry* 27, no. 4 (n.d.): 525–39. https://doi.org/10.1080/07351690701484675.

Pretty Woman. Buena Vista Film Distribution, 1990.

Pronin Froberg, Doris, and Doris Bergen. *Play from Birth to Twelve and Beyond: Contexts, Perspectives, and Meanings*. New York: Garland Publishing, Inc., 1998.

Psychology Today. "Acceptance and Commitment Therapy." Accessed September 23, 2023. https://www.psychologytoday.com/us/therapy-types/acceptance-and-commitment-therapy.

Radner, Hilary. *Neo-Feminist Cinema: Girly Films, Chick Flicks, and Consumer Culture*. New York: Routledge, 2011.

Raj, Suhasini. "India Struggles to Eradicate an Old Scourge: Witch Hunting." *The New York Times*, May 13, 2023, Asia Pacific edition. https://www.nytimes.com/2023/05/13/world/asia/india-witch-hunting.html.

Refworld. "France: Preamble to the Constitution of 27 October 1946." Refworld. Accessed December 9, 2023. https://www.refworld.org/docid/3ae6b56910.html.

Revilla, Analyn. "'The Heroine's Journey' Is Not One Woman's Journey." *LAFPI* (blog), March 16, 2012. https://lafpi.com/2012/03/the-heroines-journey-is-not-one-womans-journey/.

Rieber, Robert, and Robert Kelly. *Film, Television, and the Psychology of the Social Dream*. New York: Springer, 2014.

Rigby, S. H. (Stephen Henry). "The Wife of Bath, Christine de Pizan, and the Medieval Case for Women." *The Chaucer Review* 35, no. 2 (2000): 133–65. https://doi.org/10.1353/cr.2000.0024.

Roberts, Christine. "Most 10-Year-Olds Have Been on a Diet: Study; 53 Percent of 13-Year-Old Girls Have Issues with How Their Bodies Look." *New York Daily News*. Accessed December 3, 2023. https://www.nydailynews.com/2012/07/03/most-10-year-olds-have-been-on-a-diet-study-53-percent-of-13-year-old-girls-have-issues-with-how-their-bodies-look/.

Robinson, Belinda. "Worrying Trend Reveals 80% of 10-Year-Old American Girls Have Been on a Diet." Daily Mail Online. Accessed December 3, 2023. https://www.dailymail.co.uk/news/article-2925600/Worrying-trend-reveals-80-10-year-old-American-girls-diet.html.

Rogers, C. *A Way of Being*. Boston: Houghton Mifflin, 1995.

Rogers, Michele. *The Wounding and Healing of the Mother Daughter Relationship* (Thesis). Carpinteria, CA: Proquest Dissertations and Theses, 2010.

Ronnberg, Ami, and Kathleen Martin, eds. *The Book of Symbols: Reflections on Archetypal Images*. Cologne, Germany: Taschen, 2010.

Rose, Gillian. *Visual Methodologies*. Thousand Oaks, CA: Sage Publications, 2003.

Roth, Veronica. *Divergent*. New York: HarperCollins, 2011.

Santhosh, Hyma. "Diving into the Subconscious of Women and Nature: Margaret Atwood's Surfacing as an Ecofeminist Novel." *SMART MOVES JOURNAL IJELLH* 6, no. 10 (October 10, 2018): 12. https://www.researchgate.net/publication/350940414_Diving_into_the_Subconscious_of_Women_and_Nature_Margaret_Atwood's_Surfacing_as_an_Ecofeminist_Novel

Santmire, H. Pall. "The Genesis Creation Narratives Revisited: Themes for a Global Age." *Interpretation: A Journal of Bible and Theology* 45, no. 4 (October 1991): 366–79. https://doi.org/10.1177/002096430004500404.

Sarigöl, Pinar. "Foucault, Sexuality and Biopolitics." *Dokuz Eylül Üniversitesi Sosyal Bilimler Enstitüsü Dergisi* 24, no. 1 (March 30, 2022): 245–59. https://doi.org/10.16953/deusosbil.1010762.

Scala, Elizabeth. "The Women in Chaucer's 'Marriage Group.'" *Medieval Feminist Forum* 45, no. 1 (2009): 50–56. https://doi.org/10.17077/1536-8742.1766.

Schlumpf, Heidi. "Who Framed Mary Magdalene?" *U.S. Catholic* (blog), March 30, 2016. https://uscatholic.org/articles/201603/who-framed-mary-magdalene/.

Schlüter, C., Kraag, G. & Schmidt, J. "Body Shaming: an Exploratory Study on its Definition and Classification." *International Journal of Bullying Prevention* 5, 26–37 (2023). https://doi.org/10.1007/s42380-021-00109-3.

Schuessler, Jennifer. "Chaucer the Rapist? Newly Discovered Documents Suggest Not." *The New York Times*, October 13, 2022. https://www.nytimes.com/2022/10/13/books/geoffrey-chaucer-rape-charge.html.

Searson, Hannah. "Star Wars and the Hero with a Thousand Faces." *Film Obsessive*, December 13, 2019. https://filmobsessive.com/film/film-analysis/star-wars-the-hero-with-a-thousand-faces/.

Sedgwick, David. "Winnicott's Dream: Some Reflections on D. W. Winnicott and C. G. Jung." *Journal of Analytical Psychology* 53 (2008): 543–60. https://doi.org/10.1111/j.1468-5922.2008.00745.x

Sex and the City. New Line Cinema, 2008.

Slater, Glen. "Archetypal Perspectives and American Film." *Spring Journal: A Journal of Archetype and Culture Cinema & Psyche*, no. 73 (2005): 1–19.

Sleeping Beauty. Animation, Family. Buena Vista Film Distribution, 1959.

Smith, Jen, and Andrea Cavallier. "Lori Vallow Is Sentenced to Life without Parole for Murders of Her Kids JJ and Tylee and Her Husband's Ex-Wife Tammy Daybell." Daily Mail Online. Accessed May 6, 2024. https://www.dailymail.co.uk/news/article-12356641/lori-vallow-daybell-Idaho-sentencing-updates-killed-children-Tylee-Ryan-JJ.html.

Smith, Melissah. "Why Successful Women Need to Be Submissive." LinkedIn. Accessed May 2, 2023. https://www.linkedin.com/pulse/why-successful-women-need-submissive-mellissah-smith.

Snow White and the Seven Dwarfs. Walt Disney Studios Motion Pictures/RKO Pictures, 1937.

Solomon, Charles. *The Art of Frozen*. Burbank, CA: Disney Enterprises, 2013.

Spencer, Erika Hope. "Research Guides: French Women & Feminists in History: A Resource Guide: Witch Trials & Witchcraft." Research guide. Accessed May 5, 2024. https://guides.loc.gov/feminism-french-women-history/witch-trials-witchcraft.

Specter, Emma Why Are Women Now Required to Cover Their Arms in the Missouri State House?" *Vogue*, January 18, 2023. https://www.vogue.com/article/missouri-state-house-bare-arms.

Spigel, Lynn. *Welcome to the Dreamhouse: Popular Media and Postwar Suburbs.* Durham, NC: Duke University Press, 2001.

Star Wars: A New Hope. Twentieth Century Fox, 1977.

Stein, M. "The White Snake: A Psychological Hero's Journey." In *Psyche's Stories: Modern Jungian Interpretations of Fairy Tales*, edited by M. Stein and L. Corbett, Vol. 3. Wilmette, IL: Chiron Publications, n.d.

Sternlicht, Alexandra. "Miley Cyrus Is a Rebel for Her Own Cause." *Forbes*. Accessed February 23, 2023. https://www.forbes.com/sites/alexandrasternlicht/2021/12/12/miley-cyrus-is-a-rebel-for-her-owncause/.

Stone, Merlin. *When God Was a Woman.* New York: The Dial Press, 1976.

Substack. "The Witch Trials of J. K. Rowling." Accessed February 14, 2023. https://substack.com/inbox.

Sullivan, Mark. "The Analytic Initiation: The Effect of the Archetype of Initiation on the Personal Unconscious." *Journal of Analytical Psychology* 41, no. 4 (1996): 509–38. https://onlinelibrary.wiley.com/doi/abs/10.1111/j.1465-5922.1996.00509.x.

Tangled. Walt Disney Studios Motion Pictures, 2010.

Tanner, Itsa et al. "Images of Couples and Families in Disney Feature-Length Animated Films." *The American Journal of Family Therapy* 31 (2003): 355–73.

Taylor, Elise. "A Timeline of Prince Charles and Princess Diana's Tumultuous, Tragic Relationship." *Vogue*. Accessed February 9, 2023. https://www.vogue.com/article/a-timeline-of-prince-charles-and-princess-dianas-tumultuous-tragic-relationship.

The Exorcist. Horror. Warner Bros, 1973.

The Free Press. "Has the Sexual Revolution Failed?" Live Event, n.d.

The Heroine Journeys Project. "Maureen Murdock's Heroine's Journey Arc," February 12, 2015. https://heroinejourneys.com/heroines-journey/.

The Little Mermaid. Buena Vista Film Distribution, 1989.

The Princess and the Frog. Buena Vista Film Distribution, 2009.

"The Role of Women in Church, in Society, and in the Home." Accessed May 6, 2023. cbeinternational.org/resource/role-women-church-society-and-home/

The University of Toledo. "What Were You Wearing Art Installation." Accessed December 5, 2023. https://www.utoledo.edu/studentaffairs/saepp/what-were-you-wearing/.

Toews, Miriam. *Women Talking*. London: Bloomsbury Publishing, 2019.

Turner, Marion. *The Wife of Bath*. Princeton, NJ: Princeton University Press, 2023.

U. S. National Science Foundation. "Supporting Women and Girls in STEM: Broadening Participation in STEM." Accessed May 5, 2024. https://new.nsf.gov/funding/initiatives/broadening-participation/supporting-women-girls-stem.

Ulaby, Neda. "A Wife of Bath 'biography' Brings a Modern Woman out of the Middle Ages." *NPR*, February 4, 2023, sec. Author Interviews. https://www.npr.org/2023/02/04/1146691833/wife-of-bath-canterbury-tales-chaucer.

UN Women. "The Paths to Equal: Twin Indices on Women's Empowerment and Gender Equality." Accessed August 7, 2023. https://www.unwomen.org/en/digital-library/publications/2023/07/the-paths-to-equal-twin-indices-on-womens-empowerment-and-gender-equality.

US Department of Labor, Women's Bureau. "Facts Over Time: Women in the Labor Force." United States Department of Labor, 2022. https://www.dol.gov/agencies/wb/data/Facts-over-Time.

Vagianos, Alanna. "Art Exhibit Powerfully Answers the Question 'What Were You Wearing?'" HuffPost Women. Accessed December 5, 2023. https://www.huffpost.com/entry/powerful-art-exhibit-powerfully-answers-the-question-what-were-you-wearing_n_59baddd2e4b02da0e1405d2a.

Vaz da Silva, Francisco. "Red as Blood, White as Snow, Black as Crow: Chromatic Symbolism of Womanhood in Fairy Tales." *Marvels & Tales: Journal of Fairy-Tale Studies* 21, no. 2 (2007): 240–52. https://www.jstor.org/stable/41388837.

Via, Esther et al. "Self and Other Body Perception in Anorexia Nervosa: The Role of Posterior DMN Nodes." *The World Journal of Biological Psychiatry: The Official Journal of the World Federation of Societies of Biological Psychiatry* 19, no. 3 (April 2018): 210–24. https://doi.org/10.1080/15622975.2016.1249951.

Violence Policy Center. "When Men Murder Women: An Analysis of 2020 Homicide Data." September 2022. https://vpc.org/when-men-murder-women/.

Von Franz, Marie Louise. *Individuation in Fairy Tales*. London: Shambhala, 1970.

———. *The Feminine in Fairy Tales*. Revised. A C. G. Jung Foundation book. Boston: Shambhala Publications, 1972.

Wade, Renee. "How to Be Submissive in a Relationship." *The Feminine Woman—Dating, Love & Relationship Advice for Women* (blog), October 27, 2022. https://www.thefemininewoman.com/how-to-be-submissive/.

Waska, Robert. "Catching My Balance in the Countertransference: Difficult Moments with Patients in Psychoanalytic Treatment." *International Forum of Psychoanalysis* 20, no. 3 (2011): 167–75. https://doi.org/10.1080/080370 6X.2011.553632

Weber, Samuel R., James W. Lomax, and Kenneth I. Pargament. "Healthcare Engagement as a Potential Source of Psychological Distress among People without Religious Beliefs: A Systematic Review." *Healthcare (Basel, Switzerland)* 5, no. 2 (April 5, 2017): 19. https://doi.org/10.3390/healthcare5020019.

Wellman, Billy. *The Black Death: An Enthralling Overview of a Major Event in the Middle Ages (Europe)* eBook, n.d. Accessed May 6, 2024.

White, T. H. *The Once and Future King.* Kindle Reprint. New York: Ace/Penguin Group, 1987.

Widawsky, Rachel. "Julia Kristeva's Psychoanalytic Work." *Journal of the American Psychoanalytic Association* 62, no. 1 (February 2014): 61–67. https://doi .org/10.1177/0003065113520041.

Wikipedia. "Echo and Narcissus," May 17, 2023. https://en.wikipedia.org/w/index .php?title=Echo_and_Narcissus&oldid=1155163474.

Windle, Gill. "What Is Resilience? A Review and Concept Analysis." *Reviews in Clinical Gerontology* 21, no. 2 (2011): 152–69. https://doi.org/10.1017/ S0959259810000420.

Wolkstein, Diane, and Samuel Kramer. *Inanna Queen of Heaven and Earth: Her Stories and Hymns from Sumer.* New York: Harper & Row, 1983.

Women Talking. Drama. United Artists Releasing, 2022.

Wonder Woman. Action/Drama. Warner Bros. Pictures, 2017.

Woodhead, Linda. "The rise of 'no religion': Towards an explanation." *Sociology of Religion* 78, no. 3 (2017): 247-262. https://doi.org/10.1093/socrel/srx031.

Woodward, Amanda L., and Sarah A. Gerson. "Mirroring and the Development of Action Understanding." *Philosophical Transactions of the Royal Society B: Biological Sciences* 369, no. 1644 (June 5, 2014): 20130181. https://doi.org/10.1098/ rstb.2013.0181.

World Health Organization, English. "Levels of Domestic Violence Increase Globally, Including in the Region, as COVID-19 Pandemic Escalates." World Health Organization, Regional Office for the Eastern Mediterranean. Accessed May 5, 2024. http://www.emro.who.int/violence-injuries-disabilities/violence-news/levels-of-domestic-violence-increase-as-covid-19-pandemic-escalates.html.

World Health Organization. "Female Genital Mutilation." Accessed February 11, 2023. https://www.who.int/news-room/fact-sheets/detail/female-genital-mutilation.

World Health Organization. "Violence against Women." Accessed December 6, 2023. https://www.who.int/news-room/fact-sheets/detail/violence-against-women.

Yalom, Marilyn. *Birth of the Chess Queen*. New York: HarperCollins, 2009.

Yousafzai, Malala, and Christina Lamb. *I Am Malala: The Girl Who Stood Up for Education and Was Shot by the Taliban*. Kindle Edition. First. Boston: Little, Brown, and Company, 2013.

Zhou, Li. "The Sexism of School Dress Codes." *The Atlantic*, October 20, 2015. https://www.theatlantic.com/education/archive/2015/10/school-dress-codes-are-problematic/410962/.

Zhuang, Peina, and Siqi Weng. "A Comparative Study of the Body and Power between Han Feizi and Michel Foucault." *Neohelicon*, August 21, 2023. https://doi.org/10.1007/s11059-023-00705-w.

Zipes, Jack. *When Dreams Came True: Classical Fairy Tales and Their Tradition*. New York: Routledge, 1999.

Zoladz, Lindsay. "Ridicule Is Resistance." The Ringer. Accessed May 6, 2024. https://www.theringer.com/2017/1/22/16040964/report-from-the-womens-march-protest-washington-dc-e29c9ccd75e6.

ACKNOWLEDGMENTS

This work has been a labor of love, joy, heartbreak, and sacrifice for over a decade. It could not have happened without love, support, and critique. My family have supported me through many iterations of this work, especially my husband, Ched Hover; my daughter, Danica; and my nieces, Avery and Zoe. Avery took beautiful photos at events to support this work, and Zoe has been my editorial assistant on this and other writing. My best friends in the world—Patricia Hunter McGrath, Laura Voglesong, Mary Gelfand, Jane Henrickson, Marie-Dominque Verdier, and Cathy Huddleston—have listened to and helped me organize my thoughts on this work since the beginning. They are my chosen family and have never failed to support me. The original group who heard the words and gave me the first critiques at the Queens Brunch: Chris Spitale, Shannon Dorothy, Rachel Helding, Gretchen Bangs, Lou Allene Mallory, LeAnne Matthiesen, and Lisa Dawn. I am deeply indebted to you. My writing group made this book possible. I will always be profoundly grateful to Selene Castrovilla and the writers of Writer's Pinnacle for their contributions, support, and thoughtful critique. The team at Roadmap Writers was instrumental in getting my work seen. Thank you, Joey Tuccio. My agent, Mark Gottlieb, has been a steadfast champion of my work. He has brought deep and thoughtful consideration in everything I've done and has talked me off the ledge more than once. I will always be grateful. My editor, Sally Mason-Swaab, has been an amazing collaborator, reading drafts and always making meaningful suggestions and offering thoughtful critique and encouragement. Allison Janice believed in this work from the beginning—thank you! There are too many other people to thank, but a few deserve acknowledgment.

The incandescent Steven Pressfield believed in me early on, and his encouragement kept me going for years. The Association of Women Directors and Donna Bonilla Wheeler have supported my classes and workshops. My UK friends have been amazing supporters, including my friend and fellow writer Lorna Partington, and my friend and resilience coach Helen Soutar. I am grateful to the women who participated in the first FemmePyre workshop, especially speakers Deborah Hurwitz, Kate Neligan, Helen Soutar, and Dr. Valerie Rein, and the women who agreed to be interviewed on camera, Danielle Lajoie and Susan Cross. Thank you also to all my clients who have graciously shared their stories and stepped onto the Queen's Path with me! I am deeply grateful that you have invited me into your queendoms.

ABOUT
THE AUTHOR

Stacey Simmons, MA, Ph.D., LMFT, is a licensed marriage and family therapist and certified psychedelic therapist. Her clinical practice focuses on helping creative professionals with everything from early trauma to creative blocks. After a debilitating few years being haunted by nightmares, Stacey left a career in entertainment to become a psychotherapist. She is a clinical supervisor at Hope Therapy Center in Burbank, California. Stacey is a leader in women's spirituality, having co-founded a church for Wiccans in her native New Orleans. She engages with spiritual seekers on TikTok as Your Witch Mom **@WitchDaily,** where she has over 300,000 followers. She is a volunteer researcher with the Integrative Psychiatry Clinic at the Semel Institute for Neuroscience and Human Behavior at UCLA, as well as an affiliate researcher with the TranceScience Research Institute in Paris, France. She holds a Ph.D. from the University of New Orleans and a master's degree from Pacifica Graduate Institute in Santa Barbara, California.